GREEN SPIRITUALITY

Green Spirituality
Magic In the Midst of Life

Rosa Romani

Foreword by Rae Beth
Illustrated by Poppy Palin

Green Magic

This edition is published by
Green Magic
The Long Barn
Sutton Mallet
Somerset
TA7 9AR

Typeset by Academic + Technical, Bristol
Printed and bound by Antony Rowe Ltd.

Cover image by Poppy Palin

Cover design by Chris Render

Cover production by Tania Lambert

ISBN 0 9542 9636 2

GREEN MAGIC

'The tree is my church, the tree is my temple, the tree is my mantra, the tree is my poem and my prayer.'

Satish Kumar, 'No Destination – An Autobiography'
(Green Books, 1992)

Dedication

This book is for the wise ones of the bark, whose bodies are the medium that carry my words into the world. I thank the trees with all my heart for the gifts they bestow.

Contents

Acknowledgements

I would like to thank Pete Gotto of Green Magic for being so supportive and understanding during the completion of this project. His partner Chris Render has also been wonderful, as has Tania Lambert their assistant. They all do an excellent job and I wish them every success.

I would also like to offer my gratitude to the following people who have all been great supports to me in their own myriad ways over the years: Germaine Helen (formerly Knight), Marion Pearce, Jill Smith, Flick, Sue MacDonald-King, Elly Frelly Phillips, Alan Richardson, Mike Prince, Lisa Tenzin-Dolma, Amber and Jon House, Ashley Pascoe.

Thanks to Helen and Harry Knibb for being generous, gorgeous web-weavers.

Big thanks to Rae for taking the trouble to write the foreword and for her friendship.

Immense gratitude to Poppy for her inspirational and green-spirited artwork.

Thanks to Tim Willmott for introducing me to West Penwith.

Thanks to Marc and Rick for some great conversations!

Also to the divine Naomi Kosten of the pagan/green oriented gift shop *Inanna's Festival* (see the resources section at the back of this book for more details). Naomi gave me my confidence back and I thank her for having confidence in me in the first place.

Major thanks go to the hairiest of all honkiest tonks, Becky Haynes, for being just wonderful in general. Also to the gorgeous and much loved Jennie Smith and the infinitely talented, caring Celtic hero Davey Kendall. They are all very special people indeed and I am blessed to have them in my life.

Thanks to the band U2 who proved to me, once and for all, that personal creativity, be that in music, words or art, can make a difference.

Last (but by no means least) I offer a whole heap of special thanks to Gary Howe and the rest of my band, Gypsy Moon, because they have changed me and my life for the better and given me so much pleasure. So cheers Dec, Jon and Jer . . . but especially super-drummer and all round ace pokey person Gary, as without his fire, vision and natural talent the band never would have happened. He is a beautiful gift *and it makes me so high to be me.*

A Note from the Author

The aim of this book is to be inclusive. Therefore if I have omitted any reference to those with disabilities when I describe the suggested practical activities in this text then please do assume that I am aware of the fact that not everyone has the ability to see/walk etc as I do. Please do adapt the work as suggested in other parts of the book, or to your own specifications.

Similarly I am aware that I use the term 'it' to describe trees when this work is centred in respect for the wise ones of the bark. If it sounds like a dismissive or derogative term then it is certainly not meant this way, rather to denote that trees can chose to be seen as either gender or none at all. It here simply denotes that neutrality or fluidity of gender rather than a sense of dismissive denigration.

It's hard to get everything right in this way and I do hope that the overall feel of warm inclusiveness this work hopefully promotes isn't overshadowed by the occasional omission due to restrictions of chapter size etc.

Think globally, act locally and feel deeply...
Rosa Romani, South West England, 2003

Foreword

Within the tapestry of the Earth's spiritual traditions, green spirituality may be the least acknowledged and most important strand. It has no churches, no hierarchies, no organisations, yet all the world's religions and traditions partake of or include it. And now, when the human relationship with plants, creatures and the land is so badly ruptured, with such potentially disastrous consequences for all life, it is clear that we must remember and embrace beliefs that are rooted in nature. Where else, after all, should a sane spirituality be rooted?

Within the newly reconstructed European Paganism, as well as in the Paganism of Native Americans and Australian Aboriginals, there has always been this central green thread from which all else develops. Indeed, it would be true to say that green spirituality derives ultimately from these, and other, similar Earth-honouring religions. But it is also present in Christianity, within the works, for example, of Hildegarde of Bingen and Matthew Fox and in the teaching of St Francis. If I knew enough about the other mono-theistic faiths I have no doubt I should find it there as well. And in Buddhism and Hinduism. Besides that, many who may for all I know call themselves agnostic, have written about it from a scientific point of view. James Lovelock comes

xiii

to mind as an obvious example but there are many. (Not that I mean to imply all scientists of a green spiritual persuasion are necessarily without structured religious belief. Think of Tielhard de Chardin.)

Green spirituality is not, when it comes to religion, mainstream, but it is beginning to attract many adherents including those who do not call themselves 'religious' at all. There is no dogma within it. Instead each person upon the Green Path may create their own approach from an eclectic blend of traditions. Or may work to restore the green thread within one tradition whilst acknowledging others.

Rosa Romani's book is a first-rate introduction to green spirituality in practice. Skilfully she leads the reader to an understanding of how to experience this potent magic – the spell of being on Earth in fellowship with all beings. 'The Spell of Living Well' to quote from an ancient prayer to the Goddess Isis. And this is what green spirituality means really. Living well, not in a materialistic sense, but in the happiness of finding the meaning in all that is. And of seeing the sacredness in the land. In a world where a sense of the sacred is almost non-existent for many, this brings back life. Green spirituality can also show us how to help and heal both ourselves and others. And how to progress in wisdom and to experience life more keenly, our full range of awareness, including the psychic, restored to us.

This, the spirituality of the environment, is about giving the Earth Mother Her dues and other species their right to live. It is about not desecrating the land we live on. Or other lands either. But it is also about another magic 'as old as the hills'.

Rosa's book is a major contribution to her subject. It points the way forward for us all and contains many fresh insights while staying firmly rooted in tradition as well as in nature. And in practicality as well as theory.

Rae Beth
Somerset 2004

Introduction

A Journey to the Wild heart of Being

There is often a reluctance to express our true spiritual nature, and the values and behaviours that stem from that nature, openly in modern western society. If we chose to do so then our actions and expressions can be interpreted by others as something bewilderingly nebulous at best or downright embarrassing at worst and so either way we become unworthy of a sensible response and the appropriate measure of respect. Alternatively, a spiritual impulse and the actions that stem from this can be mis-read as a statement of religious allegiance of some kind. The latter is the more usual response, as it is easier to explain away spiritual expression in conventional terms than it is to explore any other possibilities that lead to unfamiliar territory. Therefore our authentically profound, and completely natural, spiritual impulses are usually pushed into the shade of the nearest convenient religious umbrella and any uniquely wild and joyful experience of the divine is so tamed.

To separate out religion and spirituality is something that the majority of us rarely do, yet if we begin by engaging in that process now then we will be better served to explore the more balanced way of expressing our soul-selves that this book shares. It is a process that will enable us to make the journey to the wild heart of being that green spirituality inspires and gives us the ability to discern what is wholesome, instinctive and free and what is a synthetic construct. It allows us to identify that which gives effective shelter yet insists we live in its shadow, stunted.

So, what *is* the difference between religion and spirituality? Well, we could state that religion is something that has been fashioned by men, for men . . . it is a construction that categorically answers a basic human need for meaning. Even if it is claimed that it is based on the word of God it has still been filtered and moulded by a human source, built upon or added to like an ancestral home over the ages until it dominates its

1

surroundings with its impressively imposing solidity. Religion can certainly be quantified immediately as something tangible like bricks and mortar and because of this robust familiarity we may establish an easy allegiance to it, a tie. Indeed, the root of the word religion in Latin is in the verb *ligo* meaning to bind or tie, which then becomes *religio* meaning god-fearing. Such a description is in itself enough for us to perhaps understand the difference between religion and the organic, free-flowing soul-expression that the words 'green spirituality' suggest.

Religion is a fixed proposition that promotes an unshakable adherence; it is not about resurgence or growth in a natural verdant sense but about continuity and steadiness. It has little of the spontaneity or unpredictability of a living spirituality; rather it is a rigid structure that shelters us from other more unrefined ways of being. It may have its basis in truth and contain a measure of the original dazzling vision that inspired it but essentially it is a yoked and plodding donkey as opposed to a glorious white mare pounding through the surf at twilight. It has been domesticated and certainly won't do anything astonishing – and indeed many do prefer a sturdy workhorse to a flighty and charming one.

Religion requires us to be similarly domesticated and give over our personal autonomy to the belief system or master. Moreover, it does not link us directly to the divine but instead ties us into a chain of command by which we may communicate with the sacred . . . these we call priests, rabbis, imams etc. We are roped, like men on a mountain, to the next highest figure, in a line of such figures continuing upwards out of our sight. We only know that the furthest invisible being is up there above us as we are kept from falling by the chain that stretches out to them. We are kept safe yet effectively disempowered, unable to observe for ourselves what may be above us, or all around us. It offers a structure with reassuringly solid walls and obvious boundaries, not a flexible framework which allows us to peer through.

Religion certainly makes life easier for us in many respects; it offers us a means of unwavering support in a changing world that can be very reassuring. If we are willing to accept its ethos wholesale then it provides all of the answers for us and we need not tax ourselves by looking any further for 'the truth'. Therefore it is possible to be protected and comfortable but never to be a pioneer or explorer in a religious sense. There is nothing to seek as someone else has already found it for us and will offer us the map that will lead us to life's treasure with no surprises. The price of the feeling of security we gain from it means that we must put the exotic blooms of our spirit in a tiny plant pot on someone else's windowsill.

Through religion we may keep our spirit's foliage nurtured to some degree even if we cannot then flourish, as we should. We can rely on being watered and offered a little sunlight at least. The real problem with religion is that when we, as living energetic beings, grow too big for the pot that its belief system has placed us into we will simply find ourselves transplanted in a slightly bigger pot of exactly the same design rather than be dug directly into the rich loam of the land. This is where spirituality comes in; it allows us to choose our own type of soil and to use our own knowledge and instincts to pick the best sort of positioning to allow for our growth. We may not have the security of someone else providing us with water but when the rains come we feel twice as refreshed.

Spirituality has little to do with the tenets and laws that bind with their security ropes and has everything to do with individual exploration and personal feelings. It is an experiential way in which we can feed directly from that which is sacred in order to reach our fullest potential and so blossom accordingly. One may be a spiritual seeker where it is not so easy to be a religious seeker as we may only ever seek truth within our religion's framework. This can make our search for enlightenment rather like taking part in a treasure hunt in a small fenced and cultivated field when we could be out on an open heath turning over every lichen-patterned rock with wonder. Preordained religious parameters provide us with a foregone conclusion whilst with a more flexible spirituality the quest is ongoing. Religion both protects and restricts whilst spirituality has wide-open spaces that challenge us with their unfamiliarity. Spirituality is, by its nature, gloriously limitless and unconstrained.

There are no firm universal beliefs that one must subscribe to in order to be spiritual. Spirituality is more about having an active faith in the existence of the sacred than in a hard and fast belief in it and a desire to label it conclusively. Faith, perhaps, is about hope and searching whilst religious belief already knows and feels safe to shut the door on other possibilities. Faith knows that it does not know but has a willingness to learn. When we believe, in a religious sense, we are all too ready to draw lines in the sand which say 'us and them' or 'right and wrong'. Good and evil are the artificial divisions which polarise us, for and against, using limited criteria to judge others and elevate our own posi-tions in accordance with a religious doctrine that gives us full permission to act in such a manner. Such divisions are the tools of separation, not of ongoing transformation. Faith is a gentler concept that speaks of broader truths as well as personal ones in a way that allows us to be willing to amend our views. Therefore there can be a fearless interchange and colloquy...a free-flow of ideas and feelings, an ongoing soul-poem, a natural unfolding. Spirituality speaks not in complex concepts but in our daily lives. When man-made or intellectual constructs end there can be a constant stream running through our days, a stream bubbling up from the cool depths of ourselves, unpolluted.

Another fundamental difference may be this...that religion is usually linked to the State or with patriotic fervour whereas spirituality is aligned with liberty and choice and is a matter of personal preference that sits well with us at a deep level, regardless of race etc. Spirituality of any kind may be the way of the freethinking nonconformist who values the right to change and grow unhindered, like a wildflower. Their only limits are self-imposed, those of personal integrity and acquired empathy, the result of unhindered personal interaction with the sacred.

In its simplest form, spirituality is about acknowledging spirit. This starts with our own eternal spirit and ripples out in an understanding of the spiritual nature of other people, be they living or currently discarnate. Part of spiritual exploration may be working with these latterly mentioned 'unseen ones' who we ourselves can learn to perceive through various techniques as well as via a natural ability or openness. Perhaps, in some cases, it is this innate ability to 'see' (or look beyond that which we are told is 'real') that drives us to nurture our spiritual impulse. From there we may gain an acceptance, by direct experience, of a greater unseen spirit, a motivating quality in our daily lives, the life-force energy or Creator energy. It is wholly up to us how we attain communion with spirit, as there is certainly no-one there to mediate or correct us if we are simply seeking our own truths. Perhaps this is why so many folk today class themselves as 'unspiritual' (or, more usually, non-religious) as the whole area of spirituality can be perceived as rather vapid and insubstantial, an area without the blessing or security of conventional authority, with no hierarchy to monitor it. However, the burgeoning interest in a wide array of practices loosely affiliated to the seeking of truth beyond conventional or customary ideas, practices such as divination, healing, clairvoyance etc., reveal a thirst for greater meaning within the general populace.

So how may we quantify spirituality at all, how are we even able to name it? Well, spirituality is open hearted and has a wide embrace. We cannot spot it by its doctrines or creeds but rather by the authentic compassion one person may show to another, by the level of attunement a person has to the subtler emanations of a situation. When one is unafraid of revealing one's spirituality there is a genuine expression of inter-connectedness, of a deep union with all other beings who are soul-kin under the skin regardless of temporary boundaries imposed by gender, age etc., and a sensitivity to the energies that unite us all. A spiritual life is one with kindness at the core, a boundless benevolence that comes from that faith in the life-force energy that runs through each of us and is a gift born of the greater spirit.

To live a spiritual life can include active service to the world alongside prayer and meditation, retreat and contemplation, as can a religious life. This is what spirituality and all world religions share, the desire to be a more compassionate and contemplative human being. But once again we can observe the difference. There are no masters in a spiritual sense, as all people act as our teachers and life itself is the temple. The only bonds in spirituality are to our enspirited brothers and sisters on Earth, in service of the spirit that created us all, with love, in peace. It is blending the faith in that unseen energetic aspects of being with purely manifest acts of kindness and care.

So, where does *green spirituality* take us that pure spirituality does not? Why do we need it?

Green spirituality looks beyond the human spirit and considers all beings as ensouled, from the adorable dormouse to the snapping alligator. A green-spirited person knows that it is not only the two-legged being that is animated by the life-force energy, the spark of the Creator, but also the four-legged, the furred, the finned, the feathered etc. We may find this easier to contemplate when we consider mammals rather than when we think of reptiles, fish or insects yet this way of being does not exclude one creature because it doesn't find favour with us aesthetically. Green spirituality looks beyond the purely physical into the realms of the life force behind *all* beings. Furthermore, this green spirituality considers those who may not normally be classed as beings at all as spirit-full also. By this we refer to the land, the trees, the herbs, and the rocks . . . to the inanimate and growing ones alike. To white water and forest fire, freezing air and marsh mud. All of these are possessed of the same Creator energy as we humans and although the energy does not animate or motivate them in the same way as it does the two-legged folk of the planet it does give them a sentience, a unique awareness, a sacred point of view. The rowan trees, the purple sage, the pebble of serpentine stone, all are spirit-full.

This is green spirituality in essence, that we live in a world that is truly alive and so filled with numinous possibility.

This way of viewing the world enlivens our existences, filling them with magic of a wild and beautiful kind. We are not walking in a relatively dead place that serves a suitable backdrop for human existence, rather we are sharing a living and cognisant planet with a whole variety of fascinating fellow spirits made manifest in ingenious and captivating ways. That boulder you touch, that bush you pluck at, that sapling you water, all are spirited beings in their own way. The cat that sits in your lap therefore is no longer your pet but your companion on life's journey. There is no hierarchy of importance; we are all part of the same dance of life...all unique and vital parts.

Not only does this new way of looking at things make us able to live well, with a renewed sense of enchantment and wonder, it also makes things harder. Now the carrots we crunch upon, the tiny beetle we accidentally crush, the grass we mow...all of these share the Creator's energetic inheritance with us. Isn't it hard enough when we just wish to avoid suffering, taking care not to crush snails on wet pavement or overcoming a fear of creeping crawling beasts in order to place that spider outside rather than on the underside of our shoe? How are we to cope if we consider that all creatures, plants etc. have that spark of spirit with in them? How can we avoid cruelty?

Well, we need not enter into a resurgence of green-spirited being with a heavy heart and a sense of failing before we even begin. The way to approach this way is to have an *awareness* of the sacred aspect of all who share this verdant place with us and a willingness to do all we can to show our appreciation. Part of our spiritual journey is to foster this way of looking at the world, to give credence and value to the wild heart of every being, not just to see them as ornaments or hindrances to a more important human existence. To have respect in a wholesome healthy way that allows us to walk gently, but realistically, is enough. It is only the wilful ignorance of this that makes us cruel.

If there is any core aspect to a green-spirited way then it is to have an attitude of gratitude to our fellow beings and so, by direct reflection, to the Creator spirit in whatever form we choose to perceive them. We can thank each creature we encounter for its unique being and for walking with us on the journey of life's learning. It is through our fellow creations, from the most bullying dictator to the scuttling shrew, from a mega-tsunami wave to a tender rosebud, that we come to understand the Creator spirit and therefore to establish a direct link with the divine on a daily basis. Our lives become an ongoing spirit-song or prayer when we live this way. Our gratitude and awareness from moment to moment is a paean of praise in itself and an act of the holiest communion. Here is a way of living ideas...of us actually living our understanding from moment to shining moment, and of our growing through this understanding. This we know as 'walking the talk'. In Native American terms it is known as the 'beauty way'. When we walk the beauty way we can awaken to the inherent wisdoms of our own land, wherever that may be, with a heightened awareness and reverence for its energies, its ancestral heart and its deep rhythms.

Green spirituality is about the Earth and our magical lives upon her and so it is organic and alive, unpredictable yet cyclical, subject to the same spurts of growth and periods of dying back, famine and flood, as are all things in nature. Where religion seeks to separate us humans from the Earth, from our fellow beings and their unique and powerful energies, this burgeoning way seeks to unite us once more, reminding us each step of the way of our relationship with the divine. Green-spirited living is about relating to the qualities and attributes inherent in nature, seeing ourselves as having the flexibility of a withy, bending with the winds but never breaking, and the receptiveness of a bat, bouncing its sonar off hedge and wall so that it may find that which sustains it. We know that as humans we are not above these things, that they are our relations in spirit and our equals on this planet.

This green aspect speaks of our experience of divinity as expressed through our response to our environment. It is born of an active respect and deep love of the natural world and a direct appreciation of our part in its ever-unfolding beauty. It therefore involves *eco-activism*, that is, the direct participation of the green-spirited individual in maintaining the right of our living host, Mother Earth, to be treated with respect. This goes for all of her children too as this eco-activism encompasses all aspects of abuse, cruelty and neglect as regards any fellow being. With a green-spirited understanding we know that to hurt one is to hurt all, none of us stand alone without responsibility and equally all of us have access to the wild magic of being. The spiritual dimension of this way is about acknowledging the unseen energy behind each terrestrial (and extra-terrestrial) being, about working with this glorious mystery and not using it for selfish human ends. It is also about learning to travel beyond that which is commonly seen to the Otherworldly levels of existence where enchantment dwells behind the human façade.

Both the manifest and unseen elements of green spirituality weave together seamlessly as we begin to live a more integrated magical life. *Here is a way which combines green issues with magical living . . . natural enchantment meets hands-on working for positive environmental change.* We can learn to cast simple healing spells with the waxing tide of the year, using specially nurtured organic herbs to facilitate increased health. We can dedicate ourselves to writing letters of protest under a dark moon, to banish certain destructive practices such as factory farming. We can chant our wishes for clean air to the wind on a dramatic cliff edge or on a swing in the local park. We can make green-spirited vows to clean up the clogged cave at a local beach and then journey, in deep meditative trance, to the Otherworlds to fulfil the vow in all realms, seeking assistance from the spirits who dwell there. With all that we do we can make 'unseen' and seen gestures, one strengthening and inspiring the other, a deep magical interaction and profound manifest commitment. By this we reinforce a relationship that is often overlooked to the detriment of modern man, a relationship which is as old as the hills, that which bonds the mother and the child, the Earth and ourselves.

Green spirituality is therefore earthy and unearthly. It is holistic and fantastic, at once grounded and yet filled with mystery and wonder. We can bring enchantment into our kitchens as we cook, resonant magic into our gardens as we dig, bring Otherworldly meaning to our routine journeys and a spiritual context to our familiar tasks. With this life-enhancing way we can bring a wild delight into every aspect of that which we once considered to be ordinary and uninspiring. There is no separation, no us and them, no division between what is sacred and what is profane. Our experience is that everything is as the Creator intended: gloriously alive, throbbing with possibility.

So this simple, yet profoundly affecting, green spirituality is about connection, collaboration and celebration. It is about ceasing to think of our fellow inhabitants as resources but as partners in a fabulous dance of being. It is about feeling and experiencing the life force that thrums and hums through each twisted tree and spiral shell, about recognising and exchanging sacred energy for positive purposes. It is a living way, day to day, of finding magic in the midst of a life we once considered to be mundane. By it we experience a much-needed greening of the soul and of the land we live on, and through it we may come to know the wild heart of being once more. With our roots firmly planted in the Mother Earth we may allow our spirits to soar like a buzzard on the eddying currents of profound personal insight, for the good of one and all.

1

Finding the Greenwood

So, how may we begin our own journey to the wild heart of being? Well, our main source of support and guidance on our quest will be the wise ones of the bark, the trees themselves.

Before we begin it may help us to consider the following. When we search for deity, for a source of divine fatherly or motherly support which lies above and beyond the human realm of existence, we usually look to the heavens. To somewhere 'out there'. If we have a modern pagan outlook (pagan in this work meaning 'of the country', a natural green-spirited way which acknowledges the traditions of the ancestors) we may also look to a place deep within the Earth herself, to the hidden regions of ancient myth, the Underworld. Rarely do we ever look to the level of manifest being that we all inhabit on a daily basis for our deities, yet it is here that I will encourage you to look for a true embodiment of divinity. In keeping with the whole ethos of the spiritual expression we are discussing, that which knows verdant magic to be inherent in day to day life, we may look no further than our own back yards, parks, fields and moorlands for the god-like beings we seek. They desire no worship, elicit no sacrifice, and are not among us to condemn or to grant boons. They are simply there to give lovingly, unconditionally, as is the role of any god-like being. The trees, they that bring us clean air to breathe, they that offer us a means to shelter, to find shade, to access deadwood for our hearth, these are the ones we seek.

Their nuts and fruits bring sustenance to many beyond ourselves. Their leaves give nutrients to the soil which in turn yields our harvest. Their very bodies bring us the ability to share the words and images of others, translated onto paper. Their manifest selves, from bark to bud, bring healing, being the source of remedies like the willow's natural aspirin or the hawthorn's heart tonic. More than this they have inspired the artist and the poet with their timeless beauty and simple grace, brought comfort with the solidity of their bodies and reassurance with

11

the unending cycle of their seasonal transitions. They give life, enhance life and support life. They are our sustainers and also our teachers, the wisdom keepers with the knowledge of how to *be*. They are perfect examples to us green-spirited humans of how to express our own true nature effortlessly, as do they. With their flexibility, stability and approachability they offer us the opportunity to interact with the greatest gurus that ever were . . . themselves.

To put this into perspective, it is important to remember that as little as two thousand years ago Britain and most of Europe would have been covered by a lush green woodland, broken only by swathes of gorse-strewn moor, heathery heath or rocky hillside. Trees were once the dominant species of the lands of our ancestors and so had far more right to the title of 'indigenous inhabitants' than say the Celts or the Neolithic builders of the great henges and barrows. These human tribes, and their ancestors, lived in a Europe that was deeply forested and they relied heavily on the trees for their basic needs. Their dependency on the wise ones of the bark was not purely selfish, however, and the tribal peoples felt the power and enchantment of these incredible original inhabitants. Oak, ash and thorn were among those they revered, and for the longest time they were afforded the same respect as the grandmothers and fathers of their tribes, if not more so. The native peoples of European lands knew the sacred had manifested most profoundly among them as the tree-beings, their benefactors, and therefore a great magic was associated with them and paramount importance given to their well-being. Trees were certainly not treated as the expendable, albeit attractive, commodities that they are today. In those times, the times we need not seek to emulate but rather to honour, the land and the native trees were not seen as part of a glorious stage on which humanity may enact its dramas. No, the land was an integral part of the tribe, not a backdrop apart from it, and consequently there was a sense of interconnectedness which gave rise to a quiet responsibility. This responsibility was based on the premise that '*what we do to the land we do to ourselves*' the two were considered inseparable, the people being bound to the soil which was enriched by their predecessors' blood and bones. The trees which grew most eloquently from this soil were valued as part of the people as well as being considered excellent role models and magical guardians.

The trees are still our finest examples of living well that we have among us. If only we take the time to observe and understand them, as our tribal fore bearers did, we will have immediate access to the great mystery of life made manifest with simple fluidity. With effortless grace and great ingenuity the tree-beings reach towards the heavens and yet remain rooted far into the earth with unfailing certainty, their bodies acting as the conduit between soil and sky, matter and spirit. They unite us, above and below, they are the links to both the airy levels of insight and idea and the profound levels at the wild wise core, deep within. Our green spirituality leads us to a place where we too may be as connected to the sacred land as the trees themselves whilst remaining in tune with our own human spiritual selves and staying receptive to the greater universal energies. Trees are the bridge builders (both literally, using their physical bodies to span rivers or chasms, and in terms of their ability to link the seen and the unseen, above and below) that allow us to see how we can be grounded whilst reaching for the stars. If we need to seek that which is beyond us yet part of our daily experience, a transformative being which has access to the transcendent as well as the dark primal womb of the Earth, then here are our gods.

We may well have heard of the maxim that 'all the gods are one god', meaning that although we may acknowledge the divine source by one name, or via one set of attributes, we cannot so limit the ultimate expression of the sacred and should therefore acknowledge that we are witnessing but one face of an integral being. We can apply this truth here and say that all the trees are one tree, that the tree we witness with our eyes is a representative of a greater force. Although each has its own resonance (as do we) and its own innate soul-type (for each is as spirit-full as are we) the trees are so adept at being themselves, so fully attuned to the natural way and the ebb and flow of the universe, that they are as one with each other. They are representatives of *Tree*, with a capital T. We can refer to this collective tree-nature as the World Tree.

There is no singular World Tree for us to go and commune with *physically* (although we may do so spiritually in the Otherworldly realms) yet the divine attributes and wisdoms of the World Tree are inherent in all trees. The ash in the local farmer's field may express its own uniqueness, its *soul-song*, in a variety of ways (to us it may seem cheeky, mysterious or any variation on the theme of a singular person- ality) but beyond that it is a representative of the World Tree, part of the larger collective *Tree*. Indeed it was the ash that the Scandinavian peoples revered as the World Tree, referring to it by the magical name Yygdrasil. The Bodhi has the position of the World Tree in the Buddhist faith as it was under a Bodhi tree that the Buddha once sat to achieve enlightenment. So passionate was Ashoka, Emperor of India, about this tree that he asked each citizen to plant and nurture five trees per

13

year...not only for their own benefit but for universal inspiration and the enlightenment of all. The Tongan myths refer to the World Tree as Akau-lea, the Tree of Speech. It is also referred to as The Tree of Life in the Jewish or Near Eastern Qabalah as well as the Tree of Knowledge, a term it shares with the Celtic perception of the apple tree. In Celtic myth it was from three apples growing on this primary tree that three precious drops fell into a cauldron belonging to the formidable mother goddess, Cerridwen, bringing the inspiration from which all beings derive their life-force or creativity...the *Awen*. The Celts also revered the oak as the World Tree, due to its longevity and consequent great size, not to mention the wide variety of life it is able to sustain in its boughs and trunk. The oak is indeed one of the most widely revered trees in the world due to its obvious strength and ability to protect. Indeed, King Arthur's round table was said to have been made from a single giant slab of oak. In many Native American traditions the World Tree is seen as a pine and it also has the beautiful names of the Tree of Peace or the Great Earth Tree.

It is important for us to understand these ancestral ways in a poetic sense as we can again access our own sense of rootedness by knowing we are continuing an ancient understanding, a globally accepted wisdom. However, we need not get too bogged down in any one version as the rowan in a neighbour's garden or the elder by the busy road have just as much access to the great tree spirit and are to us as much a part of this unifying energy, this 'World Tree-ness', as the ash, oak or the Bodhi. We need not hold one species above another like this although through the course of our experience as green-spirited individuals we may have experience of hearing each tree's unique soul-song as well as the soul-song of its species and the greater song of the World Tree. Just as we have the singular melody our own spirit brings along with an overlay of our current manifest gender, race or creed, we also carry the traits of humanity as whole. This blend is a kind of three-part harmony that all beings emit and something we will return to throughout the book. Trees are particularly adept at expressing their innate energies, this three-part resonance, being wholly unconcerned with the clutter and artifice of modern 'civilisation'. They bring us back to the wild heart because that is where they dwell, abidingly. They are the teachers of magic that is spontaneous and gloriously undiluted.

As we have already considered, as we walk on our green-spirited way we will blend the manifest and the ethereal, combining that which we can do now, in this moment (that which is concerned with the land and her eternal greening), with the unseen or Otherworldly aspects of being (that which may be deemed of the spirit). We can learn to access this latter more nebulous aspect through techniques such as the trance journey. This book, and the work which stems from it, is all about this seamless weaving of three magical strands into one shining cloth of gold, of taking the threads of what we do in the world, who we uniquely are and what spiritually lies within and beyond us and passing them lovingly back and forth, under and over, the loom of our lives. So, let us begin now by blending a manifest journey and a spiritual trance journey in order for us to understand the concepts we discuss fully, not only intellectually but as a deep inner reality, a heartfelt truth. We will go on a quest to find a special tree in nature, locally in our area, and we will also become acquainted with the World Tree, that representative of all trees that dwells in the Otherworldly realms.

INNER AND OUTER JOURNEYS TO MEET THE TREES

The combination of contemplative inner (spiritual) exploration with active working, be it in service of others or as personal creative expression, means that we are living our way, not just talking about it, or even thinking about it. *Prayer in practice* is one of the simplest ways to put this, our Earth-honouring spirituality which blends the corporeal with the more transcendental aspects of existence is a way of being; it is meditation on the move. In the next chapters we will look more at this vital combination of 'soil, soul and society' (a phrase first used by the peace pilgrim Satish Kumar) that is our prayer in practice. However, even though our way is an interactive one it doesn't mean that we cannot pray in a more traditional sense also. Before we begin this exercise it may be beneficial for us to do just that.

What follows is a suggestion for such a prayer. As we are going to be engaging in an exercise which allows us to forge deeper relationships with the wise ones of the bark, via one special tree and the World Tree, the prayer should have a sylvan feel. Without such feelings our prayers are dead things, done out of duty. We are not praying here to God, or the gods in a specific sense (as we are probably used to doing when we think of prayer), but to that which is inherently sacred, to the divine as it is expressed in leaf and branch. We are sending a message of love and of loving intent to a valued part of creation and, in so doing, are honouring the Creator also. We are not praying to beseech or petition for favours, we are simply creating a paean of praise that expresses our gratitude and appreciation and tells of what we wish to do and how we wish to do it.

'*Oh tree, ever-growing, all-knowing,*
Tree at the heart of all being,
Whose fruits are as the kernels of truth I seek,
Whose roots are as my own veins,
Whose trunk is as my spine
Whose branches my limbs, reaching ever higher,
Whose singing sap is my blood, free-flowing,
Please witness my yearning for the wisdom you keep,
My honest desire to touch treasures beyond gold.

Oh sentinel, born of the first seed-fire,
Lover of loam, caresser of clouds,
Generous host who offers safe haven,
Sustainer of both grub and bright bird,
First dweller, gathered in glade and grove,
Hear my affection, softly spoken,
See the purity of my intent, shining like leaves after rain.

Oh tree, I seek the sanctity of your eternal mystery,
The magical reality of your endless charity.'

It is an inbuilt urge for some of us modern westerners to end such a soul-prayer with 'Amen'. However, we are not obliged to do so here, especially if this has no real meaning for us. Too often we are encouraged in our secular society to repeat, parrot-fashion, words which have no resonance with us! Now would be a good time to consciously rid ourselves of some of that baggage, carried from childhood, and create our own ending to a prayer. What is it we are saying as we end a prayer? Are we beseeching, dedicating, wishing? Well, when I created the above prayer I thought of saying 'as it is, so may it be', thus establishing that 'my hopes shall become reality, in accordance with natural way of things'. As further examples, 'as I have spoken between all realms, let it be so' or 'in the name of all that is wholly holy, I give up my prayer', or even 'in the name of truth and love let my prayer be heard and accepted'. A particularly green-spirited way of ending our heartfelt plea or celebratory piece may be 'may all that crawl, fly, swim, grow and stand hear my words and accept them as gifts'. Any variation on a theme may be employed and this can be as personal to you as you like, as long as it has meaning and resonates with us as individuals. One size does not fit all in a spiritual sense; we can and should create a bespoke service which gives us pleasure and fulfilment. Prayer without any sense of personal involvement or emotion is a prayer bereft of a reason to exist. I believe it was the Native American medicine teacher Sun Bear who exhorted us to leave behind our 'canned prayers'. Fashioning our own prayers, no matter how simple or poetic, means that we have begun to engage with the subject, our thoughts being gathered and honed into one profound outpouring. That effort, that interaction, is worth a great deal.

Now we have a prayer, or an idea of how to lovingly create our own version, we should decide where and how we wish to release it. For the purpose of our work here we will be making a journey, on foot if physically possible, to a place of vibrant green energy, a place where trees grow. This is for the specific purpose of meeting a special tree, a tree that will act as our teacher and inspiration for a time. Offering up our prayer before we leave on this journey is a wonderful way of stating that we are about to undertake something which means a lot to us, something which marks our stepping away from our old way of interacting with the world. We can integrate this offering into a simple pleasing ritual and I will suggest how we can go about this shortly.

This journey is a wild pilgrimage of sorts, albeit one which will take us hours rather than days or weeks, and should be approached with a light heart and focused intent. We should designate a time when we will be entirely free without pressures of time etc. and give this undertaking the space it deserves as a valid act. If we have the ability to walk then it is vital that we make this journey on foot, or if we cannot walk then we should travel via any manner of transport that allows us to take in our immediate environs without a pane of glass between us and *it*...it being nature. When we put a window between us and nature, as we so often do, we immediately reinforce that separation, that 'us and them' attitude which is so prevalent today and is endemic in the abuse of the land and her inhabitants. We can, by undertaking such a journey (however short), make the commitment to spending as much time 'up close and personal' with nature as we can, resisting the temptation to placing an artificial barrier between ourselves and the 'outside' as much as possible. By this we state *'we are one another, part of the same wild spirit, I am the land and the land is me.'*

As an aside here, I am writing this piece out of doors with my bottom firmly on the floor and an ant crawling over my left knee on which my laptop is balanced! I wouldn't preach unless I too was fully committed to practise this myself!

17

The purpose of the walk is not only to find a special friend but also to strengthen our ability to be 'in the present' with all that is happening around us. It is for us to be observing how the local plants and creatures behave at that moment, for us to re-learn how the gift of that day, at that particular time, feels to us. The walk therefore can be any length as long as it gives us a chance to re-acquaint ourselves with the exquisitely performed dance of the natural world with no external pressures to distract us. It is a time for us to return to that way of being by which we feel included in the dance. Ultimately we will, as our green spirituality blossoms and blooms, understand that the dancer and the dance are one and the same but for now we should actively pursue that idea until it becomes a reality.

So, is it enough to aim for a local area which is home to a variety of tree-beings? Well, no. The way we walk as green-spirited individuals also may be said to be 'off the beaten track', that is, it is the road less travelled which leads us to the wild heart of being and not the well lit, overly manicured route. Therefore our track may take us to urban waste ground where a single magnificent, but entirely forgotten, holly tree grows. Or it may lead us to the windswept side of a lonely moor where a twisted hawthorn shrugs its gnarly shoulders against the prevailing winds. It may lead us to the stunted alder which grows in the park away from the footpaths or to the crack willow, full of rotten hollows and cankers, which stoops over a local stream. Where it will not take us is to the most obvious human-centric place which will be highly populated by tourists, and it will not necessarily lead us to the most visually impressive copper beech or magnificent old oak. The trees in such places are obviously as sacred as any other tree but their location will not afford us the quiet personal space that we need to establish an ongoing bond. Also, trees in such frequented places, or trees which are obviously attractive or impressive and so gain much attention, may be so used to humanity as to feel disinclined to engage in such a close friendship. Such trees will probably spend a great deal of their time giving to people as it is. My advice is instead to be soul-led to the places where you may know that trees grow (on the overgrown banks of a disused railway line, for example) and actively seek out those which may be entirely overlooked by the majority. Seek a friend off the beaten track whose resonance, rather than appearance, calls to you.

Before we set out we will also need to consider taking a gift with us on our journey, a gesture of friendship for the tree. When we get to know our tree companion we will learn to ask what it is that it would like us to bring, but for now it is for us to decide what would be an uncomplicated biodegradable present. In my own experience, trees like a gift of a beverage which can be poured around their root area so that they may taste it. They also generally appreciate a token for their own companions, the birds and small creatures who find a home with them. Remember also that we are considering very earthy beings here and so consequently a gift of beer and oatcakes can go down well. In the past I have been asked for orange juice and banana so that the tree may get a taste of unusual flavours. Milk is often requested and I know that whiskey is acceptable also, as well as any light homemade cordial. For now a safe bet is a good organic ale and a wholesome oaty cake or a chunk of home baked wholemeal bread. Certainly do not think of anything artificial or carbonated: this would be rather insulting unless we genuinely believe that such things are beneficial to ourselves or others. A tree is, after all, used to water and sunlight; we do not wish to shock it with harsh chemically enhanced gifts.

Why take anything at all? Well, besides it being polite as we are going to be introducing ourselves as guests in that tree's personal space (and visitors often take tokens of gratitude), it also serves as a symbol that we are willing to give as well as receive. Our taking an unrefined, unsophisticated and wholly natural gift to the tree states that we are hoping for a relationship which is a two-way process, not typically another way for a human being to take, take, take and never replenish. Green spirituality is primarily about replenishment, about the rejection of selfish short-sighted greed which leads to depletion and ultimately extinction, and part of this is the practice of compassionate courtesy to our fellow beings. Everything we seek in the world begins with us and so if we decide to gift every being we meet, be that with a word of praise, a listening ear, a helping hand or an offering of sustenance, then we become generosity, we embody the spirit of open-handed clear-hearted kindness that the world so needs. All we need ask is 'how may I be of service to you this day?' not in a fawning way but with an authentic desire to share what we have. When we freely give of ourselves, as do the trees, we keep the energy moving, allowing that which is good to pass unhindered from one to the next, as nature intended. There is much wild magic in this flow, and all sorts of remarkable things happen when we become a part of it ourselves.

With this in mind is it then appropriate to take *things* to a tree, or to a special place like a waterfall, or to a spirit we encounter in the landscape? Here in the UK we often see trees, especially hawthorn, tied with 'clouties' ... pieces of cotton rag which are wished upon for healing purposes. This is simple sympathetic magic, as the rag biodegrades so the healing spell is released and the sick person gets well again. Hopefully this is always done by those who first consult the tree and ask its permission to tie the cloutie. However, in recent times these gentle symbols of country magic have been joined by other gifts or offerings, ranging from crystal jewellery to glittery mobile phone cases, plastic key rings to car air fresheners. It seems as if the ancient custom of cloutie tying has been expanded to include anything one may have about one's person at that moment in time. Yes, we could say that these may be gifts left with a good heart and should be acknowledged as such but that which does not break down into the soil to replenish it is less of a boon and more of a burden. Petitioning for healing by knotting a small piece of natural fibre certainly isn't in the same league as leaving our detritus hanging on a branch in order to ask for something in return. That is just as rude as taking an inappropriate gift to a friend in the hope that they'll give you something better!

As we will discover soon, each tree not only has its own spiritual essence but it has accompanying nature spirits too, independent beings who guard and cherish their partner-tree. Just as each of us has a familiar companion spirit, or indeed several such companions (as we will discuss in chapter three) so do the trees, rocks etc. Similarly each area of land has its resident protective spirit . . . more of this in the next chapter! By inappropriately adorning green or non-human beings with gifts which will not break down into the soil we are probably offending both tree, rock, river, etc. *and* the accompanying spirit. This not only because their existence was ignored but because the object is manufactured and not easily assumed into the site to replenish it. Remember, trees (and obviously their companion nature spirits) are completely a part of the bionetwork and will not readily accept 'things' which were created apart from the natural way, things like plastic which remain intact despite the administrations of water wind and sun, insects and bacteria. To them it compounds the notion that humans are inconsiderate, polluting creatures who have no respect, no compassionate courtesy. I myself have witnessed the nature spirits who guard places getting hopping mad over human insensitivity and I have had to concur with them! Although occasionally we may be asked to bring something special as a gift to a place, like a piece of silver jewellery for instance, please do keep to simple personal offerings like hair or hand-dyed cotton velvet which can easily be absorbed or reused by birds in nest building. Steer away from that which is artificial or created away from the wild spirit.

So, we have our organic gift ready and have decided in which direction we may wander on our tree walk. Now on our appointed day we may step outside and release our prayer. What follows is a suggestion for how to do this. As with all exercises in this book, please do adapt it in any way to suit your own physical abilities. If our own garden affords us no solitude, or if we have no garden, then we may move to a place nearby where we may gain a little privacy. There we should find some earth, avoiding concrete or tarmac, although natural stone or wood would suffice if there were no soil and grass. If it is at all feasible, remove shoes and socks and plant the feet squarely on the earth. We should then take three long slow deep breaths, allowing the abdomen to inflate with each in breath and deflate with each exhalation. Feel the ground beneath our feet and know that this is the skin of the mother, of whom we are a part. We can be aware of all those who inhabit the soil beneath us, just as the trees know the writhing ones in the darkness at their roots. Now we can feel our own roots growing, snaking down the taproot of the spine, sprouting from the soles of our feet and pushing down into the earth below, seeking purchase in the rich damp loam. Now stretch our arms to the sky and spread the fingers, seeking sunlight, clean air and water. Remain like this for a few moments, allowing that connection above and below to become established. Now is the time to release the prayer, whilst feeling that link between trees and our human selves. Now stoop down and rest on one knee and touch our fingers to our forehead in a gesture of reverence of our own being and then touch the earth lightly with the tips of our fingers to give her reverence also. See the soil, our fingers, and any other beings such as blades of grass or insects that share that moment with us.

We are now ready to begin the walk!

Here is an opportunity for us to really be ourselves, in the precious present, absorbing the sights, smells and sensations inherent in that unique experience. Endeavour to keep our breathing deep and our senses keen. If possible walk tall and straight, remembering our spine as a tree trunk or a great trunk-mirroring taproot, supporting us. At first this may be a struggle but if we persevere it will come more naturally to us. Note anything or anyone that crosses our path, observe that which takes our attention away from the simple rhythmic act of walking with full awareness, and consider that which makes us feel elation or revulsion as we encounter it along with anything which inspires or angers us. Keep tuning yourself in to the sounds and smells that are around us and away from busy human thoughts about work etc. Think of this walk as being a meditation in which we simply have an awareness of such cluttered invasive thoughts but can let them float away. Do take the time to stop, stare and touch but when walking aim for a rhythm which suits. It is beneficial for us to slip into our natural pace and not always be governed by dictates of time and the avoidance of traffic, both human and otherwise. It is a rare treat perhaps for us to find this innate rhythm at all, so we can enjoy moving to our own beat!

How will we know when we have reached the right tree? Well, there is no right tree, only the one that draws us to it, rather like a person whose voice we single out beyond all others in a crowded noisy room because we like its pitch or tone or the sentiment of its speech. If we continue to keep the message of the tree prayer in our hearts then we will attract the attention of one who wishes to assist us, as trees are adept at responding to such emanations. They hear voices on the wind, in the rustles, murmurs and creaks of their bodies and those of others. They are attuned to the vibrations in the earth of each passing creature, be they rumbles or barely perceptible patterings, so they will know we are there if we send out our silent energetic call to them. And how will we know when our message is responded to? Even for those of us who think we are unable to pick up on atmospheres or feelings there will be a deep and very real sense of knowing for us, as if someone very familiar has just greeted us yet we do not yet know their name. A very real sense of 'oh, it's *you*!' a joyous reunion. If we insist on ignoring or dismissing such intuitive messages we may even find that the tree will trip us up with a root to gain our attention, or tangle our hair or whip off our hat with its branches. If in doubt, we should close our eyes for a moment and sense the environment around us. Then we should mentally send out the call from our prayer, the genuine request that we are looking for a teacher tree, and then listen and feel. An idea that we perhaps should walk a different route could occur to us, or likewise a notion that we should retrace our steps. Anything could happen so be accepting of it and follow, within reason, any gentle prodding or advice!

We may already have a tree in mind but when we reach it find that it is not responsive to us at all. If this happens then do not be disheartened. This is a valuable part of our green-spirited work, to know that we cannot plan everything to the minutest detail and that we have to have some flexibility when we work as part of nature. During the course of our lifetime as magical seekers of truth we will encounter torrential rain and gale force winds when we have planned an outdoor ceremony or find that footpaths are closed, streams dammed up and that fruit and flowers we wanted to work with can appear late, early or not at all! To be like a tree and bend a little when the need arises is another lesson for us. So if we find that on our first journey we encounter no such tree then do not be discouraged. We should simply take the opportunity to enjoy the chance of being in the moment with nature and concentrate instead on strengthening our powers of observation, as being *in the now* with what is happening around us is an invaluable skill for the green-spirited person to re-acquire. Then we can vow to take another walk when the time is right, perhaps to a new area which will suggest itself to us if we have a more relaxed approach about the whole affair. The light heartedness of our being does not mean we are being disrespectful or not taking matters seriously, rather it means that we know we will get more benefit if we are gentle on ourselves, as well as on our fellow beings, and take life as it comes, minute by minute.

Whenever or however we find our tree we can then spend some precious time introducing ourselves and giving the tree space to respond. This encounter is no different from us meeting a new human being socially. Perhaps it is more like a blind date! We wanted to meet this tree but have no real knowledge of its unique character or physical make up. With this in mind, we don't need to spend the whole time chattering on about ourselves and what we want or need from such a relationship. If that is how we behave with other people we are intro-duced to then we probably don't get to see them again as such behaviour, even if it is done from nerves, seems self-absorbed. Instead sit or stand in front of the tree. Now do the equivalent of looking it straight in the eyes, take in the features that are closest to our eye-level. We can, if it seems right, now make a bodily connection, resting a palm lightly on the bark in a gesture of greeting. Unless we are in the habit of rushing at folk you have just met with a great hug we shouldn't wrap ourselves around the tree just yet! It may or may not like such contact so soon and it's best, as ever, to be courteous to its needs as well as our own. Not all trees like to be hugged on the first date! All beings have a personal space that should be respected, after all, and a nature which will make them respond differently to physical contact. What makes us feel better may make them feel infringed upon. This is not a typical human encounter with nature. We are aiming to move away from that human-centric approach to re-establish our sensitivity to the feelings of other species.

If this seems a little daunting, putting us on our best behaviour, then relax! Being ourselves, albeit a gentle, responsive and courteous self, is the very best way to begin and maintain any relationship. And here's something really important to remember when we are out on our own, engaging in a dialogue with a tree...we have full permission from now on *never* to feel foolish about talking to non-human beings! If our green spirituality is to be a truly living way, a viable alternative to modern conventional thinking, then we should be proud to acknowledge that we do not see the wise ones of bark and branch as being dead. Just because other beings have no human voice, or human ears to hear, it doesn't mean they are deaf and dumb. We live in a realm of sentient beings who speak in other languages, by other means, and that is all. The fact that our world is alive is a cause for celebration, not shame or embarrassment, so let us all find the strength to commune openly and with dignity with whomsoever we please!

A Romany once said to me that trees find it impolite when humans sit with their backs to them, i.e. resting on them, when they are talking and in my experience trees do prefer to be related to directly as do any of us! So, for this meeting do remain seated or standing facing the tree. If we want to look up, or around it, to get a full measure of its physical stature, then ask if we may, or, if we feel that we won't be able to tell if it's right or wrong at this stage, inform the tree what we are doing and ask its pardon if it minds. We could ask for the tree to show us its response in quite a physical way if we are convinced we cannot pick up subtler signs or emanations to begin with. Perhaps we will find ourself pelted with nuts by a squirrel high in the branches or showered in blossom. However the interaction progresses the main thing is that we do not spend the whole time doing what we want but rather just be with the tree with a clear mind and an openness to receive its messages. Take some silent space to just feel what it feels like to be near this wise being. This feeling is more important than anything as it is beyond words and enters the deep realm of soul-to-soul contact. Breathe deeply of the scent around the tree, note who and what lives on and near it. Witness the smoothness or creases of the tree-being's skin; see if it has any signs of growth on the trunk, like human stretch marks. Is it healthy? How has it grown towards the light and what does that tell us about its nature and immediate environs? Hold a fallen leaf or twig and enjoy its colour and texture. Perhaps we will be given something like this as a gift of our budding friendship, to take away with us.

As a word of advice here, many of us are exceedingly out of practice at using our listening and observational skills. A basic course in counselling training, run at a local college, can give these tired skills a boost and give us a heightened awareness of what it is to be fully present for another being. With elementary training we will learn to look for visual cues as well as sensing what is happening for someone beyond what they say: we 'listen' with far more than our ears.

Perhaps on this first visit the tree will give us a sense that it is male, female, indifferent to gender, young, old, genial, stern or any other number of characteristics that are not available as purely visual cues but which can be picked up, or intuited, nonetheless. Consider that we may be the first human to give it time and space to communicate and it may therefore either be a little unsure of such communication or so effusive as to bombard us with images, feelings and messages straight away. This is an individual matter and again do not think that because our tree said little or too much that this is the wrong tree or the wrong way of going about things. We may be given a name to refer to the tree by at this stage although this is quite rare in my experience. Trees are beings that rely on resonance and vibration and so their names are usually sounds rather than human titles. With this in mind do not feel frustrated if you know no name to give to the tree in question. Persevere with our open and generous attitude and relate to it as 'tree' or 'oak' or whatever it suggests – don't let expectation of a wholly human-style interaction, complete with names, discourage us.

When we offer the tree the gifts we have brought give it time to respond. Consider what it may like next time; hear what it may have to say. Only repeated visits and much 'tuning in', in quiet repose, will give us the insights we desire from this green being. Afterwards thank the tree and ask it if we may visit it again.

Let us go against the mode of modern humanity, going instead with the natural flow, and give our interactions the time they deserve. We may take this opportunity to decide that we can no longer go full pelt as society encourages, impatiently discarding that which is not instantly gratifying. Anything worth having or knowing needs a measure of perseverance, a willingness to stick with it unconditionally. Perhaps we can make a simple pledge to honour this way of being more fully in our lives. We can then consider how this pledge may be fulfilled as we walk homewards. Following our new ethos of *soil, soul and society* (the concept which is the weathered, mossy but infinitely reliable cornerstone of our green spirituality) we can begin to understand the following:

Soul

Being more attentive and giving all things the time they deserve will fulfil us more deeply at a *soul* level. We can consider our walking in nature's (not society's) time as a gift to our spirit, a way of authentically valuing this life of ours and the fabulous insights and experiences that are present in the moment, if only we take time to appreciate them. This means having all our senses switched on and not running on 'automatic pilot' any longer, adopting a pace of life which allows for an 'attitude of gratitude'. This is the difference in experiencing 'life through a window', or through the lens of another's direct contact as we witness it on television, and honouring creation as we alone can perceive it. We can create a small prayer to reflect this, saying something like:

> *'In the eternal sacred round of existence,*
> *There are always returns.*
> *May there be a return now, to valuing that which is found*
> *In the gift of the now, the present.*
>
> *May this return bring an awakening of appreciation,*
> *A fecund joy at the bounty of creation,*
> *A walking in time with the beat of life,*
> *An awareness of the steady pulse of all being.*
>
> *May there be a greening of the senses,*
> *May there be a knowing of wonder,*
> *And may there be the time taken, always, to pause and give praise.*
>
> *May all of these things begin with me, today.'*

Or if we prefer a more vibrant active affirmation we can fashion a rhyming chant to be spoken or sung as we walk, thus echoing our steady 'inner' beat of our footsteps. Repeated rhyming chants set to a beat are a wonderful way of making what we desire a magical reality. The benefit of chanting like this is threefold: (i) The *repetition* 'fixes' the wish into our consciousness. (ii) The *beat* allows for a meditative state to come about in which such fixing occurs at a more profound level. (iii) The *releasing* of words by vocalising in a pleasing melodious way, aided by the rhyme and metre, allow the words to be carried onwards and outwards into the wider world.

Here is an example or such a simple green-spirited chant for this purpose. Note the pattern or cadence of the chant which would become stronger each time we repeat it. It may suggest a tune to us as we read or speak it aloud:

> *'Let me know each vein and hair,*
> *Each movement in the fox's lair,*
> *And in the greenwood stand and stare,*
> *At that which nature has to share.*

26

Let me know each seed and shoot,
Both prickled stem and velvet fruit,
With senses searching like deep roots,
I'll hear the voices of the mute.

Let me stroll as others run,
And raise my gaze to the blessed sun,
This is no race but I have won,
For I see the land I walk upon!'

Soil

We can then consider the matter of *soil*. How may we give a pledge to the land that we will endeavour from now on to walk with more consideration, giving time to that which is valuable in terms other than money or prestige? We could vow to plant a tree from found seeds this autumn and spend time nurturing it and observing its progress from tiny sapling to full grown adult. We could begin to make our own organic compost, closely watching the process of rotting and returning to the earth which occurs.

Society

What of *society*, and how may we honour this pledge in a wider social context? Well, we could gift some of our precious time to a conservation project that was primarily associated with trees or woodland management. If this is physically unfeasible then we could join a conservation body as a supporting member rather than an active one, or we could raise awareness of conservation issues by writing letters to the local press etc., something which is time consuming but highly worthwhile. We could talk to others we meet at work or offer to give a small talk in our child's school on the importance of trees and their lifecycle etc., encouraging personal observation through tree planting. Whatever we do now it will make a statement of intent that is honoured in the spiritual and physical sense, one backing up and supporting the other, thus making it a very real thing on all levels of existence. We are saying *'my values are different now'* and acting on that.

This brings us on to the keeping of a journal for the purpose of noting down all that we experience in magical terms, a record of how we act in that vital blend of spiritual and manifest green-spirited work. Such a journal helps us to understand how we have progressed and can be used to note down ideas as well as to log all of our interactions. It is so easy, despite all the good intentions in the world, to forget how we celebrated a seasonal transition one year ago, or to recall any spiritual guidance we may receive as we move on to working with our unseen mentors (more of this in the next chapters). For now, consider what sort of book would be fitting for such a journal, that which is to be a diary of natural enchantment and environmental action. Although any paper and ink would plainly do it may be nice to invest in a special bound book made of beautiful recycled paper and a pen which could be dipped in a natural ink. However, anything we can do to manifestly reinforce our spiritual ethos of homespun reverence for the environment is important so we can feasibly make our own paper and ink too, if we feel that is an area we would like to dedicate our burgeoning love of the green beings, and our time, too. Here are some very basic suggestions for paper and ink creation which fits with our path of complete respect for our Mother Earth whilst celebrating the fact that she gives us the resources to create everything we need.

PAPER MAKING

This is a very messy but satisfying process! To prepare we can collect used envelopes and paper that are not too heavily ink-soiled. These should be shredded or torn into small fragments and soaked in water. Along with this, collect anything beautiful and natural, petals, leaf skeletons, crushed bark or twig, wool caught on a fence etc. A special magical walk could be taken to find such items. We can also incorporate any old scraps of cotton material too tatty to give to a charity shop, thus recycling them. Old newspapers should also be kept also but not shredded and soaked.

We will also need to create a frame the size that we require our paper to be, a simple rectangle covered with stretched fine mesh in metal or nylon. Any suitable framed mesh will do for this, if we can find one ready made. Think of a tennis racquet's head, only square with a finer mesh! (Of course we can use a round or oval frame but we will then get round or oval paper sheets!)

Two or three handfuls of our soaked recycled paper should be liquidized (with water) in a kitchen blender until a 'gruel' is created. Tip this into a large plastic container of water, such as a child's storage box, along with some of the natural found material. Then do then next few handfuls etc. until all of the material and recycled paper is in the container of water. We should stir it well, focusing on any outcome we desire. This maybe as simple as the desire to create stunning paper or it may be a wish for all beings to recycle and re-create. At this stage we may also add an essential oil, for scent, or a little grated natural soap which gives a smoother finish to the paper and so aids our writing upon it in the future.

Dip the frame into the container and allow the water to run through. Tip the fame slightly to encourage full drainage. The material should be only slowly dripping when we are ready to proceed.

We then need to fashion a 'couching mound'. On a flat surface fold a large (broadsheet) double sheet of newsprint in half. Then take a second double piece and fold it three times and place in on top of the first. Then add another folded twice and another folded once on top again . . . this should make a mounded effect, raised in the centre. On the top of all these sheets place an unsoiled cleaning cloth, the sort referred to as a 'j-cloth'.

We should hold our frame over the cloth and then flip it carefully so that the material is directly pressed into the cloth raised in the centre. We can then gently encourage the material to part company with the mesh by smoothing our fingers over the back of it. Now flip the frame gently back again.

What remains should be an intact sheet. If it isn't then tip it back into the tank and repeat until the process is successful. If we are happy with a sheet that isn't ripped then place another j-cloth over the top for protection so that the prospective paper sheet is in a sandwich of cloth. Place another cloth over this covering one and begin again. We can have up to five sheets of material before we will have to begin a new pile. With the old pile, cover the top sheet with a cloth and lift it off the paper mound carefully.

Now fold some more newspaper and cover an ordinary wooden kitchen chopping board. Place the pile down on the paper and then cover the top j-cloth with another sheet of newsprint. Now use a second chopping board as a pressing weight to remove any remaining moisture. Place it on the top. This can be further evenly weighted using any heavy available object . . . the aim is to make a successful 'press'.

The final part of the process is drying, as to make it as natural as possible peg the sheets on a line, indoors or out.

INK OR DYE MAKING

Here is a beautiful and ancient art that our ancestors would have been entirely familiar with.

First we need to identify our need and then safely and ethically select and identify our plant.

So, what do we need the ink to write about . . . for example, is our subject matter to be love, strength, protection, green vows etc.? In future we may need to identify just one aspect but here we are discussing our journal writing so it is not specific but can include all of these aspects of being. Therefore we are fairly open and can allow instinct to draw us to the sort of colour we would like, or to the magical/medicinal properties of the plant which will provide us with it. Here is a basic guide to some of the green beings who can help us in this process:

- The elder gives us blue-violet from its berries.
- Dandelions give orangey-brown from their roots and yellow from new flowers.
- Nettles give greeny-gold.
- Onion skins give a bright golden-brown.
- Ash leaves give a subtle yellow.
- Woad leaves give the familiar blue of ancestral body art.
- Madder root gives a lovely red, hence 'rose madder' as a hue for paint. Its Latin name is *Rubia tinctorum*, the *tinctorum* of which gives us the knowledge that it was used for dyeing: think of 'tint'.
- Walnuts or coffee grounds for a rich shiny darkish-brown.
- Weld gives yellow.
- Work with calendula for a sunny glow.

And there are many more easily found or grown plants and vegetables such as dock, red cabbage, forsythia, sloes, blackberries, oak bark, bracken and camomile which give good results. Some are obvious in the hue they will provide, others less so like the oak gall (created by wasps) which, although reddish-brown, make a black colour when boiled up and steeped which would be excellent for ink. Experiment with any non-poisonous plants, non-endangered, with their permission. We can grow our own especially for the purpose, from organic seed in a peat free compost, and see the process through from beginning to end.

When we have responsibly harvested the plant we wish to work with then we should crush the gift we have been given, be that root, leaf, flower or stem, and steep it in water in a large stainless steel pot or pan. After boiling it for an hour, allow it to steep again for as long as we wish, for up to three days, stirring occasionally. All sorts of variables can affect the result as well as this part of the process. These are natural affects wrought by the nature of the growing season, current and past weather, time of day/month/year upon gathering etc. and go to impress upon us the delicate, meaningful interactions of the natural world. Making ink or dye is an education in itself and a great way of becoming more profoundly acquainted with the green being in question as well as with the seasonal fluctuations that affect us all.

When we have brewed ourselves an ink that we find pleasing we can then store it in a lovely bottle, perhaps one we have recycled or found in a second-hand shop. Even if the bottle itself is plain we can decorate it using glass paint with a personal symbol or a favourite design. Better still we could create a glyph that represents the plant person that donated us the leaves/bark etc. in the first place, to honour them and add in our own motif, to represent a relationship between ourselves and the green beings. The bottle could then be sealed using a specially cut cork, recycled from a wine bottle perhaps, a recognition of a natural material and the tree that donated it originally.

The whole study of natural dye making is an exciting one and can lead into a whole new area of exploration when we consider colouring our own unbleached cotton or homespun wool. A material that has been treated with care using home-grown or handpicked leaves, barks etc. would be so much more powerful (or personally resonant) than a poor old chemically treated piece that had 'been through the mill' in more ways than one, rendered quite soulless as part of a wider commercial process. As we seek to bring the magic back into our daily lives it would be a satisfying thing for us to engage in the process of what we wear or use in such a way. Indeed, if we cannot weave, spin or sew (or have no inclination to engage in this area of crafting) then at least we can hand-dye a piece of recycled cotton to make a simple folded magical pouch to be tied with a cord or to make a healing 'cloutie'. We can then oversee the process from start to finish, a very healing thing to do as it gives us back a sense of connection and further removes us from being merely a 'consumer', a truly dreadful word which suggests a heedless consumption of Mother Earth's generous giftings, treating them as mere resources for humanity to plunder.

Consider now how consuming what is mass-produced also makes us powerless. We cannot say how the component parts were obtained, treated etc. Making a vow to only buy what is absolutely necessary through mass retailers is to make a vow to empower ourselves, allowing us to reconnect with what is local to us, and therefore real and not removed. Buying locally from small ethical traders or making what we need ourselves is a way of ending separation; it stops us living life through a window and makes us fully appreciate how we and others are a part of all there is.

When we complete the full cycle of such a project we also give it a sense of enchantment born of the wonder we experience as the plain

31

material goes from neutral to a beautiful hue by our own interaction with nature. We bring it to life, imbuing it with spirit in a way that buying from a shop does not. If we are fully present in each moment as we find the plant, pick the leaves (asking permission first of course), stir the dye etc. we can ensure that our desired outcome is focused on as we do so. As we infuse the fabric so we infuse it with our green-wishing. This should be done with an awareness of the energies of the plant etc., as to go against what is inherently present is fairly pointless and quite insulting to the plant energy we have been gifted with. For example, it would make little sense to infuse a sunny, zingy dye of marigolds with the intention to make a pouch to aid better sleep as one energy would clearly contradict the other! However, it may be an excellent dye with which to colour a plain t-shirt to be worn to elevate mood and restore vitality. We will look at the principles and practicalities of such sympathetic natural enchantment in each subsequent chapter, enabling us to integrate life-enhancing magic into our everyday doings with ease.

It is vital to add here that for dyeing fabrics, as opposed to simply making ink, we need to give the fabric concerned a 'key', just as when we paint a chair we need to have roughened it with sandpaper to get the paint to cling to the surface. In dyeing terminology this is called the *mordant* and this comes from the Latin meaning 'to bite'. A common mordanting agent is alum, which is safe and environmentally friendly. This can be purchased from a local chemist in small quantities and can be dissolved in boiling water and then poured into the pot before the dyestuffs or plant parts go in. If we are dying fabrics then they are added after the alum and the plant parts. Therefore the pattern for dying is:

Mordant – dyestuff – fabric – boil – steep.

To steep, we can also leave the mixture in a large clean glass jar in a sunny position for as long as we feel is valuable. This can be trial and error and so quite an enjoyable experiment but perhaps not a method to adopt if predictable results matter more than using a low-impact, no fuel way of dyeing! And do not leave the jar longer than a week. It is well to be aware before we leave this subject that this method may smell a little pungent, depending on the dyestuffs involved. Plant parts that give a strong colour tend to smell similarly strongly!

*   *   *

So, we have now hopefully fashioned or purchased a journal, a book which is intensely pleasing on all levels. If we have made our own paper, we can hand-sew the sheets together using hemp twine or naturally-dyed ribbon. If we have bought the book then do personalise it in some way, using images, found items or drawn symbols to embellish the covers. Perhaps the first page should be marked with a statement of intent, a green-spirited personal declaration which gives a visual/poetic reference to the time when we began it as well as the actual date. This may be something like:

'It is the new moon of the sixth month and elder blossom is falling like tiny stars into the river made more fluent by the recent rain.

On this day I walk with purpose into the greening of a new dreaming, And I vow to catch the essence of my journey here on these pages, Not trapping the magic but allowing the memory of it To flow on, like a river filled with swirling stars. For the trees who gave their bodies willing so that I may now commit my words to their honour, I write.

And I write that I may know myself and remember the power of my own path, This day and all days, may my words ring true On the page and in my heart.'

When writing up the account of the tree walk in the new journal it is important that we consider not only what happened literally but *poetically*. This does not mean that we have to suddenly start thinking of rhymes and sonnets but rather that we begin to look at life on another level beyond the physical and actively seek out that which moves our spirit . . . the poetry we are looking to express is soul-poetry. We are not only working towards manifest change but towards regaining the romance inherent in life, becoming aware of the profound lyricism of being incarnate on a beautiful planet. Therefore do describe in both straightforward and expressive terms what happened, including any sights, sounds, smells and impressions. We may not, at this stage, consider ourselves to be particularly 'psychic' (a rather off-putting term which suggests a special gift rather than an ability to experience life on many levels, including the unseen) but we can indulge our own innate ability to feel that which goes beyond what is readily tangible. For instance, one need not be considered actively psychic to pick up sensations of melancholy, passion, mystery, joy etc. or to become aware of presences belonging to non-humans. Most of us have experienced things that

33

make us shiver with delight or cringe with distaste, for instance, and most of us have sensations of being covertly watched or listened to occasionally. This is just an inherent sensitivity which can be enhanced by our vow to observe more. The more we perceive visually, audibly etc. the more we become aware of how each encounter makes us feel. Sensitivity, that psychic or uncanny ability, is an emotional response to our environs and one not a rational one.

We can note also in our journal the 'nuts and bolts' of what was accomplished, the time of day, weather conditions, moon phase, month and anything else that will help build up a pattern or make connections when we look back through the book. What seems insignificant now ('it was a wet Saturday in March, the moon was waning, I had a headache') can give us great insight as we move farther down the wild path, helping us to realise patterns of behaviour in ourselves and in the natural world. A good journal is like a hybrid of the following: a recipe book, a map, an instruction manual and a collection of favourite song lyrics which move us!

When we have written up our account of the tree walk (and any other exercise we have spoken of subsequently, like making ink) we can now engage in the more spiritual aspect of this work, a trance journey to the World Tree. This will not be the one and only World Tree but our version of it, how we uniquely find and experience it as a force of nature in our lives. And also as a universal symbol of regeneration, balance and wisdom. We will travel to it on regular occasions to connect with the strength and harmony it brings and to attune with that which is so important to our own development, the collective spiritual 'tree-ness' which aids communication with all manifest trees.

What is a trance journey and how do we go about it?

A trance journey in this context is a guided meditation (sometimes known as a path-working) which we may engage in for a specific pre-planned purpose. It gives structure and form to working in the other realms, the unseen levels, and so makes it a safe and reliable method of accessing hidden truth and profound magical insights. Through a relaxed but focused state it allows us to understand, by direct contact, what lies beyond the dense levels of being we experience most regularly. It helps us to work with energies, a vital part of our green spirit-craft, as here we truly start to appreciate the interconnectedness of all life as we learn to recognise the energetic ebb and flow which inspires and fires all of creation. It is a part of the development of that eternal spiritual aspect of ourselves, the aspect that enhances our ability as humans to be compassionate and creative as well as visionary.

34

The first consideration for us as we step into what may be the unknown is that we should be safe. We are about to travel into territory which is very much like our own manifest level and therefore it is both deeply beautiful and highly unpredictable due to the free will of the many and varied inhabitants. We can never really predict what a human stranger may do and likewise we cannot predict what the Otherworldly denizens may do. Just like people, some Otherworld citizens are hangers-on who drain energy, cause mischief and wish us ill, for whatever reason. Even those who wish good things for us in their terms may not be compatible with our own wishes or feelings. For this unpredictable aspect we need adequate protection and can practise a simple ritual to assure this. As we are green-spirited individuals we can tailor the ritual to fit our own needs but the basis of our protection should centre on the tree as a means of visualisation as it is tried, tested, effective and appropriate. As we proceed farther into the work described in this book we will get a feeling when we need to be protected thus and when it is fitting to engage in this ritual. The general rule of thumb is this:

If we are going to open ourselves up to unseen energies outside of our own then we should be protected.

We could apply this manifestly by saying that if we are about to open up to physical energies outside of our own (traffic, germs, electricity, poison etc.) we should be protected.

So, think of protection as following an instruction manual before operating electrical equipment. We cannot always see electricity but we know that it is there and is therefore to be taken seriously. Electricity is a powerful tool but also formidable force, therefore adequate precautions are needed before we engage with it. Similarly we need to know the rules of the road before we cross it or the principles involved in accessing deep water when we go diving. We are about to engage with an unseen energy, to open up to unpredictable outside forces, and we need to follow these guidelines. Here is what we should do before beginning any trance journey.

PROTECTING OURSELVES – THE WAY OF THE TREE

Find a quiet time and place, preferably out of doors in a safe space. If it is indoors then unplug the phone, ensure you will not be disturbed and use foam earplugs if necessary. Find a comfortable place to sit, preferably on the floor. The idea is to connect with the earth, even if this is not the soil directly. If we are living in a flat or apartment which is not on the ground then please do sit on the floor so as to not place yet another obstacle between ourselves and the Earth. If we have difficulty sitting then lie down straight and adapt what follows as feels good to us.

Besides being in direct contact with the Earth, the most important thing here is the spine for it is to be our trunk, the conductor of the flowing life-force which flows up through us like sap. Because of the spine's importance then we should aim to have as straight a back as is physically possible for us so that the energy can flow up and down it unimpeded. Even if we are lying down we can try to ensure this.

Good seated postures are: straight spine, legs spread 'frog fashion', soles of feet touching each other, fingers loosely steepled in the lap as in diagram (a). Or fingers connected index to thumb with palms held upwards in a position of 'receiving' as are the tree's branches and leaves, as shown below in diagram (b).

(a)   (b)

It is important for us to understand why this posture is appropriate. Well, we are aiming to be a conduit, a conductor of energy as is the tree, and therefore the connection of hands and feet makes a symbolic uncluttered circuit for us. Symbology and reflecting natural patterns is important to our work.

Alternatively we can sit with a straight spine, knees bent, feet planted squarely on the earth, hands resting on the earth, as below.

This is so that we maintain that vital connection with the soil/ ground on as many levels as possible.

Obviously sitting cross-legged in a classic meditation pose is also fine, especially if that is what we are used to doing and feel comfortable with. However, from the point of view of our green spirituality it isn't necessarily a good thing to 'cross our wires' or fold our limbs as we are aiming for the free flow of energy that the tree has. Also adopting things wholesale from another tradition, without thought but with blind acceptance, is not perhaps the way for the questing green-spirited person to go. We should get used to challenging what we do and why we do it. With this in mind do come up with any variation on the theme as long as it upholds the concept of clear connection and Earth contact... in other words, so long as it emulates the tree teacher's way.

If we are lying down then we should have our arms spread wide if possible (like branches) and the palms upraised (receiving as mentioned above) or have the fingers making a circuit (as above) or have the palms flat to the ground (connected).

Now we have found a position that is comfortable and appropriate for us we should take three deep breaths to steady and centre us in the moment. What do we mean by a deep breath? It may seem obvious but we rarely take this sort of breath consciously. Here's how to do it well.

With shoulders back and tummy in:

- Inhale slowly through the nose, feeling the abdomen inflate as the lungs fill. The chest should visibly rise. We should hear the sound of the breath as it fills us: it should sound like the sea being sucked out from the shore, pulled by the moon's inevitable embrace.
- Hold the breath in for a count of three with eyes closed, being fully aware of the moment, of the life giving breath inside, sustaining us.
- Release the breath through the mouth with a slow rushing sound (like the sea reaching the shore) feeling the abdomen draw in and the chest fall.

Now we should run through the protection routine as we continue to breathe deeply, slowly and evenly. If engaged in regularly, it will become second nature and not as involved as it may appear on first glance. Here's what to do.

Considering the self as a tree:

- As we breathe in imagine the sap/life force energy as a shining stream that is drawn inexorably upwards through our spine to the top of the head and then beyond. This light extends upwards and outwards, reaching our uppermost branches, above and around us.
- As we hold that breath for a count of three we should keep seeing this shining force radiate up the spine, through the skull and outwards and upwards in a corona like the shape of branches.
- As we breath out, feel and see this force being pulled down again, along the spine and deep into the Earth below us. Feel the spine elongate as this force pulls it, creating a great glowing tap root that snakes and twines deep into the soil below. This primary root anchors us to the manifest level.
- Now as we continue to do this exercise, breathing in and out, see the fierce brightness of our life-force now extending out beyond our body, so that as it moves up and down the spine it shines beyond it, shrouding us in a glow. See tendrils of light shooting from the spine's central tap root, forming luminous vein-like roots as it does so. These roots seek to anchor us further into the soil.
- As we continue to breathe, with the force moving up to the branches and down to the roots of us, we should have full awareness of the central column of our spine that connects us above and below, to Earth and sky, matter and spirit. We now know ourselves to be completely surrounded by living light, sparkling life-force energy that protects us . . . the same energy that courses through us, up and down. How we envisage this should be something like this:

38

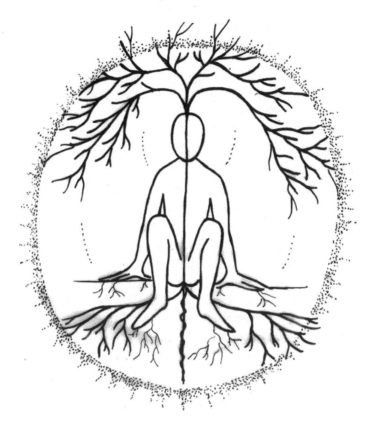

- Now say this simple affirmation to will ourselves protected between the realms of body and soul, seen and unseen:

  'I am rooted and connected,
  Like a tree, strong and protected,
  Spine to trunk I keep my centre,
  Unless invited let none enter!'

Is it really that simple to be protected? Well, yes because we are making a manifest symbolic gesture and giving it resonance with the power of intent. Obviously one could go on for hours using ever more complex rites to ensure we were hermetically sealed before we engaged in anything, but our spirituality is something more impulsive and responsive (or wild) than that and we don't need to tie ourselves in knots over it when we can simply use the will, with conviction. The above is a tried and tested method and although it is basic it will work for us, always, as long as we imbue it with enough passion. Just as we can ensure that when getting on a bicycle we don our crash hat and adopt the Highway Code, we have done all that we can reasonably do to be responsible for ourself.

There are gestures we can employ to cover ourselves more fully but these are for more advanced work and situations and we do not need to focus on them here. What is worth mentioning is that we can do this protective rite in a truncated version (excuse the pun) if we need to protect ourselves in a hurry. This could be done as:

- Take three long deep breaths.
- Find our spine/trunk centre and feel the energy flowing there.
- Envisage the energy glow around ourselves.
- Say the affirmation with certainty of its effectiveness.

Such emergency measures probably won't be necessary at this stage of our green spirit-craft but can be useful if we ever feel uncomfortable in an atmosphere, be that out of doors or in a social situation. Energies which we find difficult or hostile can be present at any time and it's nice to know that we have the power to calm and reassure ourselves that nothing unwanted or unbeneficial can infiltrate our energy field when we don't want it to.

Now we have our means of protection we can engage in our first trance journey of this book.

WORLD TREE JOURNEY

Keep breathing deeply, slowing the breathing as much as possible until it becomes a comforting rhythm. If we are lying down then it is easy to drift off to sleep at this point. This is another reason to avoid lying down unless it's necessary, although perhaps sleep is just our body's way of telling us we haven't been resting enough and should be welcomed as healing in itself. Many interactions of spiritual importance happen during valuable sleep time anyway, so we needn't think of it as a wasted opportunity or chastise ourselves if we do drop off occasionally!

We are now about to use the mind's eye and 'see'. We are entering the Otherworlds through the realm of the imagination; one smoothly segues into the other if we are open enough to the possibilities inherent in both. Do not worry if you think that we can't visualise anything. We can experience the journey on many levels and it is worthwhile to undertake it however we manage to engage in it. However, it is pertinent to point out here that those of us who flatly deny being able to visualise anything quite happily picture seemingly ordinary things, such as what we are having for dinner or the faces of our loved ones, with our mind's eye every day. A denial of being able to 'see' comes with that same misunderstanding about those with psychic gifts being special; we all use visualisation quite spontaneously to some degree in daily life. With our more grounded green-spirited approach we can now perhaps understand that we all use our gifts of 'sight' and sensitivity as a matter of course. We just don't elevate them to the status of special powers!

So, using the mind's eye and the senses we have, follow these directions. To do this we can roughly memorise them, have a trusted friend read them to us or tape them on to a cassette and play them back to ourselves, being careful to leave suitable gaps so that we may have time to act on what is suggested. If we memorise the journey's directions then it certainly need not be word for word, instead getting a feel for what's happening and picking up any cue we can give ourselves like 'grass, owl, moon . . .' etc. Alternatively, we can get a good feel for the journey by reading it over and then 'ad-libbing' to some degree when we go into trance. This is fine as long as the basic structure/purpose of the work remains intact and as the book progresses we will find the confidence to do this more and more. The journey is described very poetically here but it can certainly be pared down to its bare bones for us to recall it simply. The evocative poetic feel is to get us to enter into the experience fully; it is a tool to help us access the Otherworld. We can certainly flesh the skeleton of the journey out in our own unique ways once we know its structure.

To begin, we should have our eyes closed and be breathing very deeply.

'I am standing in darkness. There is grass beneath my feet; I feel it, dew-damp and springy-soft between my toes. I look up and above me there are a few glittering stars studding the velvet night, but the moon is low and has sailed behind a cloud so there isn't much illumination. As my eyes become accustomed to the darkness I pick out a shape in front of me, huge, broad. I want to walk towards it, to touch the shape that stretches skyward and brushes the tips of the pearly lilac clouds, but I am afraid as it is so imposing and I cannot see it fully, not yet. I stand and wait.

My senses heighten by the second now and I can smell freshly turned earth and the loamy perfume of the land, so darkly rich I can taste it. I hear the sounds of this place, of this night; the distant bark of the dog fox calling for its mate, the scuffling passage of the mouse through undergrowth as it eludes the swooping barn owl. And rustling. The whispering of a million leaves, spilling secrets to each other under night's mantle of black velvet. I feel the breeze that stirs the leaves

41

as it touches my face, gentle and caressing, almost warm, scented with the last of this year's honeysuckle. I turn my face to the stars and a smile plays across my lips. This is wonderful!

Then suddenly I am standing in the presence of a god. The moon slips off her gown of cloud and reveals her fullness and so the scene before me is backlit, showing the giant for what it truly is.

I am standing before the largest tree that has ever been.

I sink to my knees in the long wet grass and acknowledge this being with my own instinctive awe. Here is the source of the many leaves rustling. Here is the source of everything. The World Tree, magnificent, its boughs reaching to heaven, its roots spreading out and down to the hidden places below. I imagine the roots of such a mighty being would surely be directly below me now as I kneel, so huge is the canopy that rises from its sturdy trunk that the root system must echo this graceful sweep, this extensive graceful arching of leaf clad limbs.

May I approach, I wonder? I voice this wish.

The answer comes not in one voice but with all voices. I hear the response rushing in the wind, rumbling through the soles of my feet, rising on the back of the ghostly barn owl as she hunts the mouse.

I may approach.

As I get nearer the sheer size of this being is made dauntingly apparent. I can no longer determine the uppermost boughs nor get a sense of the scale of the root system. All I can see is the great girth of the trunk. The moon does her best to show me each lesion and ripple, each stretch mark and hollow on the bark-skin. I long to put my hands on this skin and know its solidity, to confirm the aching familiarity I feel when I look at it. I know this tree, this place . . .

Don't I?

Up close the bark is an intricate maze, a busy world of labyrinthine twists and turns inhabited by tiny iridescent creatures. Each segment is uniquely scored and grooved; I could dissolve into any bit of it and end up lost in its folds and creases like a minute beetle. The bark presents a world within a world, a new universe to study, complete within itself. I notice it almost imperceptibly moving as grubs and their creators shift beneath its surface. Can I touch it?

I can but ask.

I feel a pull towards the bark, my hands rising to meet it, to feel the sensation, skin on skin. And my palms are resting upon it, resting upon the body of an unknowable but deeply familiar being. Resting on hard wood, living tissue, skin that is gnarled and ancient, glowing with a youthful energy. And as I touch and stroke and learn this being through the life-lines of its bark I realise that someone else is calling to me. I glance up and see a bright beetle, bigger than the others. I watch its antennae twitch and hear its message.

Follow, it says.

Finding the Greenwood

How may I follow, you are too small and I am . . .

 I am shrinking down until I too am beetle-like and scuttling in its wake, knowing the bark now as the ground beneath my tiny feet, feeling myself undulate as we travel rapidly over its rippled surface. The beetle ahead of me crests a ridge of wrinkled brown and vanishes over the other side. I follow, curious, all fear forgotten now. All is natural and right on this fateful night. Now I am at the top of the slope of bark and I balance for a moment, antennae waving, before I descend, going down into the tree, through a knothole which is now a tunnel for me. We move swiftly and surely into a darkness unlike that which lies outside of the tree. I scent warm resin and fresh green blood and the pulpy wood-flesh, a tinge of wet organic rottenness which excites my new beetle-senses. We continue, moving through white wood into green wood, pulsing and vital. I sense veins and capillaries carrying juicy life to every part of this being. I hear the overwhelming hum of its vigour, the thrum of its senses, honed and glowing. I hear the displacement of soft wood, the knawing of hard wood and I hear the knowing of the whole being.

 And then I am at the centre, the trunk's living core.

 I am as myself now, no longer a beetle, and I am in a column of green gold light which stretches upwards and downwards from me as I hang suspended in the heart of the trunk itself. I am caught in the stream of energy which travels up the spine of the world, the axis mundi, the trunk of the Tree of Life. I can move either up in this energy or downwards, away from the manifest levels of daily life and into the unknown regions below or soaring to the celestial realms above. I look downwards and see the column becoming a serpent of light, undulating away from me. I too become snakelike, writhing, and move in waves and coils towards the base of the trunk, twisting.

 My snake-self sees itself reflected in the roots at the base and like these roots I push deep, thrusting forward into the earth, feeling the resistance of soil and small stones against my skin. The cool damp welcomes me and covers me as I squirm and wriggle with the roots, down, down. Past sleeping seeds and pallid grubs, carapaces left to crumble and broken fragments of shell and cocoon I push on, picking up the pulse of the Mother now, the throb of the land. I taste bitter loam and feel the fibrous bodies of many blind white roots, all pushing to the pulse, seeking the hidden depths, the darkest soil, the heart of the matter. Here in the Underworld I seek that which is hidden, I touch that which is primal. I descend, driven, towards the womb of the Mother, the tomb from which I may rise again, restored. I aim for the point of returns and regeneration found in the darkest hour, prepared as I am to meet my own dry husk in the endless cold blackness as it crowds around me. Tiny things that have never known the light of day slide over me and still I push for my own centre, for the world's end that is the beginning . . .

I stop. I am surrounded by ancient stone and wet loam, fed by subterranean streams. I am in the region of old bones. If I wished at this point I could enter the cave that is to be found in this place, the cave which is the hall of the Underworld realm where I may find answers to that which is buried deep within me and so within all things. If I look I may discern the entrance to this Underworld cavern even now, should I wish to enter it. But I do not, not yet. Instead I savour the sensation of being in this place. I feel what it means to me to be so far under the ground, hidden.

When I am ready I look upwards into the ebony of the depths and realise I can see stars.

With a whoosh I am travelling upwards, moving on the flowing beam of life, caught in its wave, propelled. I shoot through the earth past worms and buried treasures, sleeping rabbits and withered beech nuts hidden by squirrels and long since forgotten, until I am connecting strongly with the tree's essence again, pulled by its presence just as the great tap root is. I surge upwards and am inside the tree again, suspended in this column of light. But I do not stop here. I continue to rise, flying up through that intensely bright beam of energy, up through the centre of the oldest, wisest tree that ever was. As I rise I feel the tree's presence all around me, its awareness, its gentle strength, its nobility and its stability. It has no discernible gender, as I travel upwards in its powerful energy I experience its being as unsentimental and as sure of its own self, its own purpose, as both male and female elders can be. Yet this is no human presence, rather one which is a natural force with an impersonal yet deeply affecting air. One which states 'I will be here for you as I am here for everyone, because I AM.' I feel it observing me without judgement, with an innate curiosity and deep sensitivity. Travelling in its inner light I touch the tree-spirit, knowing the way it works, letting myself move to the constant harmonious beat of its green blood. I feel the thrust of roots below me and the stir-ring of new shoots, already seeking sky, above me.

I travel faster still, hearing the pounding of life in my ears and then I am outside. The column of light exits the tree high in the branches and travels onwards into the night, a pure ray of energy. I gaze down now, seeing the leafy canopy below me, diffused in the healthy glow of this vibrant green-gold energy. I pick out each leaf in sharp relief, each telling its own story whilst singing the song of the tree itself, the harmony of the individual and the collective. I notice that some leaves are in full health, glossy and verdant, whilst others are in autumn's thrall, umber and amber. I witness also that some of the leaves are from the ash, others from the oak and still more from the pine or apple. The whole canopy is made up of representatives of every tree that grows and the overall effect is one of balance and harmony, not confusion, as holly nestles in close to lime and aspen is a good neighbour to sycamore.

The light holds me far above the World Tree; I float in the sparkling life-force, observing the sky turning from indigo to violet. I know that here is the gateway to the Upperworld, a place of great inspiration, of enlightenment. From this point high above the Earth I can ride on the back of an eagle or owl to a place where I may hear of universal law and wisdoms, see bright visions and know transcendent beauty. All I have to do is travel up the World Tree's trunk in the beam of energy that sustains the world, the axis mundi from which all Earthly balance comes.

Dawn comes.

The sky blushes and all is song, pure and clear as the winged ones celebrate the sun's eternal returning. Plaintive, fluting, sweet and true I am caught in the moment, in that daily celebration, the thanks-giving of the birds. I let my prayers for health and healing rise with their trills and whistles. I witness the first rays of sun catch the shimmer of a starling's wing as she rises; I know the simple glory of being in that moment. Thank you, thank you, thank you! And to think, this is what the tree experiences every day, this communion. I watch as below the buds unfurl on the World Tree even as the acorns grow from green to brown and the blossom is already falling. The World Tree is the dance of all life. A symbol of returns.

And with this realisation I descend slowly, sated, transported by a beam of pure energy down through the air, through the leaf canopy, into the living wood. I am in the spine of the world, propelled down by its ebb even though this day I have also known its flow. And for this I am grateful.

Without knowing how I am no longer part of the tree but once more outside it, observing its magnificence, its vast and all encompassing presence. It is now full daylight and I must return to my own time, to my own place. But first I drop low to one knee on the dew soaked grass. Beside me I see a young doe, trans-fixed by the beauty of this new day, unafraid of me for I am no threat, just a vital part of the dance, as is she. In the distance I see a badger trundling contentedly homewards after a night's foraging. I offer my thanks now to the Tree, to All That Is, in whatever way I see fit.

Does the tree have a message for me now?

I listen.

Then I stand and slowly I become aware of another reality, the human realm of 'the now'. So I open my eyes and return.'

It is important once we have returned from a trance journey to become fully grounded in the reality of this world again. For this we should first take a few minutes to get fully back into our bodies, wiggling fingers and toes, moving the head from side to side to release any stiffness there. Once we feel a connection with the manifest again we should eat and drink a little, preferably something light and nourishing but a cup of tea and a biscuit are fine! As we progress and get used to journeying we can ensure we have a glass of water and a snack next to us for when we finish. Ditto our journal and pen. The action of immediately writing up the journal is a grounding one too.

We can employ this journey many times in the future to regain that deep sense of connection with *tree-ness* that it engenders. We can, when we have the experience, also work from the World Tree as a starting point and travel to the realms of the Upper and Lower (Under) worlds for specific purposes. Once we have the framework and the confidence we can be creative and shape our own journeys as long as we keep personal spiritual safety and a valid reason to travel foremost in our hearts and minds. A journey with no real direction or point is rather like setting off into unknown territory without a map: it could be exciting but we could also become horribly lost, confused or out of our depth. All journeys, both manifest and spiritual, do need some degree of planning and a consideration of our personal levels of competence. This isn't to say that they shouldn't be fun though; just that things are usually more enjoyable if we don't feel totally out of control.

*   *   *

So, now we are familiar with some of the key concepts of green spirituality and have a real awareness of what it means to live a magical life. In the next chapter we will broaden our knowledge and enhance our direct personal experience, primarily through our contact with the wild ones of the land, the green guardians.

2

Taking on the Green Mantle

As we are now conversant with the key concept of *magic in the midst of life* it seems appropriate to begin this chapter with suggestions for how to begin each new day in a green-spirited way.

To do this we may first consider how we currently begin our day. Many of us are tied to the constricts of conventional living as mainstream society dictates and precious few of us are able to fit in with our bodies' (and nature's) innate way of doing things. Consequently our day may begin with the shrilling of distinctly unnatural sounds such as buzzers on radio alarm clocks which haul us up from the deep well of sleep with all the subtlety of a rook snatching a duckling from its mother. We suffer the dual indignity of being woken before we are indeed ready and having the gentle rhythm of our slumber rudely interrupted by man-made alarms. Consequently our way of greeting the day may range from grumpy mumbling or bleary confusion to downright outraged ranting! Even if we can manage to wake a little more gently we may be forced to be 'compos mentis' at an hour which feels quite alien to us at some deep level. It has long since been an accepted fact that some of us are early morning folk whilst others are night-owls or semi-nocturnal by nature. Our biological make-up, as well as perhaps our unique soul-preferences, predetermines this.

So, what, if anything, can be done about such disharmonious waking conditions? Can we all simply leave jobs, reject our routine lives and spurn 'the system' in order to go with our own flow more effectively? Would we even want to if we could? Few of us would be willing to forego the creature comforts of a modern age in favour of a completely natural existence in greater accord with the Earth (and consequently ourselves). The alternative is a green-spirited compromise, a balancing act which allows us to remain in mainstream life while accepting who we are, knowing what we need and catering to that unswervingly with complete reverence for all fellow beings. Acting on self knowledge, with regard for nature and regardless of society's mores, can at least lead us to modify our lifestyle if it is currently in flagrant opposition to our long-held and sacred rhythms. Not being seduced by any other group or individual's pressures but adhering to what we hold true is hard enough in today's world without us all trying to 'opt out' by living in a hazel-framed unbleached canvas tent on a hill! We should never feel the urge to beat ourselves up because we do not immediately do the most dramatic thing possible to show that we care for ourselves and the land and understand their profound connection. A thirst for walking our talk and living out our love of nature will surely be enough to inspire subtle, yet just as far reaching, changes in our daily routines so that they no longer become routines but rather wonderful dances. Here, then, is a gentle wake up call so that we may ask ourselves if we are beginning our day in a way that is appropriate to our wild nature. Are we willing to make the changes needed in order for us to live in greater balance?

If we have addressed our daily waking patterns or if we are fortunate to be able to follow our own body clock and wake naturally then we can consider how we can turn something that appears mundane into a magical experience, something that gives our day renewed purpose and ourselves renewed vigour. Even if we are resolutely not 'a morning person' we may find the edge is taken off being awake if we have a sense that we are entering into a day which from its very outset is filled with an air of enchantment. For a start, how many of us currently recognise the miracle of sight, smell and hearing when we open our eyes (if we are fortunate enough to be able to do this)? Do we enjoy the sensation of clean sheets? The touch of a loved one's skin? The rasping wetness of the cat's tongue as it licks our face? Do we draw back the curtains and truly marvel that we can appreciate what is outside . . . not because it is a beautiful day, although it may well be, but because we have the privilege of experiencing it at all? Is our first thought ever 'thank you!'? Personally speaking, when I took time to consider the absolute joy of still being present in this body, at this time, in this place and after I had surrendered to sleep the previous night with no guarantee I would ever wake then I was suitably touched to offer up my gratitude every day. Certainly sometimes it is easier than others, when a pleasant day seeing people I love lies ahead, or when the sun is out, but with practice it gets easier to recognise the simple beauty of just being conscious to all this wonder for another day. It is a start in counting blessings, part of our green spirituality.

If it seems impossible for us to feel pleasure upon waking at a particularly 'down' time then engaging in a simple altruistic act which takes us out of ourselves is beneficial. Having a companion plant to tend and water on the bedroom windowsill can help in this way: we can pour our respect for the blessings we have been given into the compost and focus our love of the natural world on to this one green being who shares our space. Any sort of mild depression is well treated by tending our leaved and stemmed companions who really do offer a very gentle reminder of how to be, in the simplest and most effective terms. We should never berate ourselves for becoming down at certain times; instead we could simply recognise our own innate patterns and cycles which give rise to such feelings, as well as considering any external factors. It isn't only the time of day that can see us at a low ebb; we can be influenced by greater cycles too; for instance, is the moon waxing, waning or full when you generally feel low? What is the time of year? We will consider such influences in chapter four. Meanwhile it may be well for us to start noting any such personal mood shifts in our magical journal. If we find that we are generally more down than up, emotionally speaking, then we can perhaps take time to consider where in our lives we may be going against our own flow or inherent inner rhythms besides just forcing ourselves to get up at inappropriate times for us personally.

If we feel more groggy than depressed upon waking then perhaps we could engage for a few minutes as we rise on a craft project especially designed for the purpose of welcoming the new light of day. The very act of focusing on something physical which we have specifically chosen can serve as a good way of grounding us back in manifest reality. This can be as simple as you like...how about constructing a seed necklace or bracelet? First we should choose the fruit we wish to work with, thinking of something that resonates symbolically with the task we are to engage in. So seeds from 'upbeat' plants such as the sunflower could be employed. The zingy golden honeydew melon is another likely candidate or perhaps we may see the pumpkin as being ideal with its welcoming roundness and warm orange skin, so reminicent of the sun. It is, as ever, vital that we understand the beings we work with from the beginning to the end of the process; buying a packet of dried seeds from the supermarket means that we are once again removed from nature's way and the energies involved. Once selected, we can then prepare the seeds by removing the pulp and juice from the fruit that created them and leaving them to dry out on a flat dish in a warm place like an airing cupboard or on a windowsill above a radiator or in a sunny position. If possible we should chose somewhere in our bedroom.

As the seeds dry we can talk to them, informing them of what we wish to achieve, in this case making a simple threaded piece of jewellery that will remind us of the blessings of each new day. Then when we are about to string them, select each seed individually and focus on that attitude of gratitude and on a particular bright blessing that each morning represents for us personally. See each seed as golden and light, infused with the sun's kind cheery rays. Each morning we could string three more seeds, by using strong thread and piercing them, grounding ourselves fully in the new day by a simple act of creativity, enhanced by our magical wish that this will be a necklace or bracelet with a particularly positive energy to it. The seeds could be interspersed with acorns, small holey stones, pierced shells and perhaps even simple hand-turned wooden beads. Tiny bells or meaningful charms may also be incorporated but it is more beneficial for us, especially at this stage, to stick as much as possible to a hands-on approach, working with home-grown/found items rather than bought ones. However, if we happen to be a silversmith or jeweller it would be wonderful to employ our skills in making additional charms! We could rub a suitably sunny essential oil, such as lemon or sweet orange, into the finished piece, thus making it a treat for the senses. Or stain alternate seeds with a natural dye such as wild angelica which gives a yellow hue.

Another valuable way of grounding ourselves in the physical is to immediately write up a dream diary upon waking. This could again be a notebook that we create ourselves in the way described in chapter one and could be suitably embellished with colours, collected images, pressed found objects such as petals, illustrations and even impregnated with scents that suggest the realm of sleep and the gift of dreaming to us. For instance, the pages could be infused with lavender oil and we could incorporate camomile flowers into our paper making, both being herbs which help with deep refreshing sleep. Even if we insist on stating that we either do not dream, or do not recall our dreams on waking, then such a diary could be used to write about our initial feelings upon opening our eyes, any lingering impressions or sensations we have which could be meaningful when referred back to or looked at over a number of months to reveal a pattern of behaviour. The wonderful thing about a dream diary is that it not only 'earths' us after sleep but it allows our dreaming to become more relevant in the waking world. Part of green spirituality is to bring through the subtler unseen energies, the magical Otherworldly aspects of being, and ground them in our daily reality; keeping such a diary helps us to do just that.

Furthering the idea of collecting evocative images, an 'inspiration board' is a lovely way to brighten our first waking moments and can be a welcome point to focus on if the view from our window isn't too inspiring. We have the ability to bring our own window into the world we want by using a large corkboard with a painted frame and pinning on photographs, news clippings, words, swatches of fabric, photocopied images etc. that bring us joy or make us remember who we are and what is important to us. In fact this board can be themed to represent how we wish the world was... healed, honoured, celebrated... and we can perform a little powerful magic every time we wish by dwelling upon it. Imagine if everyone did this first thing in the morning rather than dwelling on the images of war and destruction in newspapers! My own board has a sunny golden frame and includes pictures of people I find admirable, such as animal rights activists, along with photos of favourite natural sites, other people's artwork which honours nature, samples of beautiful paint colours, words such as 'impeccability' and in the centre a prayer-piece I wrote to help me count my mornings blessings. Here is a fragment of it, for your own inspiration.

> *'This day has been generously granted to me*
> *So I may walk into its beauty with no guile,*
> *Living my truth creatively,*
> *Unafraid to witness the lessons hidden under each leaf and rock*
> *Or over the brow of the next hill.*
> *I am as I am, so may I rejoice!*
> *May I have the grace to thank all others for being.*
> *With an open heart and mind may I grow and unfurl,*
> *Like a wildflower, like all creation.'*

With considerations of time available and matters of privacy we can make the simplest most resonant gesture of all and offer up our own prayer of acknowledgment of the blessings of a new day upon waking. As we know we may pray in our minds or turn our heartfelt offering into a soul-song. We can sing it on the patio or in the shower. We can whisper it upon opening our eyes or as we take the dog out. Every action is a sacred part of the journey; we can say it anyhow and anywhere as long as we *feel* it too. It could be something like this, amended to suit the particular moment:

> *'The day is a hedge-blossom, full of wild beauty,*
> *Delicate, singular, radiant,*
> *That once was bare twig and will be bright fruit,*
> *Kissed by dew and blessed by sun.*
>
> *I breathe of its pure scent,*
> *I cup it in my hands, unpicked,*

I give thanks for its honouring me,
With simple grace, endless possibility.

May I be like the blossom this day,
And know how to be, pure and open,
For to myself I have awoken,
My thread of life remains unbroken.'

For a really simple and beautiful magical morning pick-me-up which can be re-established throughout the day why not seek out and carry a prayer pebble? Obviously with our renewed attitude of courtesy and inclusiveness we would have to focus on finding a small stone that wishes to accompany us for this purpose. It would be highly inappropriate (or not green-spirited) for us to grab a pretty pebble because it appealed to us aesthetically without so much as a by-your-leave as to its own sacred point of view. We should therefore send out a wish-thought asking for the pebble that will be our prayer companion to reveal itself to us in due course in the midst of daily life. When we think we have the right stone we should do our very best to ascertain if it *feels* right for us to take it. If it does then we can take it home and sing or speak our sacred prayer into it, asking it to hold its energy for us. Such a prayer could be:

'*I honour the divine within myself,*
I respect the sublime within all others,
I acknowledge the blessings within this moment,
I cherish each moment that I am given.

My heart and soul with thanks do swell,
By this small stone where beauty dwells.'

Then we an place the prayer pebble in a safe pocket or specially made pouch of recycled fabric, cut from an old dress or shirt, and carry it with us at all times...or until we have the feeling that its time with us is over. Stones, like all beings, are not ours to keep captive. Let all beings we work with move on when the time is right, let the energy be one of sharing and never ownership. Therefore it isn't really apt to paint symbols on our stone-friend unless in some transient medium such as blackberry juice or our own saliva (which is quite definitely sacred not sordid!). While the prayer-pebble is present in our lives we can touch the magic it holds for us, feeling that prayerful resonance all day long, reminding ourselves of our blessings and the enchantment at the heart of all we do. And wouldn't it be wonderful if we felt moved to touch that stone both in the presence of a rosy dawn and a flaming sunset but also when faced with poverty, disability or discord? Be creative, be innovative, think symbolically and feel free to work with a seed instead of a stone (a kernel of truth in your pocket!) or perhaps a spiral shell or shiny russet conker. It is, as ever, the intent behind what you do, with love, which counts for everything.

Of course, such praise-prayers can form part of a much more ritualised gesture of gratitude and acknowledgement which we may want to indulge in on holidays, which are after all *holy* days, and give us more space to explore our connections to the land. For these we may break our fast outside, sharing a meal of local wildflower honey, organic butter and home-made wholemeal bread with the birds and pouring a 'libation' of an energising pick-me-up herbal tea, such as peppermint, rosemary or lemon balm (which gives a gentler lift) to the very soil which allowed us to partake of her bounty. We may also honour the sun, even if it is not visible, and the rain, likewise, for their part in the creation of our sustenance. By doing this we see ourselves as part of a cycle, partnership of creation, we being the part that treasures what grows and tends/harvests it accordingly. We could circle or spin with our bodies to reflect this cycle, moving in a clockwise, or sun-wise, fashion with arms uplifted or outstretched and then stoop to touch the earth, acknowledging the above and below aspects of creation with ourselves as the grateful link between each.

As an aside here, when I mention herbal tea I certainly do not refer to pre-packaged herbal brews in small white bags, rather an infusion of the leaves or flowers of a plant we have grown ourselves and so have full energetic knowledge of. We may then know the plant and how it *feels* to us personally, as opposed to just relying on the attributed medicinal qualities we read about in books. When we ask its permission to harvest it etc. we form a relationship. In green spirituality there are very few shortcuts. We should endeavour to cut out the middle man and get 'down and dirty' with the beings/plants etc. we choose to ingest or imbibe. Such a way of life engenders everything as special, nothing as dead or ordinary. It is worth every ounce of effort to change the way we approach such apparently humdrum matters as tea making, since if we give the small things credence and care the rest will surely follow. By having this new way of approaching life we can then appreciate more fully what we have to celebrate first thing upon waking . . . the good things become much more apparent!

Note that the suggestions I am making are really simple as I do not believe that green spirituality is about complex ritual or meditation but rather about how we can bring the childlike enchantment and wild connection back into daily chores; it is truly 'grass-roots' spirituality. This book is about down-to-earth hands-on magic in the midst of life and so the suggestions are primarily for things we can do to enliven and enrich our daily patterns. As Mother Theresa was quoted as saying 'we cannot do great things; we can only do small things with a great amount of love'. Clearly if we have time to meditate to welcome in our day then this is wonderful but I shall remain within the flexible framework of wholesome uncomplicated practicality for now.

So we have looked at a few ideas for activities to begin our day. Now here is the next truly vital part of our transformation into green-spirited individuals; that we spend a little time at the start of our day being *in the moment*. As with all the things we talk about in this book it may seem deceptively simple. To be *fully present,* however, is perhaps one of the hardest things for the average human being to be in modern society. This means the following.

- Have no extraneous thoughts, agendas, desires. Let the nagging voices, expectations, judgements, advertisement jingles and songs that all fight for our attention every waking minute of every day be muted into silence so that we can hear what is being said to us right now. Or what isn't being said.
- Be aware of each sound, smell, sensation etc. that we experience and of each personal feeling (not thought) that we have at any one time. This is both drinking in the moment and distilling through our own personal filters so that we know how it tastes to us.

If this sounds easy then try doing this for a minute right now. We can try being aware of everything that is happening around us and inside us as we read these words. Just read the words and do not think about them, absorb them. We can feel our bottom on the seat beneath us, sniff the scent of the air, become aware of the fabric of our clothes against our arms and legs, and listen to the rustlings and creaking around us.

Does that feel alien, unusual? Can we honestly say that we do that with such perfect attention regularly? Well, here it is being suggested that we try! Begin by doing this each morning when we sit on the train, walk to the newsagent's shop, make the bed, water the garden, feed the cat or whatever it is we often do. Now experience this activity fully. *Really be there.* Realise how often we have half a mind on something else and do something to reverse this trend of being absent from daily life. This can be practised as a kind of active meditation for it shares the same principles of stilling the mind and maintaining full conscious being without the associated relaxation and trance aspects.

Instead of becoming relaxed we will attain wakefulness, being alert and absolutely vitally in the here and now. Once we have the measure of being present then we can expand upon it, allowing ourselves to be *in the now* for five minutes a day, then ten, until we can say that we are more actively aware in our lives than on 'automatic pilot'. It is an exercise in habit breaking and gives us immediate access to a new reality that was actually there all along.

Why is this so valuable to green spirituality?

Because if we live like this then we feel a part of nature, of the All, for we then realise that we share each moment with the whisperings of leaves, the clicking of our bones, the insistent voices of both seagull and sparrow, the creaking of bark and the eternal hum of the universe as well as with the clinking of glass, the revving of engines and the chattering of televisions. We fine tune ourselves to hear the smaller subtler voices. We allow ourselves to perceive our own resonant presences upon the sacred Earth, to witness our own intuitive feelings rising up, and we prepare ourselves to witness the voices of the spirits who we will be working with from hereon in. We become more open, more able to engage confidently. And besides, is it not better to learn to be present than to continue being semi-absent?

What better way to give thanks than offering a prayer of our being fully present (or receiving the *gift of the present* as Jamie Sams, the wonderful teacher of Native American Spirituality, so eloquently puts it in her own work).

Here are two suggested prayer-songs:

'I dance alone but my partners are many,
Each tiny movement I share with the moment,
I step to the beat of creation's wings,
I hear the soul-music the present sings,
May I move and be moved by the way of things,
May I always receive what the here and now brings.'

Or:

'This day is a bursting ripe fruit longing to be tasted,
Its flesh soft and yielding, its sweet juice on my lips,
The hairs on its skin ready to delight my tongue,
Its seeds hidden, waiting to be discovered in its sweet centre,
May I savour the flavour, may I relish each bite,
May I swallow deep, may I drink it down,
May the tang of this day and its fragrance be mine.'

If the latter prayer poem seems a little too sensuous for that which is conventionally considered prayerful then let us re-establish here that we are singing the praises of creation in earthy terms. There is no separation, no higher and lower, no trying to rise above the body, not in our green spirituality! All is holy in this living verdant way, a way that is essentially about the swelling fecundity of nature and the powerful surging of the wild spirit that animates it. It is not about talking in tame or even abstract terms for the sake of politeness! Here is a chance to be authentic and passionate about how we feel what we experience and how we express our divine connection to the land. So yes, I make no apology for being sensuous in this way or encouraging you to be so either!

Let us get back to our way of beginning the day for a moment. In symbolic terms, dealing with how we begin our day is important, it makes a statement of intent to ourselves and others, and it sets the tone of things to come. Symbolic resonances are just as vital to what we do as manifest gestures, as we have previously discussed. The unseen intent of our prayers and thoughts go hand in hand with our environmental actions. Before we can progress to addressing the spirit-work to be found later in this chapter we need to shift our understanding of how things really work, both in the world and for us personally ... *as without, so within*. If we are to work with nature (and other) spirits then we need to truly take on board at the most basic level that life has *unseen* as well as seen aspects. For example, such actions as being prematurely and rudely ripped out of the realms of sleep have energetic as well as manifest repercussions ... we may well observe the baggy eyes, sore head and bad temper we have each morning but what of the equivalent damage done to our unseen spirit-selves? If we do something out of kilter with our personal ethos or nature's way then we cause disharmony manifestly *and* energetically even if the latter cannot be so readily observed. The man who casts the contents of his litter-strewn van out of his window as he drives along is making a manifest mess *and* a symbolic, subtle unseen (energetic) statement of disrespect and disharmony. His statement of intent is that he doesn't care and sees no connection between himself and the land.

Here is a good place to establish that simple yet profound maxim for spiritual living:

Everything is energy and our energies are everything!

From a purely scientific perspective we know that we are all made up of millions of tiny particles which we may perceive as distinct from

58

other such collections of particles because of the differing frequency at which they vibrate and the variations of light which they absorb or reflect. The interplay and interchange of this energy reveals shape and form. From the sturdiest farmhouse table to the flimsiest butterfly, from the police officer in Cairo to the squirrels in a London park, from the stagnant pond to the craggiest peak we are all unique pulsating collections of pure energy. Because of this we emit a singular tone or give off an ambience which allows us to be *felt* (or sensed) as well as seen and so can be distinguished from what is around us. For now it is enough for us to consider our world not as a place composed of solids which can be experienced on one level but rather as a place composed of energy which has different vibrational rates, thus giving us the impression that it is solid. If we are aware of the energetic nature of all that we perceive, including ourselves, then it allows us to recognise how these individual energies are affected by what we, and others, do to them. We are no longer experiencing the world as dense and immutable but as something which can be influenced or enhanced at an energetic level. Here are three very simple exercises to allow us to witness energy and energetic resonances for ourselves.

- Stand on top of a hill, or at an unpopulated ancient site, on a dry day and look at the sky. Don't stare hard but gaze at it in an unfocused way, rather as if looking at one of those 'magic eye' pictures that were once so popular. If we do this we will see the 'floaters' present in or own eyes, disc-like blobs. We will also see, if we look past this, a kind of static in the air, a great dancing mass of subtle sparkling energy. This can be observed as a whizzing or fizzing in the air and is always more apparent, especially for these seeing it for the first time, in wild, wide non-human open spaces (though, of course, it is everywhere to varying degrees.) This energy is the very stuff of life! With practice (and with an increased ability to be *in the now*) we may also learn to feel it in our bodies, through our hands, feet and faces.
- From seeing these energetic 'sparkles' in the air we can turn our attention to any trees that may be in the vicinity. Again stare in an unfocused way but this time at their topmost boughs where they are silhouetted against the sky. We should be able to see the fizzing energy dancing around them but also a bright white glow should become apparent, like an after-image, one that follows the trees' contours with flaring radiance. Once this bright halo has been witnessed we may then perceive colours flashing or mingling

around the periphery of this pale corona, bright aquamarine and pinky-lavenders especially. This spectral glow is the energetic aura or resonance of the tree.

- When we have seen this fantastic energetic glow around the trees we can look at the flow around our own physical selves. If we can we should hold our outstretched palm against a plain pale background. The very same kind of effect, i.e. radiance close to the flesh which may be edged with flashes of brilliant translucent colour, should become apparent. Not trying too hard is the key to seeing our own unique energy imprint and so we are best served by staring at our hand in a dreamy way, trying to look past it, beyond it, exercising our inner sight a little.

Let us take this a step further and allow ourselves to consider what follows as a profound possibility. At the absolute core of our own energetic body there is spirit, that eternal spark that animates all physical, and indeed non-physical, beings. Spirit-energy is refined beyond human comprehension (being literally 'not of this world') and is so 'non-manifest', remaining intangible to us as humans. It is so 'fast' and light as to be imperceptible to our ordinary senses although we may be moved by its presence within ourselves and others and *feel* its existence as an innate truth. Perhaps each of us can remember that 'shiver up the spine' moment when a piece of music or prose touches that unseen spirit-core of us, or the goosebumps that appear on our skin when an unseen spirit-being is close by? It is this immortal spirit, this totally unique *life-force energy*, that which gives us meaningful life along with the more physical aspect of existence; they are in partnership. With our broad pagan outlook we may recognise that this perception applies equally to the elephantine-skinned beech tree as much as it does to the robed monk, accepting as we do that all beings are equal and are composed of energy which cannot be quantified as better or worse, lesser or greater. We are all, essentially, beings made of whizzing light and at the heart of this lies the most refined light of all... the one that never goes out yet remains unseen: *spirit*.

This understanding is fundamental to green spirituality otherwise it would simply be green activism, a colder sort of practice altogether, with no greater understanding of the magic involved, the sacred fire that gives our lives (and indeed the lives of all) passion and meaning. It short this understanding gives us *soul*, it makes our actions soul-full. So our green spirituality is alive, entwined like lustrous and tenacious ivy at a deep level with who we are, rooting us into the land and connecting us to all beings, in essence. This sense of a shared spiritual source gives us more of an emotional response to all creation and impresses upon us a sense of light-hearted responsibility, really enabling us to express ourselves with dignity, honour and joy in the world.

The open acceptance of the refined energetic, or *spirited*, part of ourselves and others leads us on to the next stage of our journey, thus allowing us to meet the spirits who assist as greenwood guardians. These guardians are the unseen beings who inhabit the groves, copses, forests and wild places. It is time for us to extend our awareness and contact them. It is another step along the winding rough track into the untamed heart of being which leads us well away from old human-centric, 'civilised' thinking.

MEETING THE GREENWOOD GUARDIANS

Because green spirituality is an individual way for caring free-thinkers, a way that connects us to the untamed source of all life, we primarily work alone in human terms. This aloneness allows us the necessary liberty to do what we will when we will. If we feel moved to visit a remote waterfall on a rainy Tuesday in March then we need not gather a consensus from a committee on the matter, or wait until the next formal meeting to discuss it! And we need not toe any party line of beliefs. It is religion, as we discussed at the very beginning of this book, which tends to be a pack activity, not spirituality. Yet there are benefits to spiritual groups that we may never experience, because of our unique and possibly radical perspective. Groups offer a forum for discussion, enabling us to bounce ideas around, they offer support when times are tough or celebrate when all is going well for us and they help us raise power to perform magical acts. Groups can be a power pack as well as a hindrance. They can give us confirmation when we have unusual experiences by saying 'yes, I felt/saw that too!' or they can give us the benefit of other perspectives. We green-spirited people have the ultimate freedom of one-to-one contact with nature, we need not compromise, yet we may at times find ourselves a little too out on a limb for comfort. However, we need never be lonely for we do have allies, beings we can share our daily lives with, unseen folk who will be more than happy to offer a working partnership and even an open friendship. We have already established that the trees themselves will offer us an unsurpassed source of support if we give them the respect and courtesy of the same. So who are these other beings?

Wild spirits – the very essence of our native soil, unpretentious and free.

These beings dwell beside us in/on *and somehow beyond* the land. They are the stewards of the natural world and all the individual aspects, such as plants and rocks, within it. Let us make it clear that each plant and rock has its own spirit, its own unique animating inner force. These nature spirits are individuals in their own right and are caretakers of the plant beings etc. More specifically they can guard areas, such as bluebell woods, streams, rock formations, pools and caverns. They are like the guardian angels or spirit guides ascribed to each human individual. Having a guardian angel/guide/spirit helper doesn't negate our own human spirit, it simply enhances it; these nature spirits are life-enhancing.

The wild world is alive with their multifarious ingenious presences. They are not robustly physical but *spirit-full*, beings of pure energy which have a much less dense frequency to our own and so can only be perceived at our solid earth-level as ethereal and changeable light-forms. (Light in this instance can mean radiance but also the absence of heaviness. These beings are of an energetic essence of such a pure, high frequency as to hardly register on our scale of discernment.) It is only through our intuitive mind's-eye sight that we may ascribe any sort of form to them, filtered according to our own culture, experiences, expec-tations, imaginations etc. We basically clothe the pure energy of their being in a pleasing or symbolic shape so that we may better relate to them as individual beings; we anthropomorphise them. This is a very human trait which fulfils the mortal need to be able to recognise and categorise something as readily identifiable, or definable, within a previously established framework. The nature spirits will therefore show themselves on the screen of our inner vision as archetypal gossamer-winged flitting faery folk, lurching goblins, elegant elves or squat gnomes etc. They are, in this respect, true *shape-shifters*, unregulated by dense energetic restraint. They are not of our material plane, working on the inherent energy and not the physicality of the land as they do, and so have no need of such fixed bodies. They are willing to allow us to 'robe them' in our imaginations using archetypal disguises if it means we can relate more easily to their nebulous forms. Many will try to trip and confuse us too, wearing inappropriate shapes to beguile or revile us, depending on their mood. These are immensely bright, quick, highly refined spirits and this means they love to play with we clumsy folk who currently plod along in our great overcoats of human bodies!

It is rare to actually physically see such a nature spirit as a fixed and solid form in the 'world of men' although I for one know of some very sane folk who have. More usually we are aware of their energetic presence around a particular place . . . the same awareness that raises the goosebumps or sends a shiver through the core of ourselves. We may then 'tune in' to their refined frequency by making a trance-journey, a meditative pilgrimage into a more nebulous level of existence. If we are truly going to take on the green mantle we need to have an open mind and heart to these Otherworldly yet worldly presences for if we do our own world will be enhanced beyond all reason . . . then we will truly see the magic in the midst of life as every grass verge, field, cove and city park becomes a playground (and a potential battleground if we humans threaten nature) for these luminous, humorous, utterly fearless spirits. The following will serve as an introduction to these unseen denizens of nature. The very best lessons will come from personal experience and direct interaction (as green spirituality certainly isn't about theory over practical hands-on working) but here is a taster of what to expect and how to respond.

Elementals

Some nature spirits are strongly connected to the four elements and are therefore less attached to an individual stream/hill etc. but rather to the water and earth of which they are made. They are, essentially, the spirit of water, air, fire or earth, and both defend and express, or celebrate, these qualities. Therefore they can be attracted to raging torrents or gentle flows of water and be a fierce or gentle spirit depending on their mood. They generously enable us to commune with that which may seem uncommunicative and act as a bridge of understanding between we humans and the hill/river/tornado etc. they represent. Therefore as an example we may talk to a local brook or listen to the voice of the sea translated through an attendant watery elemental spirit-being.

The elementals are quite removed from the human realm and should be approached with a good measure of respect and caution. This refers especially to the fact that to death is not a concept the elementals can grasp as they do not die in a physical sense but rather transmute, water being a particularly fine example of this. We humans physically cease to be while water moves from ocean to raindrop to puddle to stream etc. Elementals simply *are*. Yet there is a further reason for a measure of wariness and that is that humanity is often perceived by them as troublesome at best and a pest to be eradicated at worst. This is due to our flagrant disregard for the Earth and a lack of respect for her non-human denizens. Pollution is one such issue that raises the ire of vengeful elemental energy. For example, a farmer polluting a local river with his chemical slurry may well find his home sabotaged by water spirits who would delight in bringing about a plumbing disaster, a leaky roof or presenting a pool of water on the kitchen floor for the man to slip over in. They do not wish to seek us out and cause us trouble yet they will protect their own element unswervingly. They can also detest us for the destruction of their precious habitats as they find themselves and their beloved wild places marginalised and brutally tamed.

We can do much in our daily lives to show respect for the elementals. Such seemingly simple acts as not leaving water running when we clean our teeth, visualising and giving thanks for the water that ends up in our bath tub, dedicating our abandoning of harsh chemical deodorising sprays to the spirits of air and returning an apple core to the soil, rather than consigning it to a litter bin (perhaps with a brief wish that it should nourish that which generously provided the fruit in the first place), show our willing to reverse the tide of human abuse and neglect. A Romany man once helped me further understand this green-spirited approach by showing me how he always bowed to the candle once the spirit of fire had deigned to light it . . . and the candle flame always bowed back! Small poignant acts bring about resurgence, a spiritual and physical *greening*, of reverence, gratitude and an understanding of our connection to all nature. I'm sure each one of us can think of at least a dozen more such gestures on a daily basis.

We can connect, through our Otherworldly trance-journey work or meditation/visualisation, to the elemental beings for help, advice and inspiration yet we must be prepared to honour them. If we do not we are quite literally playing with fire . . . or whichever element we choose to work with. As with all green-spirited magic, it is never wise to *use* another being. Working with permission as a partnership is the only ethical option. Once we become au fait with spiritual journeying, as we surely will by the end of this book, then we may employ very simple techniques to make this contact ourselves whenever we feel it may be beneficial to all parties concerned . . . not just to us.

As a very basic guide for how we can work with the elementals as muses and instructors, the spirits have the qualities that their element suggests symbolically. Therefore generally speaking water spirits have that liquid and flowing, profoundly lilting and lyrical aspect that water suggests and are therefore connected with all things poetic, deeply mysterious, dreamy and emotional. However, this can be in either a torrential, cascading or a drippy, dribbling sense; don't expect all water elementals to be lilting and lispy when they also have the resonance of white water and storm tossed oceans! Perhaps we may work with water elementals to both simultaneously clean up the garbage out of a local river as we focus on letting go of our own emotional detritus such as jealousy or guilt. The vital combination of the physical (making actual changes to the river) and the spiritual (dealing with inner emotional baggage) is essential in green-spirited being. Remember the idea of 'soil, soul and society' we touched on previously as well as the new adage 'as within, so without'. What we do spiritually needs a physical reflection, and an altruistic one. The elementals can, if approached with care and kindness, offer further imaginative ideas for such beneficial inner and outer work.

The element of fire suggests power and transformation with its ability to cleanse, clear and reduce to ashes. It does this in a way that can be controlled and comfortable as the hearth or as roaring and out of control as a forest blaze in summer. It has also the heat of passion, the sensuality of an undulating exotic dancer, the ability to melt hearts. There is something delightfully tricky about fire with its dual nature, the cruelly searing and the comforting and cosy. In Poppy Palin's *Waking the Wild Spirit Tarot* (Llewellyn, 2002) there is a flame-hued, spiky fire elemental wildly leaping over a small blaze while a gypsy fiddler, or representative of devilish energetic energy, stands nearby, winking at the observer. I think this expresses that wicked yet irresistable aspect of fire perfectly. We could, perhaps, work with the fire elementals to assist us in rekindling the passion for helping others or the environment in our lives as we set a fire to obliterate the deadwood that has been stopping light getting into our garden.

Air is about wafting, drifting and floating as well as being buffeted and blown apart, it is both subtle and strident. Air carries sound and so is symbolic of all manner of communication, from the whispering of sweet breeze in the leaves of the young silver birch to the mournful call of the heron as it flies over the marsh to the impassioned yelling of anti-war protestors or the encouraging shouts of football supporters. Air is all manner of speech and song, hysterical laughter and infectious giggling – it gives expression to how we feel and what we wish to express. It howls, it whistles and it sighs around and under and through our environs. Yet it is also unseen. We cannot see the breeze, only observe its effect on our surroundings and the change it brings . . . therefore air is also all communication that cannot be seen, such as thoughts and ideas. As an example of how we may work with the air elementals we could create a simple, beautiful wind chime, either by hand-crafting at an evening class or by constructing it from recycled objects, asking that as they send the wind to make the chimes sound so may people hear, at a deep inner level, the call to stop polluting the air by unnecessary car or aeroplane use. Or to abandon anything which releases unwanted toxins into the atmosphere.

Finally the element of earth. Generally speaking, earth elementals could be said to be still and slow, suggesting symbolically that which is solid and dependable as well as being somewhat deep, unfathomable and resolutely stubborn. Earth certainly has a more moody, rumbling resonance than the others, which may be why we so often see its spirit beings as clumping giants and grumpy groany old gnomes etc.! We may see the element of earth as being representative of the physical in all its aspects: health, home, family and survival on a very basic level. There is certainly a sense of that which is hidden, safe and protected. The flip side of this familiar, comfortable, resolute and reliable aspect is of course human greed and all that stifles and holds us firmly in outmoded ways of being. Therefore ideal earth work for these elemental beings to help us with would be, say, to dig over an area of land and turn it into a thriving organic vegetable patch (with great advice from the elementals involved as to what we would be best advised to grow there, what we should use to fertilise it etc.) whilst vowing to dig over our own lives, leaving no stone unturned, no matter how personally uncomfortable/ difficult it may be, so only that which is firmly rooted in environmental awareness may remain as a constant.

There is no time like the present for us to re-open a connection with the elemental ones. We may go out this very day and enjoy a walk which helps us appreciate just what a presence they are in our daily lives. The magic can be immediately brought back when we realise that each gutter and drain, rooftop and chimney, electricity cable and pylon, brick and slate has an elemental correspondence and therefore has an elemental spirit connected with it which will meander, fly, stride or leap into our awareness if only we ask politely, with a complete under-standing of its individual nature and with a strength of feeling that these powerful beings can relate to!

Nature spirits

These beings are not embodiments of the elements but rather nature's own embodiment, separate spirits with allegiances to the wild world who protect their corresponding natural form, promoting growth and ensuring well-being. Your garden, if you are fortunate enough to have one, has attendant nature spirits. Similarly your window box or allotment has them too. Simply anywhere where there are living breathing plants, flowers, herbs or any manner of leaf and stemmed being will have its own network of protective spirits. This does not negate the plant's or shrub's own innate life-force energy; remember these spirits are their guardians, their life-enhancing supporters. And nature spirits certainly do not stop at, for example, being bramble or marigold guardians; rather they can be found as the champions and celebrants of whole tracts of land such as hedgerows, beaches or valleys. It may push the idea a little far to think that each individual blade of glass has a single attendant spirit (although there is no reason why not) but the meadow certainly will have its spirit-associates. There would certainly be a collective grass spirit guardian.

Your tree friend, the tree you forged a bond with in chapter one, has a personal inherent spirit and an attendant nature spirit too, no doubt. The former is the tree's *spirit*, its personal life-force, and the latter is a *tree-spirit*, that which is external yet in association. It is therefore the best place to begin when looking to make a connection with these unseen green ones as it helps us continue our friendship with this particular wise one of the bark whilst raising our awareness of the unseen. So, how may we contact the nature spirits around our tree companion?

We should by now be used to the idea of making a pilgrimage, a sacred walk with a magical purpose. We need to undertake such a physical journey before we can make the inner journey to contact the spirit of our tree companion. We can then take the opportunity to (a) be *in the moment* fully as we walk, opening the senses, leaving behind the mind's chatter and building up a rhythm with our own natural heart-beat drum, our measured stride becoming one with the land's pulse and (b) we can use our intuition, or follow up a previous suggestion from the tree itself, as to a gift to bring to it. If we have no suggestion from the tree it may be nice to send it a thought, early in the morning, asking what it would like. To do this, simply visualise the tree, link into its green energy and ask! If a question has been asked it is polite to give the person asked time to respond so do spend a little time in quiet contemplation, open and receptive, afterwards. If nothing happens during that time then be open throughout the day for any extraneous images or words that float into the consciousness from outside as these may well give us the answer we need. Of course the more we visit our tree friend the better this psychic link will become and eventually we will have no bother at all in 'hearing' the response to any message we send.

This bond with the tree should always be considered. We aren't going to the site of that particular wise one of the bark just to take from it in whatever context and so we need to show that we give it full credit for making decisions like any other individual. Offering gifts, asking questions, being responsive, these are all things we can do to reverse the notion that humans simply witness the 'great standing nation', the beings of root and branch, as resources, typically as dumb, inanimate but attractive sources of wood, paper, shelter etc.

It may be wise to undertake this physical journey to the tree several times before we consider doing the inner work as it would be beneficial to experience the tree and its environs in wind, rain, frost etc. as well as pleasant weather. We could say this symbolically shows we are more than a 'fair weather friend' to the tree and also it gives us a real opportunity to get a feel for the area and the tree's response to different conditions. We can easily become complacent if we always go there in sunlight at a certain time and therefore may switch off our inner senses to any subtle emanations and changes in energy there. So try a night visit, or a dusk one, if this is feasible. We can alter our patterns. This goes for all of our actions; green spirituality is about a spontaneity that eradicates stale energy and old conditioning, thus freeing our hearts and minds to new ways of being.

However, we do need a dry day for our actual trance-journey to meet the tree's spirit as we will need to sit on the earth before the tree and be able to sit comfortably there for twenty minutes or so. Perhaps taking a waterproof cover to sit on is a good idea anyway as the damp or chill penetrating our bones is not conducive to a relaxing session!

So, here is a safe framework for what to do when we reach the tree on the day we are to do the simple but effective inner journey to meet the attendant spirit:

1. We should make our greetings and ask if it is alright for us to undertake the trance-journey, stating its purpose and our good intentions. This journey is a way of extending our green-spirited awareness *and* getting to know the tree better.
2. We should ask our tree friend where it is best to sit to undertake this. If this is unspecific then find somewhere which is inconspicuous where it is possible to feel safe and unobserved. If this is frankly impossible at the site of our tree companion then find the nearest location that is. Or as a final option (not the greatest, as it is far more beneficial to be out there physically surrounded by the energy involved) tell the tree you are going to be doing the journey at home, if this is appropriate.
3. We have asked permission and stated our intent. Now we may close our eyes and undertake *the way of the tree,* our protective ritual as

described in chapter one. Slow and steady the breathing as previously explained. Become at peace, protected and receptive.

4. Now undertake the journey:

'I am sitting upon the sacred earth in the presence of my tree companion. Yet I sit not in the world of men but in the world of spirits which is always present behind and beyond our own perception. I sit in the enchanted landscape and witness the energy of all I survey, the life-force glow around grass and plant and my own fingers. I see the intensity of colours and hear the voices of nature with more clarity. The heartbeat of the land is my own and I breathe deeply to its rhythm, slowing my breath even more and feeling that deep connection rising and falling and pulsing within me. More than this I see the other inhabitants of this sacred land. I see the ethereal guardians, the nature spirits.

I know that one of these beings is the special protector of my companion tree. I also realise that these nature spirits are shy of humanity and so I need to call them to me gently. To do this I must create a space where they feel safe to be themselves without fear of reprisal or capture. I must also show that I am willing to be part of the same scenario, that it is no trap. So, I raise the index finger of my active hand and focus upon it. I witness a stream of blue-gold luminosity stream from its tip, like cold fire. This is a protective energy that I will direct.

Pointing, I inscribe a circle on the ground before me with this protective fire, large enough for another being to feel comfortable in and far enough from me for them to not feel threatened. This circle I extend out towards me as I am to draw a figure of eight, the top circle to be for the spirit and the bottom to be looped around me where I sit. We are joined by protective fire yet separate in our own circles. I use my finger and the streaming blue-gold fire that emits from it to make these figure of eight/two conjoined circles clear and strong whilst imaging it as something which keeps us both safe. Perhaps in time, when a relationship has hopefully been established between me and the spirit, I will not need such precautions, but for now it is apposite to have such a system in operation.

I draw a star in the air with my finger, creating a shining fiery symbol of magic and mystery above me, and ask,

'Oh guardian spirit of my companion tree,
I have created a place where we may sit and talk,
Each being kept separate and secure, with respect to our differences.
Come and let us gently join forces,
Uniting in our common love of this tree,
Sharing our desire to protect and serve and celebrate it. Come to
the space I have prepared for you,
May the true guardian come!'

I sit and calmly wait, focusing on the empty circle in front of me, being alert to any changes in energy in the area. I open myself up, knowing I am protected and I keep sending out the call to the genuine spirit I wish to meet.

Gradually I may become aware of a presence in that circle. I may or may not be able to perceive them as a figure. They may simply be a dancing light, or a misty form. As long as I have the awareness of a presence I may point at them and ask them that they are indeed the guardian spirit of the tree in question, in truth, and not a passing mischievous spirit wishing to cause confusion. As I point at them a stream of the same blue-gold liquid flame streams out towards them. It cannot harm them; only direct my will that they show themselves truly. I ask:

> *'Only the true guardian spirit of this tree may remain,*
> *All others must move on.*
> *Are you the true guardian?'*

The spirit, although not captured, has agreed to operate by my laws in my space and therefore will ascent to such a testing of their nature. If they are indeed the true spirit they will become stronger, brighter, more defined as a presence. If they are not then they will fade or vanish and I am then free to repeat the process until the true spirit shows up.

When I have made contact I may just introduce myself or give them time to introduce themselves. If there is an automatic bond and good communication I may ask three questions and see if they have any questions for me. Questions may be things such as

- *What can I do to ensure the safety or health of the site/tree?*
- *What is it that you wish me to do when relating to you/the tree?*
- *Is there anything I need to know this day about you/the tree?*
- *How may I make our link stronger and more meaningful?*
- *How can I help you by making practical gestures?*
- *How may I act magically/spiritually/imaginatively to enhance the tree?*

I may also wish to the spirits to show themselves in a more recognisable form, which they may be prepared to do if there is an instant rapport between us. They may also offer a name by which I may call them although I should be aware that they probably will not give me their true name or indeed reveal any preferred shape to me. They will simply shape-shift and say what it is that I can relate to personally. Whatever, this intimate connection must be allowed time to develop.

I should not make the first contact session too long but build up trust and time spent together gradually, with care. Obviously I should give profound thanks for their time and effort afterwards and ask if I may speak with them again in this way. I can then come back to the present/manifest reality, having made the link with the nature spirits. Perhaps in future I can bring a little of their enchantment back to my realm with me, so that I may experience it more clearly in my daily life. Eventually I may well be able to see the spirits without going into trance at all and talk to them in the place between our worlds with full consciousness.'

After this session, sit with the tree itself and write up the magical journal, sharing a simple meal and drink to both ground ourselves and enhance our friendship with the tree.

Note that this very simple journey framework can be extended out to cover meeting any other nature spirit we may feel the need to encounter for our own education and for sharing purposes, asking how we may better serve nature.

What can we offer the tree's attendant spirit by way of thanks afterwards? We could make a vow that we will take every last bus ticket, shop receipt, paper wrapper etc. to the paper recycling point/ depot. Imagine if we all did that. *Imagine*! Imagining is wild magic. So yes, imagine everyone feeling the urge to do just that. Imagine everyone valuing the gifts that the trees give us, never wasting paper or wood.

Finally, as regards this section, I must recommend an excellent selection of artwork relating to nature spirits and one man's stunning vision of their presence in his life. Marc Potts, a fine artist from Devon, England, has a particularly good eye for the hauntingly beautiful and powerful tree spirits we have ourselves been encountering. His website is at www.marcpotts.com. Obviously this is not how all tree spirits look but rather how he sees them; having a look at his work shares but one interesting and arresting vision.

Faeries

Here is a whole different race of individuals, the Fey, a word which stems from the Latin '*fatare*' meaning 'to enchant'. (I use the capital F for Fey to denote their race yet the lower case f for faery to denote them as individuals in general. Also fey with a lower case f denotes a faery nature, fey meaning 'of the faery' in this instance.) The relevance of these captivating hidden beings to us as green-spirited modern humans is enormous as our contact with their kind, should they allow it, is like drinking from the source of a pure bubbling mountain stream. The Fey are refreshing, they care not a jot for the constraints and orderliness of the world of people, preferring to remain in their own dimension of reality which is more focused on mischief, making love, merriment and, perhaps above all, magic and mystery. Therefore contact with them replenishes our sense of what is truly important, the poetry of living in harmony, and the unbridled joy of being at peace with whom and what we are and the mystical aspects of existence. They are vital, unpredictable and beautiful in terms of their completely spontaneous, liberated way. In my precious experience of these (tragically) largely forgotten folk, they can teach us, we who are trying so valiantly to care for the Earth and our fellow beings, how to have the utmost fun whilst acting with care and courtesy for this divine planet. I personally find their disdain and often outright contempt for humanity endearing (even if it is not meant to be) and I love the fact they will shape-shift, cast a glamour or do virtually all within their power to confuse, trip and tangle us human-kind in a web made largely of our own foolish, selfish desires.

These fabulous beings are contrary, wilful and cheeky and do not like to be summoned or held by any human bond. Rather like Romany Gypsies they are the outlawed ones who dwell on the fringe of our memory and consciousness and we miss their charismatic company yet know that the world we have made is not one they wish to be in. Often there is no place for their wild and flamboyant presence. However effectively they have removed themselves from our world, like may well draw to like and our shared feelings about the land may reach them and unite us. With their incredible, irrepressible sense of fun they may not be able to resist showing themselves to us in the wild places they still inhabit, albeit behind the veil of reality which separates their realm of being from ours. They prefer the 'less-peopled' land, the moors and mountains, inaccessible coves and stretches of unmanaged forest. Unlike nature spirits, their nebulous and numinous kin, they would never deign to appear in a window box in a flat on a high street. They openly spurn concrete and bustle and stick to areas which have their resonance, a particular sort of air which we can become attuned to if we have the mind to. In my experience, one knows a 'faery place' (one where the veils between their world and ours and thinner, a place which they 'haunt') not only by the degree of wild energy it still possesses but also by the 'watchful' feel it has. This can be curiosity, hostility or a particular perverse mixture, as is the want of the Fey, but there will be a sense of being observed by something far older, wiser and cannier than our human selves!

I was once on holiday in a region renowned for this faery presence, a beautiful area of babbling brooks, bogs, rocky outcrops and tangled undergrowth. The only sign of humanity was in its failed settlements, ruins of walls and foundations of cottages long since fallen to earth. I made the mistake of asking, repeatedly, to see the faery presences I could clearly feel watching me. I didn't demand but I kept on and on, I *really* wanted to see them! '*Reveal yourselves!*' I beseeched them yet they did not. Disappointed I climbed into my guest house bed that night only to find one of the faery presences was indeed with me... sitting on my bed in fact. I tried shaking them off the bed and thought that I had succeeded until I fell promptly asleep and had a rather alarming, and very vivid, dream about a strange marauding faery-beast that simply would not die no matter how many times it was shot. When I awoke I discovered that my then partner had experienced precisely the same phenomena, including the dream, in the next bed. Having met many representatives of the Fey before, I knew this to be ample warning that I was an unwanted aggravation and unless they came to me I should leave them well alone as they were far more powerful and tricky than I could ever hope to be!

The Fey are not elemental but may well have a connection to any one element or particularly elemental environment such as a hill or natural spring. For example, I once met a faery being who was extremely earthy and appeared to me as a man of twisted bark. His home was the site of a remote stone circle although he had dwelled there on 'his land' long before its construction. The only reason he ever appeared to me at all (and I clearly felt his spirit-presence as well as perceiving him in my mind's-eye as the anthropomorphised form of the bark-man) was because we shared the same anger at the human detritus left at the stone circle's site. He remained as an informative, if irate, presence in my life for some time after our encounter as our viewpoints, and indeed our energies, were compatible at that time. He was able to be present in my reality and his own at will; the faery folk can step between the realms easily. I certainly did not imagine his sharp, swift kick to my ankles if he thought that I was doing something environmentally careless. He was quite able of affecting my physical, as well as energetic, space!

These fabulous spirit-folk live behind our time, in the wild green *beyond*. They are, as the sensitive, evocative author Rae Beth suggests in her poem *Familiar Spirit*, 'of Earth's unearthliness'. Perhaps they once wore denser energetic forms, or perhaps the world we now know was less physically dense and we could move more readily 'twixt one reality and other ourselves. With our senses fully honed and open *in the moment* and in a less rigid time than we know today, perhaps we were able to flit into the nebulous world of faery and allow the faery folk to visit us also. One may believe this is so by the sheer number of tales as regards 'faery blood', perhaps those of us so privileged once lived, loved and physically lay with these fabulous ones. Yet here is another less popular idea... perhaps our own spirits used to have less human and more fey forms themselves but somehow the encroaching of humanity made it impossible for us to incarnate as faery beings in the Earth sphere any longer. We certainly know that faery-time and ours are not the same: one faery year is often described as a hundred human ones, yet the faery may not be immortal... rather have longer life spans and cycles than humans. Put simply it may well be that somehow the faery bodies we once had died and we had to come back to incarnate on Earth wearing human bodies instead. This maybe explains, to some degree, why so many sensitive people drawn to a broadly pagan path feel alien in today's culture and uncomfortable wearing a human skin; we may long for our old flexible and fantastic faery forms!

This is just speculation obviously but I personally would like to think that those of us drawn to the kind of green spirituality that mixes the ethereal with the muddy-fingered, blending the profound, the practical and the playful with ease, have a little faery blood blended in with their human lineage down through the ages. Either that or we have a fey soul which had to incarnate as a human for the sake of bringing the greening back to Earth. Whatever our link to them is, the faery beings exist. But do they wish to be contacted and worked with? For the sake of bringing magic back to life, assisting environmental repair and helping with a resurgence of wild, creative, inspirational energy the answer is a resounding yes. So, here is an idea for a simple, gentle wish-spell for making a Fey contact, should they wish it. It is like an astral, or Otherworldly, call to the Fey closest to us in temperament, needs or outlook.

When the blossom is on the trees and as the moon waxes from new to full make pilgrimages to a hawthorn, an apple and an elder tree. (There will be much more about the energies of sun and moon tides in chapter four while chapter three has more about our green allies.) Be fully present and aware of the energies of each, asking if we may work with them in a spell to bring the faery magic back to the human realm. If this is appropriate (if it feels right and the tree consents) then circle the tree three times counterclockwise, this being widdershins, the way the moon travels (the moon being a potent symbol of mystery and deep magic as well as our sister of the skies). Give the attendant nature spirits a 'faery curtsey' (or bow) by touching the left hand to the forehead, sweeping the right out in a gesture of graceful acknowledgement and, if we are physically able, with one foot pointed in front of the other bow low. Then ask if

74

a small twig may be our own for the spell to have a physical aspect to it, a *charm*. This twig will either be already freshly fallen and still full of vigorous life-force energy or it will become apparent to us that we may snap and pick one from the tree itself. We will know that it is the right thing to do by the ease with which the wood breaks and parts company with the branch. On doing this, we should vow to return when the spell has been released, with a gift of remembrance for the tree's generosity.

Allow the tree, or the attendant spirit, to tell us what this may be and memorise this message as a gesture of being fully *in the now* and attentive. We should not write it down in our journal until after we have given the gift to the tree; it is a secret to strengthen our powers of being present in the moment.

We should then offer our thanks and pledge a return when the spell is sent on. Repeat this for all three trees. We should take our twigs and keep them in a dark cloth until the night of the full moon, when the powers of enchantment are at their height. Then we can bind the three twigs with a piece of our own hair or a scrap of fabric torn from one of our old garments (if hair is not available). If we do not use hair then wiping a little of our own fresh blood or spittle on to the three twigs will suffice. It is important to give a little of ourselves, forging a meaningful bond by giving of our body. As this is done chant a simple wish-prayer such as:

> '*By living wood and moon-kissed blood,*
> *To the beyond my wish I sing,*
> *My wild heart opens to you now,*
> *The magic back to life I'll bring*
> *By power of three I call to thee,*
> *Like calls to faery like this spring!*'

We should keep this wish-bundle under our pillow and wish on it morning and evening (dawn and dusk if possible) until the next full moon. At this time take it to a place which has a faery energy and leave it where it may be found by the Fey, *not* by any passing humans... be ingenious like the faery folk are and hang it from a branch of a consenting but hard to reach tree (physical ability allowing) or place it under a willing rock or deep within some tree roots. If we do not yet know of a faery place then go to a flowing river which has a quiet bridge over it and cast it into the water, running water having a poetic mystery akin to faery energy. Whether we leave it buried, hanging or in water we should be sure to wish on it as we do so.

Certainly don't forget to return to the donor trees afterwards and gift them. This seals the magic. Perhaps a final gift would be contributing something particularly Fey of our own to the world, such as a beautiful poem or a painting of an Otherworldly/inspirational scene. A donation of old clothes, books, crockery, toys etc. to a child oriented charity shop would also be a lovely gesture with the same resonance... not only is this a 'spring clean' and a worthwhile act of recycling but also the Fey are resolutely childlike in their playful and decidedly wilful outlook and so the magical circle (that which echoes the sacred round of life) is complete.

This simple spell will give us a chance to dream about our faery contact, or be led to where they 'live' (in Otherworldly terms) or any other manner of communication that the faery may decide is appropriate. Be sure they will answer us if we contact them with the strongest and purest intent and follow up on all our promises. They Fey are particularly disparaging about humanity's lack of commitment and even though they themselves are notoriously tricky they will not appreciate *you* breaking your side of the deal! Our integrity is paramount in all our green-spirited transactions.

Spirit of place and site guardians

Site guardians can fall into two categories, the man-made and the natural. In respect of the latter, the nature spirits we have previously mentioned are site guardians. What follows is an example of what such a guardian may do.

In my locale there is a particularly fine old 'faery fort' (a round hill, often thought of as hollow, which has the ability to transport a receptive visitor to the Fey realm quite easily). Glastonbury Tor in southwest England would be a famous example of a hollow hill, a place where the seeker may encounter mystery, a portal to the nebulous realm of enchantment. I myself often visit this particular faery hill and have taken many (requested) offerings for the spirit of the place, the guardian energy, as a thank you for allowing me to walk there. It has a particularly watchful and 'heavy' presence and I have always been keen not to offend it by outstaying my welcome or making demands on its energy. However, I had noticed that there was an old van dumped to one side of this beautiful wild spot. I thought how offended the intensely private Fey and the attendant spirits of the land would be at this very ugly reminder of man's stupidity left in their midst. I was therefore not too surprised to learn shortly after seeing this van that the owner had been foolish enough to do a little impromptu 'clearing' on the hill and had set about burning the hawthorn there. As we may have gathered from the inclusion of hawthorn in the spell for a Fey contact, the faery folk love this tree very well and so this was doubly unwise. This action had lead to him promptly having some manner of serious internal haemorrhage whilst out in the wilds of the area and had only just managed to get to hospital in time.

This may seem a rather scary tale but it is to illustrate that site guardians will 'fight to the death'; it is their job description, as it were, and not maliciousness. We, as people who wish to engender a climate of renewed respect and sensitivity, should always be aware of such strong feeling and never overlook the guardian spirit/s of such a place.

Man-made sites, such as barrows, hill forts and stone circles, will undoubtedly have guardians although these will be equally man-made (although the land itself will have its own nature spirit guardians too). As somewhat unorthodox green-spirited folk we may be disinclined to follow the usual tourist trails at peak times, preferring quieter and less obvious natural sites, and so the established stone monuments may not be among our regular haunts. However, we may find ourselves in a man-made place which has been designated as sacred and wonder who, or what, is protecting it. When our ancestors fashioned the henges, burial chambers etc. they did so with infinite wisdom of earth energies and spirit-beings. They did not devote such time, effort and skill and then leave their special places unguarded. They would magically 'construct', perhaps by mass visualisation or invocation (remembering the imagination has a singularly powerful magic), an energetic presence to do the job of guarding their place in their absence. Such beings can therefore be referred to as *constructs*. This does not denigrate their power or purpose but simply denotes what they are.

I personally have encountered giant figures of formidable presence at such sites, presences which still have the power to bring a human such as myself to her knees, and would advise caution when approaching any man-made site. We have precious little idea of our ancestors' ways and cannot hope to understand the guardians they created within the framework of our modern consciousness. In this respect it is wise to know that the guardians exist and consequently 'beware of the dog', acting with quiet respect at all times.

Old Wild Ones

Here are the spirits, vast, ancient presences in the landscape, who will help us take on our own green mantle. These are the overseers, the spirit of the greening itself, the wild woman and wild man as we perceive them. How we *perceive* them, as opposed to how they truly are, is the key to understanding their essence; they are really beings of refined green energy, forces of nature and not men and women at all, but again we humans anthropomorphise them. By this I mean we witness their spiritual presence as the archetypal humanoid representatives of nature, typically as foliate men and women. They are not man-made and not of men, they are *of the land*, expressions of its primal self, stewards and custodians of all that grows and dies back, numinous native spirits. They are ancient, intelligent, strong and integrous beyond human understanding. However, they are quite willing and able to act as bridges between man and nature, much more so than the Fey or other nature spirits, and are consequently approachable and accessible as well as being awesome. Part of their core purpose is to unite all life-forms for the benefit of the land and so they will work with us if we walk gently on the Earth with them. They will always protect, nourish and show the way for their own kin, the green-spirited folk.

Let me say here that the old wild ones we are about to encounter, perhaps for the first time, are not to my mind gods and goddesses; in fact, contrary to a great deal of modern pagan discourse, there are no gods or goddesses mentioned in this work. I would like to suggest, not dictate, that in green spirituality we need no such constructs as ultimate deity figures, fashioned by human need. I have no doubt that there are forces above and beyond our Earthly sphere, beings who exist in closer harmony with the Creator, or ultimate Source energy, than we ourselves presently do, but why they should have to have human guises, names etc. seems quite untenable to me. In a limitless unfolding universe, and possibly universes, dimensions full of a myriad of life-forms, how could the ultimate Creator energy wear a singularly human aspect? Or have specifically human, Earth-linked attributes? This seems terribly human-centric again, the very attitude we are trying to move away from! I feel it would therefore be disingenuous of me to write about deities I have no experience of and am happy to stick to what can be experienced on the land and within ourselves, the mystery of the wild and its attendant energies. However, if the reader sees fit to deify such figures that is entirely up to them, obviously, and the relationship will no doubt work just as well for this. There are no rights and wrongs; I simply suggest what works for me as the person guiding the wild journey safely.

Although the old wild ones are not necessarily gods or goddesses they can be related to in the same way we may relate to such powerful energies, not by worshipping them but through prayer, appreciation and a respectful asking for guidance. How we live with a green-spirited outlook, moment to moment, can be an act of devotion and gratitude for all that is sacred and we certainly need not make formal gestures apart from this ongoing soul-offering, that which flows freely from us on a daily basis. So, once we have met these wise, wild beings we can link into their presence at any time, enjoying their care and their ability to educate us in the truest sense. This they will do in return for our own personal magical activities/thoughts; as forces of nature they appreciate balance and a giving and receiving of energy. They will act as our mentors from hereon in if, and only if, we can honour the land they represent.

Taking on the green mantle is all about making a personal dedication to the way of the old wild ones, that is, taking the responsibility to the way of replenishment on to our backs and carrying/wearing it with pleasure. We should be sure that we feel ready for this before undertaking the following trance-journey. It is a *path-working*, that is to say, a guided journey for a specific purpose. Within its framework we may feel free to change any wording that feels inappropriate to us personally. Things such as descriptions can be replaced or changed while the basic theme, pattern and meaning of the overall journey should remain intact. So, use your own imagination to embellish the framework once it has been read through.

CONTACTING THE OLD WILD ONES... A JOURNEY TO TAKE ON THEIR GREEN MANTLE

'*I stand in sunlight where there are no shades of grey; I walk under the noonday sun along the wildest way . . .*

My feet are bare and feel every ridge and ripple of the hillside I travel upon, I am skin-to-skin with the land and know her pulse as my own as I step joyfully onwards. There is sun on my face and wind in my hair, the land rises to meet my feet as I walk over the green hill to its rounded summit. All around me are the treasures of nature, pale misshapen flints, an iridescent feather caught in a tussock of grass, tiny spiral shells with their occupants long gone, the perfect little balls of dung that show me that the rabbit-kin live nearby, though may now be sleeping. I lift my arms to the scudding white clouds racing overhead and quicken my pace, moving swiftly to my own heartbeat drum as I climb steadily to the top of this gentle slope.

My feet carry me to the top and I am rewarded by a panoramic view of the surrounding area. I see the land spread out before me in all the vibrant, verdant glory of early summer, displaying its burgeoning curves and flourishing beauty with a graceful unselfconscious ease. The mature trees wear their newly bright emerald crowns, green saplings shimmy in delight in the warm sun, the tender corn sways in wide swathes and the hedgerows froth with creamy blossom, bursting with their own exuberant sap-filled energy. Beneath my feet there are celandines turning their eager faces to the equally golden sun and above my head the fluffy clouds part to reveal that very sun, concealing that beaming benevolent face only briefly as they scud fast across the cerulean blue of the sky. I note the shadows of these giant fluffy clouds moving over the green of the land below, chasing the shadows of their predecessors across bank and ditch and flat plain.

I note that in the distance the curve of the earth meets the sky in a pale lilac haze. I know that as I turn I will see the place, far distant, where the land also meets the sea. I spin slowly, taking in the land's full three hundred and sixty degrees, witnessing a lark rising high over an area of rough pasture, hearing a blackbird call sweetly and repeatedly to its mate from a lone hawthorn that has sprouted diligently or belligerently from a rocky place. I observe a family of deer running with obvious delight across a meadow to the river, disturbing a hare as they pass which in turn lopes to their left and disappears into long grass. I see the heads of cow parsley nodding in the lane where a vole runs, as yet unobserved by the kestrel hovering nearby. I spin slowly three times, noting new and glorious things each time I do so.

I stop and say: sing out:

'I'm with the land, so I am,
So I am!
I'm with the land,
With dark soil and distant strand,
I'm with the stark white feather as it falls,
I'm with the spirit that animates it all.

I'm with the land, so I am,
So I am!
I'm with the land
With the fox cub and the lamb,
I'm with the wren and the robin as they call,
I'm with the spirit that animates it all,

I'm with the spirit that animates us all!'

Then I sit down, knowing that I will soon be visited by the very spirits that animate it all, the wild man and woman. I place my hands on the back of the

Earth Mother and relish the touch of springy grass and slightly moist, firm soil beneath. It feels colder than my own skin to the touch even though the day is warm, for on this hill the wind always blows. I feel the hair tossed carelessly back from my face, the light perspiration on my brow cooling and my heartbeat slowing. I breathe deeply, scenting the rich aroma of drying cattle dung, the strange damp quality of stone, the warm sweet fragrance of gorse and the more pungent of elderflower, lifted and carried to me from the hedgerows below. I feel the chill fresh air in my lungs and relish each moment. I breathe and I wait, getting a sense of any change in the energies around me. Gradually I become aware of the hairs rising on the back of my neck, my skin pricking in anticipation as I am approached from behind. I resist the temptation to turn and look, keeping my eyes on the colourful panorama of ditch and dell and dug earth where crops wave or sprout in glossy green lines.

They flank me and sit, to my left and right, their presences giving me a frisson of fear as well as excitement. They are big, taller and broader than I; I feel that without even looking. It is like having two wild creatures drawing close to me, a stag on one side and a mare on the other, perhaps. I have the feeling that I am being sniffed and I imagine their wide nostrils flaring, lips drawn back from teeth as they take the measure of me. I wait for them to address me, unwilling to speak until they themselves are ready. I steady my breathing and take in their scents also, a mixture of darkly fertile forest loam, an evocative mineral tang like river water on stone and an overlay of faint and fleeting twin aromas; animal sweat and wet rotting vegetation. I breathe again and this time only scent a sweetness that reminds me of hay and wind fallen apples.

One speaks, the wild man.

'You have called us to you this day to take on the green mantle. We will take you to the place most suitable for this. But first we must travel together. In so doing we will witness what it means to wear the mantle. Will you travel?'

I nod my assent, still not turning to look at them, afraid I will stare if I do. The woman speaks now.

'Take our hands and rise, child of the greening. Do not be afraid, for we are only a mirror of the land you love. We and the land are one, it has always been so. Will you join us?'

This time I glance to the left and see her. She is indeed like a mare, full of grace and power, a long mane of hair blowing out behind her, tangled yet shining, caught with brambles and burrs yet silky soft. Her skin is darkened and lined by sun and wind but her powerful body is reminiscent of the valley before me, undulating, all swells and long flowing lines. Her firm slender-fingered hand reaches for mine, reminding me of hazel twigs yet flexible as boiled withies. Tiny leaves sprout from her wrist below the mantle of leaves she herself wears and a rain of starry white blossom falls on us as the wind moves her russet and chestnut hair again. About her neck is a band made of interwoven horsehair and shells, plaited corn and the teeth of tiny animals long since returned to the soil. I avert my gaze from her, conscious of staring, of placing too much emphasis on her appearance, and feel the wild man take my right hand. His grip is firmer and is as warm as hers was cool. He squeezes my fingers gently, revealing the underlying strength in his great paws of hands. His knuckles are swollen and gnarled, the veins like serpentine ropes under the surface of his wrists where the dark skin sprouts coarse black hairs. I turn and take him in a little.

He is straight as an arrow and as broad as any bear. His cloak is of both hairy hide and softest down, rough wool caught with leaves and stitched with twine from the gut of a long dead boar, a creature who died a natural death at the feet of this awesome being. His own hair is matted and long, thick snakes of it swing down his wide lean back. Again his skin bears the scars of weather and age but his frame is hard as sparkling granite and as flexible as the boughs of an oak tree. His huge feet in their shaggy boots paw the ground impatiently although I know he is smiling. I glimpse his wide mouth, his flicking tongue, the crinkling of skin around fathomless eyes and above chiselled cheekbones, hewn as if from pitted sandstone.

I squeeze both of their hands as an affirmative and we step into thin air.

We are flying, not as the hawk or rook but as the eagle glides, silently soaring. We move through the air on its currents, three of us becoming as one huge and graceful bird-being, moving without motion, flowing attentively over and above . . . yet with . . . the land.

We rise in a single moment over a small mountain, seeing the sparkle of ice on its peak, breathing the purity of the air up above it. I see the tiny ice crystals in the air and sparkling energy whirring and dancing wildly all about us. My right hand is squeezed and I hear the wild man speak with the voice of a mountain breeze, cold and refreshingly crisp.

'You witness the air as it should be, unsullied by man and the ways of man, air like a sparkling river, air free to dance with itself, pristine. Do you vow to keep the air as it was when it was first breathed out of the soul of the Creator?'

I affirm my intent to do so. And for a moment I breathe not the clean mountain air but the air of the city, of the industrial area, of the motorway, and I know that my vow stands true, I do not wish for the species I represent to continue to act in this way.

We swoop down in a fluid motion as one being without wings, following a bubbling mountain stream as it swoops down from its spring source on the slopes, meandering as it flows down and on, cutting through the valley floor in a languid looping motion, bringing fresh drinking water to the green beings and the creatures who dwell within the banks and bushes on either side. I witness it swell and move swiftly over rocks, seeing the shining scales of salmon and the colourful flanks of trout pass rapidly underneath its surface. I see it act as a mirror to the overhanging willows, reflecting and refracting clouds and sky. I see an otter slip into its welcoming embrace as it flows on, singing to itself with a voice that was pure and true.

My left hand is squeezed and the wild woman speaks in the voice of a heron that would stand in the shallows,

'You witness the water, life-giving and sweet, untainted by man and the ways of man, each bubble and ripple exquisite and vital. Do you vow to keep the waters of the Earth as fresh and wholesome as they first were, perfect as when they flowed from the heart of the Source?'

I affirm my intent to do so. And for a moment I see not clear water but foaming dirty grey water, full of the tiny corpses of fish who are swept along next to tyres and cans and plastic debris. Upon seeing this I know that my vow is an honest one for I no longer wish to support a society that condones this.

And we swoop and glide still lower until we are skimming the tops of the trees and can see down through the branches as we pass, glimpsing squirrels busily negotiating the highest reaches to the chagrin of roosting owls. Spotted woodpeckers excavate holes in the healthy bark as starlings whistle. And farther down still I see, with the vision of the bird of prey I have become as one with, the other tiny dwellers of this sylvan realm . . . the badger shifting in his earth amongst the network of strong roots, the beetles and grubs hatching, the shifting of earth nearby as a pink nosed mole edges his way to the surface. All life is busy, blooming. All is as it should be in the cycle of life, the tree standing above and below, tall, strong and fundamental to the existence of so many others.

The wild man speaks in the voice of the leaves, a swift soft whispering, soothing but persistent,

'You witness the earth realm and the overseers of this realm, the wisdom bearers and sustainers of all. You see the honour that is given to these beings by all nature and the gifts they themselves bestow in return. Do you vow to hold these wise ones of the bark in highest esteem, as they were originally created, as holders of breath and givers of sustenance and true vision?'

I give my vow to the affirmative. And for a moment I no longer witness healthy wood, glowing leaves and thrusting branches but rather buzzing timber yards and furniture stores with new furniture that no one really needs. I see the mounds of junk mail and leaflets left discarded and gasp as I observe bulldozers rip down yet more tracts of woodland to build roads and new expensive houses. As I behold such terrible behaviours I am sure that my vow will remain forever true, that I shall no longer stand by and let such desecration of the standing nation happen.

We fly on, swerving around small ranges of hills and dipping low over gullies until we are out over the moors and heading for the sea. We skim over twisted trees and stunted gorse as the wind buffets us and lifts us only to drop us down again in the next breath. I see a herd of small wild ponies running with joy over the scrubland, feel the power of the untouched land as it thrusts up stony crags and shrugs its shoulders into deep ravines. I hear the wheedling cry of the buzzard and witness the miracle of colour, from purple shadow to slate grey to pale lichen green to the sunburst of flowering broom. Then we are up with the gulls and flying over the dunes, almost touching the tops of dry grasses as we move towards the sea, hearing its roar deep within us before it is seen and then we are sinking down, called by the fragrant smoke of a drift-wood fire in a sandy cove, swirling like the smoke itself, losing cohesion, being pulled by the sea, coming apart and expanding, drawing closer and uniting, invaded by wind and wave, by sand and salt, by smoke and the warmth of the small fire as we draw nearer and nearer to it.

We are standing, we three, by the flickering fire, and the wild ones steady me as I get my bearings once more. I am saddened not to be flying but the warmth from the blaze is welcome and it quickly warms me to the bones; the realm of air can be a chilly one. I witness the bright leaping of the flames, the crimson and the scarlet and the vermillion with their heart of gold. The wild woman speaks. She asks,

'Do you pledge, by the fiery passion of your soul, to keep the protective beacon of stewardship for the land burning within and without? Do you wish to turn your righteous anger against the destruction of the Earth Mother into posi-tive action, into the way of replenishment? Child, do you vow now to see a new day rise from the ashes of wanton destruction and greed, witness the rosy dawn of a healed world, with all beings living in balance again? And will you kindle that compassionate flame to a blaze within your soul this day, for the sake of all others who share the land, as honoured guests of the Earth Mother?'

I give my assent fervently.

At this she takes a single stick from the driftwood fire and holds it aloft. Sparks shower down around us and for a moment I am plunged into the despair of a world eaten up by cruel disregard and avarice, a blackened, dusty lonely place, scarred and pitted by the humans who raped and pillaged her for plunder. I know in my bones and beyond that I will strive to do all I can do on a personal level to ensure this is never the future, only the bad dream of a confused species. I vow to turn the tide, to end this separation of man and nature, and within me the desire flares brightly in response.

The wild woman lowers the burning wand back into the fire and takes my hand again, as does her counterpart. Thus we walk up a coastal path along the cliffs, all the time walking to the thrum of the land and feeling the powerful surging of the sea in our blood which pounds in our veins in response as we climb. Our route takes us over the short spiky grass, between the wind-buffeted shrubs that cling to life there and it meanders up and down the worn, exposed cliff top. Eventually we descend steadily, moving inland. The sound of the sea becomes fainter and is replaced by another sound. Running water.

We are walking down into a tiny hidden sanctuary between rocks and over-hanging greenery. There is a cool green calm to the place, augmented by the steady cascade of clear water which tumbles joyfully down the rocks, a natural waterfall. As we reach the bottom of this magical place and stand on the damp earth I feel the deep peace of my companions and of all nature flooding through me, washing away all thoughts, tensions and expectations. I close my eyes, feeling the gentle spray on my skin, hearing the water spilling down merrily. I am aware of my companions protectively flanking me in silence and I breathe deeply once more, scenting the ferny moistness of this singularly beautiful little place. I feel in a wave a new understanding for the wildness of the land in repose, the natural world in perfect balance and harmony. I know my place within this, as an active, compassionate, responsible and spirit-full being. I breathe slowly. And as I do so I feel the hands of the wild man and woman at my neck and back, touching me lightly. They are placing something upon my back.

Their voices are one, rising in a rhythmic, lilting, uplifting, inspiring cadence, voices so reminiscent of the bubbling water, the free flowing air, the flickering flames and the shifting sands. They say,

'Take upon your back this green mantle and wear it lightly just as you walk lightly on the land. Do not grasp it to yourself but know of its presence enfolding you, protecting you, revealing you as one of the beings of Earth who has made the heart-vow, the green-spirited promise of stewardship. Wear this mantle which tells of the folk of fur and feather, which shines with the glorious hues of autumn leaf and spring flower, sewn with seeds, hung with shells, stitched with hair and sinew and stem. Feel it flow around you, blow around you, glow around you and know we are with you, for the land is one with us, and we are one with you!'

For a moment I am aware of nothing but the fullness of my heart and the gladness of my spirit, sensing as I do my part in the dance of life on a verdant planet. Then we all say, as one,

'Custodian of beauty, love and truth am I, this day and all days, so may it be!'

I open my eyes and find that I am alone again, on the hilltop where I first stood waiting for them. I am back where I began my journey but I am changed, profoundly so. I feel the presence of the green mantle about me and I settle into it, with a sense of its rightness about my person. It will sometimes be a hard road I walk whilst wearing it, making sacrifices, going out of my way to make the compassionate choice, flying in the face of public opinion and swimming against the polluted flow of humanity's destructive thoughts but I shall stand firm, a green-spirited guardian who walks with the old wild ones.

I travel back home with this knowledge at the core of me.'

We should not forget to ground ourselves after this rather epic journey by eating and drinking (tea and biscuits or water and fruit etc.) and by writing up our magical journal so that we have a full record of the experience. Also, of course, by the act of writing it down we are earthing it in daily reality.

Clearly when this taking on of the green mantle has been done in an unseen, spiritual sense (within) then we must ensure that we make a suitable gesture to the without or seen world to make it real on both levels. It is for us to think of four manifest acts, one for water, one for air, one for the earth and her creatures and one for the element of fire, symbolising our passionate commitment. There will be plenty of suggestions for manifest acts coming up in the next chapters but for now it is upon us personally to think of four generous ways we can express our wearing of the green mantle in the world, expressing our environmental concerns as well as our love of all creatures and beings. As a gesture of commitment and caring we should also relate to the old wild ones as often as we can, for they are now more fully in our lives and we are, in turn, in their awareness also. To forget their presence would be not only disrespectful but also a great shame for they are eloquent, patient and inspirational spiritual guides, as we ourselves have now witnessed.

We now hopefully have a much better idea of what it means to be a green-spirited being dwelling on the living land. We know more about how we can work and whom we may work with. Our roots are growing. Now we can move on to acknowledging our own particular spirit companions as well as gaining more knowledge about the other more physical beings who share our world. Before we do this, let's think of a way to close the day in the same way that we opened it. One such way is by offering up a prayer of thanks for the day that has been. This could be something like;

> '*This day*
> *I have witnessed the promise of sunrise and the surrender of sunset,*
> *I have bathed, both in holy water and the song of birds,*
> *I have drunk deeply, like the butterfly upon the buddleia, of each honeyed moment,*
> *And I have touched perfection in my relationship with all others.*

Now do I wash my spirit in sweet starlight,
Now do I lie down in contentment,
Knowing the quiet world of bat and fox and owl to be but a breath
away,
Knowing that breath to be mine and yours and theirs.

By moonbeam and night's dream so may it be,
My thanks flow out from the heart of me.'

To echo this prayer, making a soul-full gesture of intent in the world, we could perhaps stitch a few more squares on to a quilt we are making for another person or charity organisation. We could fill up all of our wild bird feeders and the bird table ready for morning. We could drink a cup of home-grown valerian tea, an excellent and gentle soporific herb, and pour an offering to the soil. We could spend a little quiet time finding more inspiring quotes or images for the inspiration board and perhaps copy them to send them to a sick, lonely or unhappy friend in the form of a small hand-made booklet. We could write a short letter of environmental protest to a local MP (if this wouldn't make us too wakeful) or could light a candle and place it in the window as a gift of light and hope for the world. Any gesture of care and stewardship can be dedicated in such a way. If we stop thinking of our daily chores as mundane then everything, from sandwich making to shoe polishing, can have that air of enchantment, that symbolic magical significance we are now becoming familiar with.

Whatever we choose to do, we can rest assured that we are wearing the green mantle now and nothing will ever be quite the same for us again.

3

Walking the Wild Way

We were once all country dwellers. Our ancestors, the creative, intuitive, sensitive and resourceful ones whose dwellings nestled between hill and rock, tree and stream, were essentially pagan. Their settlements were rounded, like the Earth Mother and her natural cycles, their ways were unobtrusive and at one with the land. Their way was the way of replenishment and stewardship, concepts that we have previously touched upon in this book and will return to again. It is this gentle, wild one-ness with creation, with our native soil, with all fellow beings, that we seek now to nurture further. We may do this by enhancing our own personal understanding and experience of what it means to be a green-spirited individual in a modern age, with reference and respect to those who went before us. In honour of the ancestors, the ones who walked lightly on the Earth, we will strengthen our own pagan roots by first seeking a guiding spirit that shares these aims and qualities, an unseen companion who will be willing to share with us their knowledge and empathy of the land and its green energies. This companion spirit will help us translate the ancient ways into a context which flows seamlessly into our lives today.

Some call this spirit companion a *familiar*. This is because the spirit that we work most closely with in a one-to-one relationship will be as family to us, deeply *familiar*, thus allowing for a relaxed, open and intimate exchange of ideas and beneficial energies. Yes, this is, as ever, a two way process! We are not talking about a servant, genie or god-like granter of all knowledge/wishes etc.! On the contrary, here is the opportunity to liaise closely with a like-minded soul who will accompany us, behind the scenes as it were, on an equal footing. The only difference between them and us is that they are discarnate (disembodied at present) and we are incarnate, with a body. They will walk in spirit beside us as we go about our daily business and give us the benefit of their wider picture, obtained from their position of not being limited by a physical form. This does not make them omnipotent, only in possession of the bigger picture. And, once we have established this easy bond through a structured meeting (in trance-journey) we may talk to them at any time. Here again is magic in the midst of life, not something to be left for high days and holidays in a ritual formal setting; the companion or familiar spirit relationship is ongoing, unfolding and very immediate. We can, once we recognise their energies and ways of relating, tune in to them *at any time.*

Why have a spirit companion and why would they want to have a relationship with us? Well, the forming of such a relationship enables us to work more closely with the unseen aspects of being, allowing us to develop our senses and our trust in our ability to *feel* what is right. Our companion can give us the benefit of other viewpoints and experiences, something we as solitary green-spirited folk need, and also they can guide and assist us in being more aware of the most appropriate courses of action to take, in terms of energy. They help open us up, give us the overview as opposed to a narrow human view and encourage us to grow as rounded, responsive individuals. We, on the other hand, enable them, as disembodied spirit beings, to affect real change in the world, a world they love as much as we even though they are not currently living physically upon it. They have the benefit of sharing in our ability to physically interact with the land and its inhabitants. We give them manifest influence; they give us the influence of the unseen. This is the basis of our balanced relationship.

It is well to state that our companion or familiar spirit may not appear human. They may have a non-human spirit. This is fine as we have, after all, vowed not to be human-centric! They may choose to represent themselves in a faery guise, or as another kind of elemental or nature spirit. They may show themselves to us as a mythical creature or character such as a unicorn, dragon, centaur or Robin Hood-style wood-elf. They may even be clad in a form that is 'alien' to the Earth realm but only if this will, at some level, strike a comfortable chord with us. However, they could just as well be clad in ancestral form, as a village witch, cunning man, wandering peddler or minstrel, land-working peasant, blacksmith, baker or healer. They may wear the guise of another culture or age from the one we presently live in, perhaps appearing as a Saxon sorcerer, a Buddhist monk or a Native American healer. The truth is that our close companion spirit will wear either the most compatible form for their energies that will appeal to us and make us feel at ease or a form which resonates with us because we recall our own lifetime in that guise. We may well have even known them in that guise/role in another lifetime; we may have shared a physical life together. This latter suggestion relies on an understanding, and indeed acceptance, of reincarnation... the concept that the spirit moves on to other lives, other selves, after the death of this current physical body. Whatever the truth of this for us we need to feel a kinship, a deep sense of being moved or that essential *familiarity*, with our spirits chosen guise. This is the all important thing, that we feel a sense of camaraderie, of belonging, of *rightness* with the appearance of the spirit in question. It is all just a case of the spirit 'dressing up' and we need not dwell too heavily on the precise meaning of the guise as long as it sits well with us at a deep level.

However, please remember this: if for instance the spirit appears to us as a warrior this does not mean that it is just a warrior any more than I am just Rosa Romani. Why? For we are all energy, and the unseen aspect of that energy is spirit, that which is beyond physical form, that which is refined and pure. Rosa Romani, a fleshy body with physical attributes, is just a temporary costume for my soul to wear, allowing me to walk in the world in a manifest way. Our companion, just like us, is a formless spirit and therefore simply dons a guise, puts on a suitable costume, one we will find pleasing and endearing, one which allows the important work we do with them to become paramount, their apparel fading into the background comfortably. They could just appear to us as a spirit-form, an insubstantial light-body, a cloud of energy, but this wouldn't be so easy for us, as humans incarnate, to relate to. We tend to like to talk to things we can recognise as beings!

If this seems needlessly complex at present then be reassured that as we build up our relationship with the guiding familiar, a spirit that walks with us whether we acknowledge it or not, selflessly and with love, we will be able to ask it all about such matters and get responses that sit well with us at our own level. For now it is enough to know that we all have companion spirits and that we can meet ours today, with ease, if we so choose!

Before we embark on a spiritual journey, or path-working, to meet our familiar we should first consider the idea of *doorways*. We are green-spirited people who work very much in symbolic terms, psychically (or magically) and physically, one reflecting the other. Here I would like us to consider the symbolic nature of doorways as they will feature in the journey. Here are some examples to get you started. The single tower, all that remains of St Michael's church on the summit of Glastonbury Tor in southern England, acts as a magnificent doorway. If one considers walking through that windblown open arch as *stepping into another way of seeing/being* it is very effective. Similarly I used to live by a 'sham castle', a folly which was latterly just the front wall of a castle with nothing beyond it. Walking through the open doorway there was like stepping into another reality although it was literally a few steps through a hole in a wall. It is a symbolic step and I am sure that the person who constructed this whimsical edifice knew exactly the magical effect that walking through doorways can have, if we have that very allegorical state of mind. Currently I live by another rather strange structure which appears to be a very grand stone doorway in the middle of a very ordinary field, a doorway lined with columns and looking for all the world like a façade of a fine old country house... without the house! When I look through this I get a sense of looking though into another reality. Even though it looks real and solid it has the quality of peering through into another layer of existence, as if things will be different yet the same on the other side. It is a very paradoxical way of experiencing things, *different yet the same*, and is really more about how we perceive things than any physical change. Travelling under bridges, through tunnels, through hollow trees, between standing stones, under an archway of branches, into caves... all of these things have a symbolic resonance that states '*I am passing through to the other side*'. It is well for us to think of, or recollect, a few of our own stmbols now before we begin. In this journey we will work with doorways to suggest that we are travelling deeper into a state of relaxed receptivity, one step nearer to the Otherworlds.

So, we are now going to undertake a path-working to meet a companion spirit, a journey full of magical, and so transformative, symbology. All the usual precautions/protective preparations should be engaged in, as previously described. Never leave these out! As this is to be quite a long and involved journey we should make certain beforehand that we are comfortable, warm and will not be disturbed. Also, as previously suggested, we can adapt the path-working to suit our own preferences as long as we keep the essential framework. We can call this framework the bones of the story. For example, it matters not that we are walking on a moor; we could indeed be walking in a meadow if this feels more appropriate, but it is vital that we go to a village settlement. The descriptions of the land etc. are flesh on the bones and we can be at liberty to pad out or reduce this flesh as we choose. It is the symbolism of this journey, along with the key interactions with other beings, that matters. The more we engage in such journeys the more we will have personal experience of what matters.

TRANCE JOURNEY TO MEET A GREEN-SPIRITED UNSEEN COMPANION

'I am walking on the moor, alone in this high and desolate place. The land is as wild as it can be, untouched by human hands, just scarred by weather and shaped by the foraging of the creatures who roam across it, seeking sanctuary. My companions are the circling buzzards, whose high pitched calls belie their fierce magnificence, and the sparkling granite boulders which litter this place, torn limb from limb in some crueller, colder age and scattered like rough hewn diamonds amongst bare blackened gorse and wizened barbed hawthorn. Here and there a small, shaggy pony grazes on the sparse grass, ripping with relish at the spikes of green which spring, jewel-bright, amongst the fawn and ochre of this land. They do not acknowledge me as I walk silently by. I walk with care, aware that on the moor there are boggy places where a careless human may stumble and be sucked at by dark skinned bog-beings, their fetid breath pungent with rotting vegetation and brittle old bones.

I love it here on this uncompromising land. The lowering sky glowers moodily above me in hues of gunmetal and slate while an angry yellow sun hides in the midst of those roiling clouds. I feel the power of a land untouched by humanity and untamed by its very nature. Wind whips and whistles around me, displaying its wild power, and is gone. Dry grasses hiss and dead leaves cackle at my feet. I have come here to seek my companion spirit as this land is as we are... unrefined, natural, artless. Its ancient presence, uncivilised and free, unites us across worlds, across time. I head for one of the tors that rise, like the knobbly backs of slumbering beasts, from the rough-and-ready land. Above me gulls head toward the sea, ghostly against the stormy sky, and their own plaintive cry is heard briefly before being snatched away by the unrepentant wind.

I begin to pick up treasures as I climb the gradual, stone-littered slope. A hank of yellowed wool caught on a thorny bush, a brown stem of gorse with its spines no longer so sharp, a length of dried bristle bent grass and a reddish frond of bracken. As I walk I roll them gently between my fingers until they are intertwined as one loosely woven rope. This I twist and fashion into a loop and tie the end. I chant to myself, to the hard land and to the ominous skies, as I walk;

> 'Here is a ring that we both shall wear,
> A bond of gorse and grass and hair,
> The body of the moor shall speak,
> My familiar spirit here I seek!'

I hold the ring as I march steadily upwards, feeling the life-blood throbbing in my temples and the eternal thrum of the Earth-drum keeping time as I head for *the stone structure on the top of this tor. It is not a temple or a shrine but a simple sculpture cast by nature's hand, a collection of rocks that were deposited here long ago by tremendous force, to settle against each other as an imposing bench-like structure, two huge side stones holding up a third, set slightly askew and capping them both. It looks insecure and wobbly but in truth it is set in its ways and sturdy, a wonderful and powerful edifice of granite, an asymmetrical table for giants, glittering with quartz, silhouetted against the strange saturnine sky. I approach it now, carrying my ring of grass and hair, and ask*

> *'I come to you, window on another world,*
> *I come to you, doorway to another place,*
> *I ask of you, stone-being, strong and resolute,*
> *If you will grant me passage through,*
> *Old one, may I move through you?'*

I wait for a response. I become solely aware of the presence of the stone-being, tuned in to its slow deliberations. I finger the ring in my hand, circling around and around as I focus on this monumental being. Finally I hear, or sense, its affirmative.

Giving thanks I hunker down, for the doorway is too low for me to stand fully and walk through. With a hand on the earth I edge forward, moving with a slow deliberation of my own into another reality; a place where spirits can be contacted freely and safely, another world of enchantment behind and beyond our own.

I am through and on the other side I stand, surveying the scene before me. I look down on the other side of the tor and see a settlement but this is no modern place, rather it looks as if it has sprung from the Earth herself. Simple huts in concentric rings, protective ditches in circles, enclosures and natural stone embankments all fashioned in graceful curves, rise from the land with dignity and perfect fluency. It is inhabited, as fragrant wood smoke curls lazily from chimneys hidden within rough thatched roofs, and I witness figures moving unhurriedly about their business below. I scent the air, loving that evocative aroma of wood smoke that suggests comfort and safety as well as holding within it an air of mystery from the season of mists; wood smoke is as the finest incense from the altar of the land, ascending prayerfully to the Creator in sacred spirals. Above me the gulls cry and buzzards twirl and tumble in a sky that no longer looks so sullen and temperamental. The sun breaks through the clouds in a dramatic display sending golden rays shafting down on to the stony land, illuminating its curves and making it seem softer, more yielding that it had done before. I begin to walk down the slope towards this wonderful village community at its foot.

As I approach I send out my intent, to do no harm, only to meet my true spirit companion, and keep my wits about me in case the energies of this harmonious place should change suddenly. It is best to have all senses honed. To be open is a fine thing but it is well to also be spiritually prepared when one travels afar.

I am now on the flat, walking towards an opening in the low wall that skirts the closely huddled, rounded dwellings. These dwellings are so like squat, friendly beings themselves, built strongly from the very stones that are this land's sparkling bones, growing up from the soil in comely curves and crowned with tresses of local dried grasses. As I stand at the entrance without crossing over, a male figure, simply dressed, comes to meet me. This is obviously the village's representative. The man stands on the other side of the entrance and cocks his head as if listening to my energy. I feel his appraisal and I in turn appraise him. He feels friendly; warm but guarded. I send out my intent as a silent message to him, knowing he will hear me. I know that if he invites me over this threshold, through this doorway into the space of his tribe, that he will take me deeper into this beautiful realm. As we stand appraising each other I am aware that the sun is slowly sinking into the west. The contrast between the golden orb and the black clouds is breathtaking. I take my attention from the figure before me for a moment and when I look back he has gone. I feel foolish. I wait, hoping he will return, and sure enough someone approaches. It is another person from the settlement, this time a woman in clothes that are home-spun in colours that speak of the land, and she addresses me softly.

'You are welcome, we accept you into our fold for your sacred purpose. Come!'

I feel the woven ring in my fingers and am aware of stepping across that magical threshold into their time and space. Suddenly the world is alive with colour and sound and smell. Above us the sky flares apricot against indigo as the sun sets. Torches are lit and faces appear from entrances, their dark eyes dance with bright flames. Their gaze is curious, humorous and wise beyond my knowing. They reach out to me in gentle welcome. The man and woman approach me and say, in one voice, a voice of hard winters and sun-bleached summers, 'The ones you seek lie just beyond. The entrance we have in our midst will give you safe passage to their place, their time. Come and we will lead you deeper. Have no fear for we are with you. And, although you have not yet met them, your familiar spirit is with you also. They are with you, yet they are also waiting for you. Such is the mystery of the dance of life. So, come, green-spirit!'

It is fully dark now, save for the flickering of the torches held by the throng of folk around us. They follow us as we move to the very middle of that settlement, to a place where the earth falls away slightly, only to rise up again as it slopes gradually up to meet the banked up wall beyond. We move together down the small incline, walking on packed earth worn smooth, and I see as the torches are held high that I am seeing a rounded entrance, lined with stones, that leads down into the earth there. It is like the entrance to a cave but has been fashioned by these people, with respect for the Earth's natural forms and energies. It is a gateway; a portal to deeper wisdom, to transformation. I feel a little apprehension at entering it alone, so dark and damp a place, the unknown making me shiver a little. Yet I trust these folk, these indigenous land-dwellers, and allow them wordlessly to show me into the passage that leads into the ground. I know the man and woman will remain at this doorway, guarding it for my safe return, sending their thoughts of protective love with me as I travel. The others will circle this place in silent vigil, respectful of my quest, including me as one of their own in the rites of soil and soul.

I place my hands on the stone sides of this entrance; my ring is still clasped in one of them. I say

> *'I am a traveller in this wild land, a wanderer between the worlds,*
> *I stand at the threshold of all time as the universe unfurls,*
> *I am a seeker of my spirit kin, a wayfarer who walks within,*
> *May I walk into this womb of earth and touch mystery,*
> *skin-to-skin?'*

I stare silently into the darkness of the entrance and wait. I witness a tiny flare of light within it, a glow of affirmation, a beckoning onwards. Without pausing to think I crouch low once more and enter.

At first the tunnel is high enough for me to shuffle along with my legs bent but gradually the roof lowers and the floor slopes away downwards, forcing me to crawl on all fours. I am effectively shuffling forward into pitch blackness and because of this I close my eyes, relying only on my senses, my sharpened inner vision. I let my hands and knees tell me what is happening, my ears hearing at once the high pitched frequency of this mysterious place. Beneath this ululating pitch I hear the heartbeat of the land, a reassuring counterpoint, a regular drumming. These earth energies sing in my ears and pulsate through my soul in powerful waves. I feel them sizzle in my veins and prickle my skin, making me tingle, allowing me to become more alive and invigorated. I move forward, inch by inch, my knees sometimes in shallow pools of cold water, my hands sometimes touching bare stones that jut from the smoothed walls. I am not afraid but I am unnerved, my modern human self is negated here, I must rely only on my primal instincts and intuitions.

Here and there the tunnel widens into a small cavern, I reach out around me and find that the space has increased, but I have no time to sit and explore, I must move on, focused on my inner purpose. Just as I am feeling more secure with the dynamics of the place I meet a wall.

Or is it?

Using my hands to explore I find that it is not a solid wall, rather it has a tinier entrance, stone lined, lower down. To go to the next tunnel I must crawl on my belly through this damp and restrictive gap. This is daunting but I am sure of my purpose and the rightness of what I do. So inch by inch I wriggle my body along this birthing canal, this tiny channel in the deep earth. I am aware of the mud that now clings to me, coating me and making my passage easier. The ring made of hair and grass, still held in one hand, is now wet with the Earth's own spit. I move slowly, blindly onwards, as instinctively and purpose-fully as a worm excavating the soil. This happens twice more; I meet a wall and find a smaller entrance that I must wiggle through. At the third entrance I squeeze into the cavern beyond and that rather than my wriggling to get through I am pulled. A force sucks at me, drawing me onwards, helping my passage, until I am shooting through this small orifice into . . .

Daylight.

It is sudden and unexpected. I blink rapidly, blinded, disoriented. I grope around me. There is no longer a roof. Or walls. No longer am I surrounded by the enfolding darkness, filled with the rich, raw scent of the earth, the damp dankness. I have been birthed into a different land, into hot sunshine, into the green.

I sit for a moment, getting my bearings, my heart swelling with gladness that I have made it through and found myself here in this perfect Summerland, this Otherworldly paradise. I feel a mystical joy beyond anything I have ever experienced, the heady perfume of lilies surrounds me as I am lulled and soothed by the lazy hum of insects while butterflies and swirling blossom caress my skin. Birdsong and the music of the trees lifts me higher as I sit, entranced, enchanted by beauty. I sigh with the unexpected pleasure, all the chill vanishing instantly from my bones as I languidly stretch and wriggle my fingers and toes in the penetrating but not overpowering heat of this miraculous place. All of creation is singing, scenting, shining in glorious profusion. I place the ring of friendship, now sodden and stained with the land, on the ground beside me. With my hands on the earth and my face upturned to the cornflower blue sky I drink in the moment and pour out my praise.

Gathering myself, I know the time has come to meet my familiar spirit. I need to imagine the blue-gold cold fire of protection streaming from my index finger so that I may create a safe space for us both to interact together. Then, with infinite care, I direct this powerful force, drawing a circle around myself and extending this to form another circle before me, one that is joined to mine in a figure of eight style. I then ask;

'Spirit that comes for my highest good,
By dappled shade in my own heart's-wood,

Spirit that guides from the highest truth,
By feather, fin and horny hoof,
Be with me now, I say be known!
By leaf and loam, spirit be shown!'

I wait, focusing on that second circle before me until a being becomes visible in that space. When they do I point my finger at them and direct a stream of that protective light straight at them asking

'Show yourself truly spirit, only my genuine companion may remain, may any other turn back, blinded by the righteous soul-fire of my protection!'

The spirit is then obliged to show itself truly as this is my will within the natural law of the Otherworlds. If the spirit is not my true familiar, then it will simply disappear. However, if it is that familiar spirit that I have been seeking then, when the beam of light is directed at it, it will simply become clearer, more opaque or defined. It is well for me to remember that the spirit that appears there will have worn the most suitable guise so as to appeal to me. I may take a few moments to take in this appearance, as this is my own true companion and I need to be aware of the basic attributes of this guise as well as its resonance, the way it makes me feel. As this is my first meeting it be well to keep things simple, and so it will be polite for me to welcome them warmly now and allow them to greet me in their own way. When I have heard what they have to say I should keep my own questions, if I indeed have any at this juncture, very basic. Although we are close in spirit we have not consciously spoken together before and so this fledgling relationship needs to be taken slowly and carefully. Any question should be kept to a minimum and suitable questions would be such things as

- *Is there a particular name you would like to be called?*
- *Is there a particular Otherworldly place where you would like us to meet?*
- *Is anything special I need to know about you at this point?*
- *Is there something special I should know about our relationship?*
- *Would you like me to take any information back with me today that relates to my physical life?*
- *Is there something special that you would like me to do for you in the physical world right now?*
- *Is there somewhere in the physical world where we may find it easy to communicate (for example, are our energies aligned closely with water, or certain trees?)*
- *Have we known each other in a physical sense in a previous existence on earth or elsewhere?*

100

At this stage it is well for me to introduce the friendship ring that I have made. The first thing to do obviously is to offer it to my spirit companion as a gift and, if they choose to accept it and all it stands for, then for us both to decide where we may leave it in this Otherworldly place as a symbol of our companionship. It may be nice to hang it from particularly willing tree, or it may seem more fitting for us to bury it or hide it under a stone. It very much depends on the symbolic nature of our friendship, and this is one of the questions that I can ask, i.e. what is our particular connection to each other and how may we continue with that and make it stronger? When I have concluded my interaction with my companion on this initial occasion I can thank them very much and ask that I may be able to contact them at any time in the future I wish. However, I have one final question for them otherwise I am powerless to return. I must place my trust in them fully as my true guardian spirit companion and ask their help.

Because I was 'birthed' into this beautiful place by the passage through the subterranean chambers/tunnel I cannot go back the way I came, I cannot crawl back up the birthing canal as this would be pushing against the mystery of life. Instead, I need to travel in a different way back to the village settlement. I now ask my companion what the best way would be for me to travel back. They may suggest that I may travel back to the ancient moorland village on the back of a bird such an eagle. Perhaps it will be more suitable for me to travel under or across the water, either on the back of a large fish or carried between the wings of a swan. Perhaps there will be a horse nearby who will be willing to carry me back to that place. If my companion spirit deems it to be appropriate I can travel on the back of a dragon which will rise from the damp earth to greet me, breathing fire and taking to the skies. Whichever mode of transport is selected it will be the most suitable one for me, energetically speaking. The choice of transportation will reveal something to me about my own spirit's element; the bird being of an airy nature, the fish of water, the horse of earth and the dragon predominantly of fire but bearing a little of all elements within its nature. Like the swan, a bird both at home on water and in the air, it has a nature which is balanced by more than one elemental aspect.

When we have agreed upon the most appropriate means of transportation for me then I must be sure to ask the bird, fish, horse, dragon or any other creature that offers itself whether they are willing to carry me. Before I mount the back of this benevolent being I find that my companion spirit has pressed something into my hand. This is not a gift for me to keep but rather a gift for the people of the village who allowed me to pass through the sacred doorway into this Other-worldly place. I do not look at this gift for it is not for my eyes. Rather I keep it clenched tightly in my hands.

Whichever way I am to get back I will need to pass through doorways, signifying my getting closer to the manifest/physical levels of existence and leaving the Otherworldly realms behind. If I'm flying through the air then the bird that carries me will need to go through an archway, one created by an avenue of tall trees perhaps. If I'm swimming through a lake or river then that fish the carries me will have to pass through a tunnel or hollow rock formation. If I am passing across water perhaps the reeds overhang the river on both sides, creating a tunnel effect. If a horse (or other large land-creature) carries me then I will need to go through an open gateway of some kind or maybe pass through a natural cave formation.

It is now time to me for travel onwards and it will be very important for me to keep all my senses honed and alert on the journey back as there may be many symbolic things for me to take in along the way. Any personal messages in the landscape, however obscure they may seem at present, are not to be overlooked. From this point on I must truly realise that everything I encounter in life will have a symbolic magical resonance for me. I now know that there is greater meaning beyond the physical realm I inhabit.

The willing being drops me off at the village destination and I thank it heartily, wishing it well for its own journey onwards. I then find myself back in the circle of huts surrounded by the open and friendly faces of the indigenous inhabitants of that land. Their torches are still flickering although now the sun is beginning to rise and we stand shrouded by mist and veiled in purple shadows. These people are respectful of my journey and do not press me for information. However, it is my pleasure to give them the token bestowed on me by my companion spirit. I seek out the face of the woman leader in the crowds and press my gift into the palm of her hand, acknowledging her generosity in sharing her earth-wisdom with me. Again it is not for me to know the nature of the gift; it is a part of my own training as an integrous green-spirited being that I can have respect rather than intrusive curiosity for that which is not mine to know. It is by their leave now that I may travel beyond the threshold of their settlements and once again climb the tor that will lead me to the stone gateway on summit. By this I may pass through again and find myself back on the moor where I began my journey. With the blessing of the villagers I may simply now retrace my steps and go home.'

We are now familiar with the appropriate measures to take on returning from a trance journey, just as we are with the precautionary measures to take before beginning one, and so I need not reiterate the most common grounding techniques that we may employ on return. There is something else that we do need to do now, however, and that is to make a physical statement of our connection with our companion spirit. We do this because we understand as green-spirited individuals that it is appropriate to echo our Otherworldly connection in the physical realm. It is a strengthening of the bond, making it more solid and tangible on all levels. As we now have some information about the nature of our companion, which will of course by reflection tell us something more about our own spirit-nature, we can make a suitable symbolic gesture in the physical realm. When we do this it is important to remember that maxim of 'soil, soul and society' that we have established previously and so, if we can, we should consider that triad before we do anything; that is, committing a physical act which benefits the land, forging a spiritual link and offering a creative/altruistic act which enhances society/other beings. Examples of this triad may be:

- Planting a tree or shrub in our familiar spirit's honour and vowing to nurture it just as we vow to nurture our relationship with them (soil) plus firmly establishing our spiritual link by making another trance-journey of our own devising (soul) plus having a simple wooden bench dedicated to their name in a place of beauty so that others may sit there and appreciate the healing energy of nature (society). This would be a particularly wonderful triad gesture for a companion spirit that was particularly earthy.
- Similarly for a more watery/fey spirit we could clean up the banks of the local river (soil) strengthen our spiritual link with them by working on a soul-poem with them in trance (soul) and create a beautiful mural with a particularly aquatic theme in a local school or hospital etc. (society).

Now we have made this wonderful link, it is well that we make the effort to visit our companion/familiar and talk to them in the Otherworldly realms regularly. With a little hard work, making lengthy trance-journeys to spend time with them, we may establish such an energetic connection that we may speak with them literally any time we now choose to do so. By putting in the time at this stage we can quickly strengthen a bond which allows us to be aware of their energetic presence instantly. Obviously if we are dwelling more and more 'in the now' we will become increasingly aware of any energetic shift around us that denotes the presence of the companion but also we can develop a kind of spiritual code, including the manifestation of ethereal smells and sounds, which give us a wake-up call to their presence. Of course our companions are not always available but are usually around for us, not at our beck and call but as unique and generous beings who have assigned themselves solely to our spiritual and manifest wellbeing while we are alive on Earth; partners with us as we go about our 'earth-walking'. One way that I find particularly gratifying when talking to my companions (we may indeed have more than one at any time . . . it is well for us to check with the original companion if this is so!) is using a pen and paper. As a writer this obviously suits my style and so I find it easy. However, others of us may find that communication takes place more readily by thought, received imagery transmitted to our 'mind's-eye', or by messages received only in trance journey. I will briefly describe my own chosen method for those that are interested. As we will begin by visiting our companion in trance, on journeys or self-devised path-workings (more on this in a moment) from now on it is up to us to establish with them what the best method of 'instant' communication with them would be!

To communicate with the familiar spirit via pen and paper (when we have previously established a sound relationship):

1. Go through the relaxation/protection routine 'the way of the tree' etc., as described in chapter one. We are opening ourselves up to external, extraneous energies and in so doing need to be safeguarded fully. To be fully comfortable we can also imagine a circle of protective blue flame around us and a second circle before us where the companion may join us.
2. Make an invocation to our companion, a statement of intent which tells them that we wish to speak with them via our own hand, asking that they speak through us. We should invite them, *and only them*, to join us.
3. Sit comfortably with a large notebook of plain (recycled) paper and a reliable pen. The communication can be a rambling affair until we, and our companions, get used to the method and so such things as ruled lines or pens prone to running out will only make the process difficult and the transcript unreadable.
4. Write a statement of intent/invocation at the top of the page. This could be something like '*I ask that only my true companion speak with me here. I ask that their knowledge be translated on to this page for my highest good. May you speak now, oh companion spirit, and tell me what I should know this day?*' We can obviously choose a specific topic or question but it works well when leaving the nature of what we need to know this day up to the familiar guiding spirit. Otherwise if we ask questions, especially when we are beginners at this technique, our instinct is to affect the answers we are given with our inherent expectations of what the answer will be.
5. We should hold the pen loosely in our active hand and wait for the words to come. We may hear them in our head and take a dictation

of them. Or the pen may move of its own volition and we may not know what is being written until we read it back afterwards. Relax and tune into the energies of the companion, allowing their words to flow through unhindered.

6. We may, after practice, use the inactive hand, the left hand if we are right-handed. This takes some getting used to but further surrenders our will to the companion, allowing their messages to truly flow through us without being blocked by our active mind/will. One effective way is to ask questions using the active hand and let the companion answer with the pen in the inactive hand. Thus a sort of smooth dialogue occurs.

7. We should stop at anytime we feel uncomfortable, closing the session fully and grounding afterwards. If we are able to end confidently then it is always well to give thanks, by writing a statement on the page in our own hand, and asking if the companion will be good enough to speak to us again soon. Never take them for granted!

This means of communication is wonderful, not only because it is so direct but also as it provides us with a written record or our meaningful transactions. Also, it would be well to do something for the trees as an offering for their generosity in giving us the paper to do this, as it can use up reams!

Before I close this section on companion/familiars there are two final points that should be explained. The first is how we can journey to meet our spirit friends without a set path-working being prescribed here. Well, we need to create an Otherworldly haven, or safe place, in which we can meet them regularly; a place with exists in the astral, etheric or unseen realms where we may journey, in trance, to gain further guided wisdoms. To do this we should remember that the imagination is powerful; it is a tool of enchantment and a facilitator of inner and outer transformation. We need only imagine a special place that would suit us for this purpose in order for it to begin taking shape on another level. By dwelling on the imagery we give it more energy, breathing life into it by focusing on it, allowing it to become real in an Otherworldly sense. We can put together an Otherworldly haven by recalling many of our favourite natural attributes/wild features and arranging them in a pleasing way, using our imaginations. For instance, we may enjoy woodland walking, sitting by a river or climbing hills to take in the view. We can combine such simple pleasures into a seamless set of internal directions, with accompanying imagery. Thus the bones of our journey would be:

(i) Begin at the base of a hill, climb to the top.
(ii) See woodland at the foot of the hill on the other side.
(iii) Descend the hill and walk through the woodland.
(iv) Come into a clearing where a small river flows through.
(v) Sit and call on the familiar spirit.
(vi) Retrace steps and return.

We could flesh these bones out by considering the sort of flora and fauna that may grow on the hillside and in the woodland, whether there are wild creatures there, the noises and scents that accompany the landscape we are in, the time of day and weather we prefer to walk in and the textures and colours of all we encounter. We can further enhance the journey by adding in doorways to take us deeper into the trance/Other-worldly reality. For instance at (iii) we may walk through a hollow oak in the wood. Or at (iv) we may have to walk across or under a bridge that spans the river. Stepping stones also act as an effective way of crossing over to 'the other side' where things are 'different yet the same'. Any method of crossing/moving through can be made more resonant by our request that as we travel then our steps indeed take us deeper/farther in to the realm we seek. It's also good to include representations relating to the four elements, for balance, although one or two may take preference over the others as befits our spiritual personality.

In time we can allow our familiar to guide us onwards from this initial Otherworld haven to a place which is more suitable. Perhaps they will work with us to create the next part of the journey, tailoring it to the composite energies of human and spirit. Or it may be that we hit on just the right place from our own initial imaginative creation and so our first haven serves us well as a spiritual safe place for many years to come. As it is ostensibly ours then it can be actively enhanced by us at any time but the overall ambience of the place will mould itself to our energy anyway and we can expect subtle shifts in its structure to accommodate any growing needs. We are talking about a place that is as fertile as our imaginations and as flexible and organic as nature, not a two-dimensional dead zone which serves as a backdrop. As we become more used to traversing in our sacred inner landscape we can interact with it with greater fluidity, seeing it as an extension of both our own will and of the physical land...a living, responsive, energetic body. We are all creators, able to fashion the flexible etheric realms within and without by visualisation, invocation and contemplation. What magic we have access to, and what excellent personal spiritual mentors we have to help us access it!

106

The second point that may need addressing briefly is this; what makes familiar spirits different from the wild wise ones we met in chapter two? Why do we need them when we already have ample support from these elder spirits of the land? Well, our companions give us one-to-one guidance which is closely related to our own energies, life-path and spiritual nature. The wild wise ones give us a more general kind of guidance pertaining to wider ecological issues and the nature of other beings that we share the planet with. The companion is more of a best friend, one that we can trust to be honest and true, one that we are not afraid to be intimate with; they are the ones that know us best, body and soul. The green guardians on the other hand are advisers to us all and have broader answers for us that relate to the land and the energies of all. We would ask a familiar spirit about our own journey, about personal issues, while we can ask the old green ones about externals, such as the health of the land, properties of plants etc.

It is within all of our reach to have a supportive, stimulating relationship with a companion spirit. But let us return for a while to the physical side of being. What of the other beings who share our wild world, the creatures and the other green beings? How may we have respectful and meaningful relations with these folk? How may we serve, and be served by, them in a harmonious, beneficial way? For the rest of this chapter we will look at both of these aspects of wild spirituality, working both with the creature teachers and the selfless givers of healing and joy . . . the green beings.

WORKING WITH THE CREATURE TEACHERS

This section is concerned with both the spirit-full qualities of our non-human allies and with what we, as responsive, responsible magical people, can do for them and, indeed, with them.

We are talking here about the beings of fur, feather, fin, scale and wing. You'll notice in this section I refrain from using the word animal; this is because it has connotations that suggest, in ordinary parlance, a lower order to humanity. The word animal is often used to describe human behaviour which is thuggish and repulsive. Here we are very definitely discussing beings that are to be admired for their freedom of expression and lack of guile, not despised for their wildness. All fellow beings, however different they may be from us, however far removed either in terms of their physical make-up or in respect of their behaviour/habitat, are equals that share our world. There are no evil or absurd beings in this respect, only those that we do not understand or have empathy for. Those who are not human are certainly not our inferiors or slaves, to do with as we please. Each being, just like all the other beings we have already encountered, are our instructors in how to be, an inspiration to us as they go about their lives filled with the simple grace of those without need of artifice. The four legged and the finned etc. are no exception: they provide us with valuable lessons and fill us with a renewed sense of nature's quirky eloquence, and for this we will refer to them as *creature teachers*.

Part of our work with the creature teachers will depend very much on our practising being 'in the now', observing all of the creature teachers that come into our lives on a daily basis and noting the energetic and symbolic qualities for us. We are not *using* them, rather *working with* their inherent energetic and physical properties, and then noting our own personal response to them. Therefore this section is not a list of qualities pertaining to each being that we may learn by rote and utilise but rather a guide to how we may approach the creature teachers ourselves, in our daily lives, thus enhancing the magic already available to us by witnessing at first-hand those who live in harmony with nature.

Because of the importance of one-to-one, or first-hand, interaction we are primarily concerned with the native creatures of the land we live in, and perhaps even those specific to our own regional locale, as the beings of different lands that we may encounter second-hand, through television or in the unnatural arena of the zoo, do not offer us the same ability to feel their energy. Our experience of them is once-removed, something that we, as green-spirited individuals, are trying to move away from as we cease to become viewers and work towards becoming active participants in life's dance.

Another way of describing a being's energy is to call it their *medicine*, that is the qualities it carries as representative of its species as well as its own personal way of being. Each creature that we encounter is both its own spiritual self and a representative of, for instance, the 'world fox' in much the same way as the ash is a representative of the World Tree but is also its own individual self. This means that there are qualities inherent to that entire species but we will notice, by personal observation, unique traits belonging to the spirit of that particular creature, its soul-song. It would be very human-centric to suggest that all creatures behave solely as their species dictates without any individual variation on the theme, as if humans are the only spirit-full beings with unique character traits! One only has to live day-to-day with domestic cats to

108

realise that all of them have their own inherent traits as well as the general aspects of that 'world cat' nature.

To work with the creature teachers we may do three things again, utilising the 'soil, soul, society' triad that we have been working with. For the matter of soil we may actively observe these beings in their own habitat (or create an area that attracts them) and aim to enhance that area, or certainly maintain it. For the soul aspect we may journey to meet them 'in spirit', working with their personal medicine to deepen our understanding of their ways (and so enriching our own self) and for the society aspect we may decide to make changes to our own lives which have far reaching effect upon the creature teachers themselves. We may do this by focusing on animal 'use and abuse' in the wider community for the purpose of making a difference and helping to change the attitudes of those who perpetrate or inadvertently support such cruelties.

It is well to begin by studying the creature teachers directly; this being the soil aspect, the bit where we have to get our hands dirty and engage with the land! To do this, we can either work towards attracting creatures into our locale or we can deliberately set out to observe creatures in their wild habitat . . . or indeed both. Looking at the former first, it is perhaps easiest to attract our feathered companions to us for birds may be fed on a windowsill, balcony or lawn and thus may be witnessed in close proximity to our daily lives. If we have a garden then growing plants that provide food for the birds is very helpful although this requires patience and can be part of a long term plan to work with the winged beings. It is quite easy to note which bushes and trees attract birds in the wild, and in what seasons, and we can dedicate a whole year to making our own notes as to which plant or shrub attracts which bird. However, to start us off here are a few examples of green beings that we may plant to provide food for birds: hawthorn, blackberry, honeysuckle, climbing roses, barberry and elder. The obvious thing about all of these is that they all provide fruits of some kind, from hips to haws. Such flowers as sunflowers and poppies also provide a welcome source of seeds. Ivy is a wonderful inclusion to an outdoor space as it attracts insects, as well as producing its own fruits, and also offers a welcome place for sheltering both small mammals and our feathered kin when it is well established.

If we have no garden, or are limited by outdoor space, then hanging bird feeders and feeding platforms or small tables are the best options. Feeders can contain nuts such as peanuts which are full of much needed energy, being rich in protein and fat, although whole peanuts are not appropriate during nesting season as such large chunks could be fed to a chick, perhaps causing it to choke. A variety of specialist seeds can be bought to fill hoppers, attracting many acrobatic finches and tits, and we can learn much about their inherent 'medicine' of dexterity and diligence from watching such displays. If we provide a bird table for our companions then we should ensure to the best of our ability that it is safe from cats (and pilfering squirrels). Attaching a large tin, such as a family-sized biscuit tin, underneath the table feeding platform can help ward off unwelcome intruders as can a piece of smooth guttering pushed over the length of the table's upright supporting post which will prevent predators/nuisances from gaining a grip and climbing up. Suitable food for the bird table is stale cake or uncooked pastry, any form of cooked potato, porridge oats, seeds, raisins, or moistened bread although preferably not white bread as this has very little nutritional value for a bird . . . or indeed for a human!

Providing water all year round for both the birds' drinking and bathing needs is an invaluable task as many die from thirst rather than starvation in harsh weather. If we apply our own standards to the beings we wish to interact with more closely it will become very obvious what is needed; for example, we cannot overlook another being's need for water when we ourselves could not do without it. With this viewpoint it also becomes clear that not all beings of the same species are alike; there are some people who are not as gregarious or confident as others and so, by direct reflection, this is true with birds also. To respect this we may need to offer food in a position where a little cover is on offer as well as providing for the more exhibitionist of their kin. We can strike a balance between getting a clear view of our chosen being and yet giving them to option to seek shelter close by.

Obviously providing a nest box will also attract birds as well as doing them a valuable service. A look at any wooden nest box being sold ready-made will reveal to us how easy it is to construct our own, ditto with the bird table discussed above. As we know, it is far more satisfying to be part of a process from beginning to end and here we have an opportunity to construct a simple, effective, recycled and chemically untreated table or box while focusing on its purpose, adding a little enchantment to the project. We can enhance the rhythmic action of building by repeating a simple chant such as

'Wood is sawn, hammer falls,
Here's a safe place for your mating calls!
Hammer falls, wood is sawn,
Here's a safe place to sing the dawn!'

While we chant we can feel the presence of the small winged beings being drawn in to our specially created place whilst remaining 'in the now', engaged in the simple, satisfying task.

Building a specific nest box is not everybody's forte obviously and we can take heart that, as with us humans, the bird world contains many enterprising souls determined to make the best of what is on offer to them. Robins have a reputation for choosing nest sites which are 'artificial' and an old pot or bowl left in a shrub or tree can do just as well for a nest site. If we have a garden shed we can leave windows open for birds such as blackbirds to enter and so allow them to choose a suitable cosy spot amongst the bric-à-brac there. The more we witness the behaviours of our fellow beings first-hand, the more ideas of this kind will come to us. And, of course, we can always ask the green guardians for their advice along with the nature spirits of our gardens and window boxes. Also, alongside any spiritual advice we receive we can consult with any of the professional/charitable wildlife or environmental organisations mentioned in the 'resources' section at the end of chapter five.

There is much that we can do to attract winged beings of other kinds to our outdoors spaces. Butterflies and other insects will be attracted to specific things we grow and this can enable us to observe these intriguing beings at first-hand too. If we have a garden then such plants as buddleia, lilac, lavender, borage, foxgloves and stinging nettles will attract butterflies specifically but if we are only able to have a window box then primroses, cornflowers, forget-me-nots and pinks would be more suitable. Bees are attracted to lemon balm, sedum, cat-mint, globe thistle, bluebells and cotoneaster among many others. Needless to say, by planting such flowers and shrubs, especially if we insist on buying only organic seeds in the first instance and using only organic means to fertilize them, we are doing the land on which we live much good. This is not only because we are respecting and replenishing the soil, rejecting methods which are against nature's inherent way and making a stand against man-made 'products', but also because we are encouraging a wealth of beneficial, fascinating pollinating insects to share in them with us. As we plant our seeds we can imagine that our small gesture is part of a much larger one, that our hand is a global hand and our will is the will of all people, envisioning a land full of flowering green beings, a place resonating to the hum of many insects as they go about their business. We can offer up a prayer to this effect such as

'May my dream be taken on the iridescent wings of many insects,
May my hope be carried on the scent of each bloom as it opens to
the kiss of the sun,

111

*May my desire for a re-greening be felt in the hearts of all who
walk the Earth,
May my vision be clear, may the roots of it go deep,
And as I sow the seed may the entire world be sown anew by
nature's hand . . .
Pure and bright, strong and free,
By stamen and stem, so may it be!'*

Another way that we can encourage other insects, and indeed a range of
amphibians, into our garden is to create a pond but this we will look at in
chapter four.

The more insects we can encourage the more likely it is that we will
have bat visitors each night and it is easy enough to make a bat-box, a
place for them to hang, undisturbed, and give birth. These man-made
places may actually be indispensable to them as the loss of vast areas of
woodland has been meant that many bats have lost their original habitats,
these being found in hollow trees etc. At the time of writing in the UK
there are six endangered species of bat and six vulnerable ones due in the
main to loss of roosting sites and changes in feeding grounds as well as the
more alarming fact that many are still deliberately killed despite them
being a protected species.

Below is a simple diagram showing a bat box. The box should be
ten centimetres square inside and have an entrance slit of one and a half
centimetres at the bottom to minimise draughts yet allow access. The
most vital thing about the box is that it should be constructed from
non-treated wood as the smell of a preservative will repel the bat.
Beside these guidelines it is a matter of trial and error as to the height
the box should be from the ground (although around or over two
metres seems sensible) and which direction it should face, varying
obviously in summer and winter. Patience and keen observation are
the key issues. We can do little but provide the bats with a site and
wait and see what happens, noting any developments carefully. The
importance of this perseverance cannot be overstated as we may indeed
save the life of a disenfranchised bat in such a way.

It is more difficult to attract other mammals into the garden but
leaving areas wild, for instance having long grass, rough areas, overgrown hedges etc., does much to encourage any passing small creatures
such as mice, voles and hedgehogs. We cannot artificially fashion a
domain for a wild creature with the express purpose of having them
move in as they may or may not be in our vicinity anyway and if they
are have their own established runs and routes. Some of us are fortunate

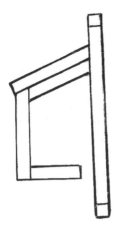

enough to live on the route of badgers and can witness a feeding display on our patios each evening while others of us can only dream of such regular close contact with these stoic creature teachers. However, we can certainly endeavour to create environments that any passing being may feel inclined to re-visit or perhaps take up residence in, with reference to the fact that it needs to provide adequate protection, food and that essential degree of unsophisticated, 'non-humanness'. Managing (or taming) a garden or outdoor space too heavily is not the best policy and although patches of tangled undergrowth may not win us many kudos in the aesthetics stakes they will guarantee a greater chance of us interacting with other beings. Ditto not tidying up too scrupulously as the old upturned bowl or large rock will provide shelter. Getting rid of areas of inhospitable concrete and creating a compost heap or log pile will make a wonderful symbolic statement of our intent in the world, as well as serving the local creature community admirably.

Another suggestion is that, as most of the native wildlife in Britain is nocturnal to a degree, one sterling piece of advice is to keep domestic cats in at night. This at least reduces the massacre of thousand of small rodents which travel in darkness and allows for an atmosphere of greater safety for other small creatures traversing our gardens at night. Not only this but it also saves cat deaths from cars on our roads and therefore the small inconvenience of hearing the cat protest vociferously is well worth the discipline!

Before we move on it is well to say that although we may dream of a family of badgers outside our window we may well be rewarded with a family of shrews instead and this, for us as green-spirited folk, is a lesson in itself. What is the behaviour of the shrew telling us personally that the badger would not have done? Nothing is a coincidence and we may gain insights from whatever comes our way if we are open enough to receive the message.

What if we have no garden or are in an area where we are certain not to witness a specific creature that we would dearly love to understand more about? If this is the case then we can actively hunt for creatures in their own habitat. By hunt here I mean that we can track them, our desire being only to observe not to intimidate. We may choose an area are to begin with where we know certain creatures go, or a type of region which usually supports such beings, and pick a time of day when we know they may be present, thus upping our chances of interacting with them considerably. Before we set out we should ensure we wear clothing that will blend into our environment to a great degree, plain dark green or brown items perhaps, and that we are not wearing any scent that may mark us out from our surroundings. If we wish we can also make a heartfelt invocation, focusing on our intent and calling to the creatures in our mind, sending out the respectful request that we would like to see them, if it is their will. We can then walk quietly and calmly to our chosen area, spending time looking at the land, noting any footprints, disturbed soil, flattened runs in the grass, droppings, burrows, scrapes, scents, discarded bones, dropped fur, scattered feathers, chewed roots or bark etc. Using our senses we can focus entirely on the moment, being fully present in that creature's reality, getting a sense of its presence, its needs, its movements etc.

We can choose to sit, if we find a suitably discreet place that feels welcoming to us and supportive of our activities, and there we can become still and wait for the creature we seek to pass by. Perhaps we could use techniques from the Way of the Tree meditation which enables us to feel our connection to the Earth Mother and to relax ourselves, allowing ourselves to be more open to the vibrations around us. We can 'tune in' to the beat of the Earth and our own heartbeat drum just as we do in our green path-working. We can become as natural a part of our environment as the bark of the tree or the turf beneath us, keeping our breathing as steady as possible and our bodies motionless except for the rise and fall of our chests. When we are calm, still and silent, yet alert, it is for us to observe each detail of our surround-ings. By doing this before any other creature arrives in that space we will be able to detect a change in the sounds, smells and energetic feeling already present. By physically feeling the textures around us, along with such things as noting the temperature, the amount of daylight left and whether any insects are sharing the space with us, we strengthen our ability to be fully present and so more responsive to change. We can then re-focus upon seeing the creature teacher.

When we observe creatures in their natural state there are several prompting questions that we may ask ourselves. For instance, what brings that creature out at that place at that particular time of day or that particular time of year? How does it move? Is it confident or wary, watchful or oblivious and how can we tell? Is it hunting, how can we tell and if so what is its prey? What sounds does it make and why? Does it detect our presence? How does it make us feel? What stage of its life is it in? Is it healthy or sick? How well is it camouflaged by the environment? Does it walk alone? Does it have a scent? Is it a tangible presence, even with our eyes shut? How would we recognise this particular individual again? Once we have identified some of these things we can return to the spot again and again to see whether the weather as well as time of day or the season affects this particular creature teacher and its patterns of behaviour or appearance. We can study the individual in this way but also broaden our research to improve our knowledge of the creature's species. For example, if we are observing a particular fox as it goes about its business it would be well to occasionally move location and observe different foxes and compare and contrast how one behaves in respect to another. Thus we are able to establish the personality of a being as a separate from its species attributes . . . its personal medicine as opposed to its 'world fox' medicine. We can do this to give ourselves a fresh perspective as we as humans tend to make assumptions based on popular descriptions of creatures. If we use the example of the fox again we may have already taken on the idea that the fox is a cunning, skulking and blood-thirsty hoodlum. Becoming one with a representative of the 'world fox' for a while allows us to observe for ourselves what the true nature of fox is; it empowers us, enabling us to begin considering our own experience as valid as opposed to always relying on received information through the media etc.

Everything that we directly observe in such a way can be translated into our own lives as we ask ourselves *'what does this creature teach me?'* This is a significant part of what we do; asking questions and making connections between our ways and that of other beings keeps us alert, open and compassionate as we witness the similarities as well as the differences, observing the pathos and the joyous power inherent in the patterns and cycles we all share.

All such information can be recorded over weeks and months in our journal, to be kept as documentation of our developing understanding. Although record keeping is important this is not an entirely practical exercise. It is also the spending of time in nature, in silent wonder and true 'holy communion', that helps us appreciate the perfect poetic symmetry and simple elegance of the beings that walk that Earth alongside us; it helps us truly feel the magic inherent in life. There is a clearly a deeply spiritual aspect to this part of our work and this leads us into the *soul* aspect of what we do.

We may already feel a particular soul-kinship with the creature that we want to observe as perhaps this creature has touched our lives already, showing up unexpectedly when we are in need of comfort for instance. Perhaps we can identify with its manner strongly, its own essential nature reflecting our own in some way. Or perhaps we have had many encounters with it before in dreams but never actually met one face to face. Maybe the creature teacher we feel the most intensely about is one not native to our own land? If we are resident in Great Britain then examples of such absent creatures may be the wolf, bear or eagle. If we feel powerfully drawn to a creature, be it resident in our homeland or not, we can make a special spiritual journey to meet the being in an Otherworldly sense. We can meet the soul of the creature, its essence, a representative of its 'world' aspect, for example, 'the world deer'. Perhaps we are not personally drawn to the being but have a need of a particular creature-quality at a particular time in our lives. For example, we could be in need of the tenacity of the 'world squirrel' or we could benefit from talking to the 'world snake' about transformation or shedding one's old skin. Other examples may be a need for the perseverance of the salmon, that valiant swimmer against the current as it struggles to spawn, or the stamina of the swallow, that tiny traverser of continents on its gruelling yearly migration. We can also ask any creature teacher at all for advice on how to *be*, naturally, as they are perfect examples of living without artifice, in the now, with full knowledge of their true nature.

In short, we can do this journey either to understand our powerful link to a particular creature teacher or we can seek out the creature which represents the qualities that we are missing in our lives at present. Therefore we can do such journeys at any time we need to throughout our magical lives. However, because of the many and varied natures of the creatures we may meet, and the complex variations of their myriad chosen environments, it would be impossible for this book to dictate one particular trance journey for this purpose. What this book can do instead is provide a quick guide to the things that any successful journey should contain. It is up to us as imaginative individuals to 'flesh out the bones' of the journey as is appropriate to the creature that we are focusing on meeting in the other worlds. Here are the bones of that journey.

(i) Find a quiet space and engage fully in the way of the tree, as we did originally in chapter one, to protect and relax ourselves.

(ii) Call upon our familiar spirits to walk with us, guide us and protect us.

(iii) Breathing deeply, relax into a trance state ready for journeying.

(iv) Visualise, in the mind's eye, the appropriate landscape for a meeting with our chosen creature, e.g. deep forest or open prairie.

(v) Allow our familiar spirit to lead us through the landscape to the safe place where we may encounter our chosen being. We should see that we pass through at least one doorway as well as travel in order for us to move deeper into the Otherworld.

(vi) Find our safe and welcoming space in this landscape, perhaps a grove or cove, depending on the nature of the creature we desire to meet and understand more fully.

(vii) Use the figure of eight, or two conjoined circles, of fiery blue-gold light as a protective measure as we call up the creature.

(viii) When they appear, we should ascertain if they are a true representative of their 'world' aspect or the true creature spirit with whom we are connected or seeking connection, depending on the nature of our journey.

(ix) We may ask either that they share with us any knowledge pertaining to their deep spiritual connection with us or that they may share with us the secret of their own gifts, e.g. if we seek strength from a representative of the 'world bear' or if we seek insights into the industrious nature of the ant then we should focus on these questions with the being concerned.

(x) We may go travelling with the creature at this stage, i.e. go deeper into the Otherworldly realms with them so that they may show us things pertaining to the question asked.

(xi) On returning to the safe space with them (if we have travelled) or after our discourse has concluded then we should thank the representative/spirit creature and ask what we can do for them in return, in the manifest world...*do not forget this part as it is, as ever, an exchange of energy!*

(xii) With our familiar we should retrace our steps and return, through doorways, to the current reality.

(xiii) When we are back 'in the now' we should ensure that we are fully grounded and write up our experiences.

(xiv) We should keep our promise/commitment to the creature afterwards!

Note that we should be aware that we are talking with the creature teachers and so communication may be quite different from our usual spirit dialogues with the familiar spirits etc. We may find we are dealing much more with shared symbols and sounds, or feelings rather than words. It very much depends on the nature of our contact with the creature and its own inherent way of expressing itself.

Finally in our work with the creature teachers we come to the aspect of *society* which brings together, in this particular case, *soil* and *soul* as it is a matter very much of our own spiritual integrity and hands-on work that will enable us to accomplish this aspect. If we do not feel strongly at the core of us that what I'm about to suggest is true then we cannot hope to accomplish the work. It needs a passion based in both our practical knowledge of the beings we share the planet with and in our spiritual link with them as soul-kin.

It is incredible that some of us, even now, may think that a creature has no soul. Or, if it has, it is somehow inferior to our own. Just because a being is more instinctive, more natural, wilder and freer (and certainly more gloriously uncivilised!) than we ourselves currently give ourselves credit for does not mean that it is somehow an empty vessel driven by its gut responses only. If we have truly engaged in tracking and observing creatures, being with them in their own space, giving them our quiet unbiased attention, then we will know in our very bones that creatures are driven also by their individual soul-spark that animates them as well as by the bodily nature of their species. To negate their soul, to give them no status or low status in a human-centric world, is something that we have to work towards changing. Such an attitude is responsible for the genocide of millions across the ages, for when we as humans deem another race, creed or species as inferior, or soulless, then we give ourselves the right, as powerful beings on the moral high ground, to perpetrate cruelties upon these groups. Human logic, couched in quasi-religious doctrine, can easily decree that an inferior being without a spirit is expendable, that such a being, being our lesser, has no ability to feel pain and no worth beyond our temporary use for them. To put our well-being above theirs, or even to deny their well-being entirely by turning a conveniently blind eye or deaf ear, is to condone and sustain an imbalanced, unjust world. We become one of the 'good people that do nothing' whilst genuine horrors are committed against our brothers and sisters, horrors such as being operated on whilst fully conscious, or being poisoned, maimed and gassed. If we are not at least endeavouring to end this organised genocide, the barbarism much beloved of pharmaceutical companies, medical laboratories, big industries, chemical corporations and cosmetics companies, then we are letting our kin down badly.

What am I actually referring to here in such emotive, inflammatory terms? Well, as of the time of writing (November 2003) here are some facts pertaining to how sentient, spirit-full beings are still being *used*, not worked with respectfully, by humanity in the name of progress. Every three seconds a sentient, spirit-full being dies in a European laboratory. Why? To provide us with washing liquids, powders and household cleaners that smell sweeter or have some more miraculous properties than their rivals. For 'new improved' shampoos and conditioners, longer lasting lipsticks and anti-ageing creams. To test drugs we already have natural alternatives for. For the military to enhance weapons performance. For organ or blood related by-products. To test pesticides we do not need, to create genetic mutations that are unnecessary and to 'just see what will happen if. . .' The total of experiments on our four-legged kin is increasing, by four percent since 2001, and currently stands at *two point seven three million per year*. There is a thirteen percent increase of our kin being used in genetic modification experiments since 1990, a fifty one percent increase for food additives, forty one percent for agricultural toxicology, an eighty one percent increase in experiments involving physical trauma, a seventy five percent increase for household products and a five percent increase in experiments that use *no anaesthetic*. Our bathrooms and bedrooms and kitchens are usually full of the evidence, the result of unbearable suffering. These are our kin. Just look at these figures. This is an insidious, unspeakable holocaust carried out upon those who have no human voice to cry out with.

But we, as green-spirited folk who respect all life and know of our sacred connection to all beings, can be their voice.

What can we do? Two things. One, we can get active by protesting with our purses and pockets as well as with our voices. The other is that we can imagine, focus, pray, use our magic. The two, the manifest and the spiritual, aspects of what we do, go hand in hand, as ever.

Firstly we can take an inventory of our own homes and discover just how many of those trusted household favourites are actually the by-products of callous testing. Then we can set about replacing them with cruelty free alternatives. To do this we may like to contact some of the organisations mentioned at the end of chapter five in 'resources' for a list of companies who are *completely cruelty free*. A statement such as 'not tested on animals' on a label is not always enough as the end product may not have been but the ingredients may well have been, either now or in the recent past. Once we have such an up-to-date list, we will find, if we look in our local supermarket, that over ninety nine percent of the products on sale there are NOT cruelty free. Therefore we need to commit immediately to going out of our way to find alternatives. The organisations mentioned can help us locate such worthwhile products, made by companies who stand as firmly as we do against the meaningless murdering of our kin. We can then write, phone or email each company that we have rejected as perpetrators of cruelty and tell them just why we have boycotted their products for good and all. Similarly we can write in support of our new choice of manufacturer – everyone needs to know that what they are doing is valued, after all. We can also get involved with the current campaigns run by the animal welfare organisations listed in this book to add to our ongoing protest.

Sadly this household inventory does not stop at cosmetic and cleaning products. Pet food is also, unbelievably, made by companies who engage in such testing for other purposes. Medicines are of course a prime suspect, with huge companies owning a myriad of cure-all products which have come to us via terrible experimentation. There is no reason why a single animal should have to die in the name of our health. Pharmaceutical tests are notoriously unreliable and we can find out much more through human cell testing and through human volunteering than we can by putting millions of creatures to a painful death each year. We have a wealth of traditional herbal remedies available to us already that could be enhanced through research, thus negating the need for new chemical medicines. In fact it was only today that I heard on the radio how beetroot provides a powerful treatment for cancer. A good working knowledge of the green beings, our herbal counterparts, should mean that (unless we have a serious or chronic condition) we have little use for such artificial products, as minor ailments can always be attended to by herbs etc. Pharmaceutical products for minor or common ailments are of little value anyway and I suggest that we all take a good look at what is really being sold under the title of a cure. For example, a cold remedy can be marketed for well over two pounds and can contain little more than a mild analgesic, some caffeine and if we are lucky a little decongestant! What sells this almost useless item to us is the overblown hype on the packaging, the brand name and the need for a quick fix! In the next section on herbs we will touch on what makes a marvellous cold remedy and it certainly isn't what comes off the shelf in an attractive box!

For more information on all of the above subjects please see the appropriate organisations listed.

We may feel, once we become active in the area of creature-rights, that we cannot simply stop at boycotting companies involved in experimentation. We may begin to question the humanity, or indeed the sanity, of putting sentient, en-souled beings through the hell of an abattoir so that we may consume meat that we no longer need when there are so many alternatives now available. We may no longer be able to purchase eggs that come from battery farmed chickens or milk from cows whose udders appear fit to burst. We may feel that buying the 'by-products' of this miserable death industry (i.e. the skin of a creature that may have been killed for its meat in the terrifying ordeal of the slaughter house) is no longer feasible for us and so we may boycott leather. Like meat, there is no need for us to have leather goods when there are so many modern alternatives. We are indeed fortunate in this respect.

Here we may argue that people have eaten and worn our creature kin since we first appeared on Earth and this is true, due to necessity. There are still indigenous peoples the world over that live as hunter gatherers, becoming one with the animal from the moment the hunt begins to the final moments of the kill and beyond into utilising each part of the dead creature's body. I was recently moved to tears by a film of a bushman doing just this, becoming one with the creature in a gruelling hunt of many hours' duration, remaining with the creature as it died and giving heart-felt thanks to its spirit. The body then sustained his family as they used the flesh, bones and skin. I was moved at his deep respect, his skill, and the tenderness with which he related to the creature as it passed over into spirit. I am certainly not advocating such a man should become vegetarian or even vegan! However, what I am suggesting is two-fold. First, there is no honour for us, nor any dignity or truth, in our engaging in the process of mass slaughter that has no respect at all for the creature being killed. Meat is an *industry* and within that industry a sentient, en-souled being is a *product*. Our receiving the end result, neatly packaged, is not green-spirited as green spirituality is about dealing with life, with others and with energies *one to one*, first hand, not several times removed through a filter . . . be that a window, screen or plastic wrapper. Second, we now have alternatives to meat, to leather goods and to products manufactured through that industry of death. We are lucky that we can make the choice and support smaller ethical companies and purveyors of healthy low fat and, most importantly, cruelty free options.

It is, of course, up to us how far we go but once our eyes are so opened we may find it hard to stop at half measures, wishing to defend our kin with our whole-hearted actions. There is no right or wrong in how much we do as long as we just do what we can. Every little helps, every small gesture counts, any action is better than doing nothing plus it is personally empowering to live our truth, to walk the talk, to live as a statement our own intent, magically. It may be time for us to stop being human-centric and wake up, taking back our power, wearing the green mantle with pride and refusing to take it off our shoulders no matter how high the personal cost or inconvenience to us.

Of course, to support any manifest gesture of protest we make we may like to engage in a more spiritually oriented project such as creating a prayer chair. This will be a particular prayer chair relating to the creature teachers. For this we need to either locate an old wooden rocking chair or build our own (or commission someone to do this to our own design, if we are able). If it is a 'recycled' chair then all we need to do is to strip off any old paint or varnish until we are back to the smooth sanded wood. By this we are symbolically stripping back our old lives, removing layer upon layer of assumptions and beliefs that once held us in that human-centric way. Then we can paint the chair with simple symbols and flowing patterns representing any creature teachers that we particularly resonate with, or have respect for, or just feel kinship with. These do not have to be in a complex artistic style, think instead of cave art and prehistoric symbols. Here are a few examples.

We can paint using natural pigments, obtained from fruits, flowers and vegetables as well as direct from the soil, as discussed in chapter one, these being dyes that will stain the wood. We could also research natural paints which are eco-friendly and not creature tested. As we paint, we can pray for the health and well being of each species that is depicted, seeing them in their own habitat, focusing on their energy, painting their particular medicine into the stripped wood. When we have embellished the chair we can rub beeswax into it to seal it or we can locate an environmentally friendly varnish for wood; I myself have already come across such a varnish but am yet to ascertain if it, or its ingredients, have been tested on our kin. The prayer rocking chair is then used to sit in and, obviously, rock. Rocking builds up a trance-like rhythm, a comforting repetitive motion that sends us deeper into 'non-ordinary reality' (Otherworldly consciousness) and in this state we can sing prayer chants and songs, focus on healing and happiness for all creature teachers and imagine a world in which all beings are treated equally as spirit-full and beautiful members of the global community. Here is a suggestion for a prayer-song that we may sing as we rock in our chair; it is an impassioned prayer to the green guardians, the old wild ones.

'Spirits who guard, overseers of sea,
Of brook and river, copse and lea,
Of glade and grove and waterfall,
Spirits, who guard, protect us all!

Keep those who slither, fly and crawl,
And those that dwell beneath the soil,
Safe from harm, forever free,
Green guardians, so may it be!

Protect the ones that hunt and roam,
And those that swim beneath the foam,
The furred and feathered, clawed and toothed,
The finned and scaled, the horned and hoofed.
Spirits who guard the wildest truth,
May those who harm feel your reproof,
May your protection thus be known,
From mountain peak to deepest loam.

Spirits who watch in dead of night,
Release those who cower in fright,
May no wild creature be so caged,
May those who witness be enraged.
Green spirits from a kinder age,

With you I pledge to so engage,
May we reach out and end their plight,
May every being have equal rights!'

Some may say that a prayer does little good when every second a creature is suffering, somewhere. Well, I say that we need prayer alongside
action, as it honours that which goes beyond the evident physical,
revealing our faith in spirit and thus re-affirming our connection to all
spirited beings. Prayer is a way in which we may give so that others
can receive; it is an energetic expression of intent, a loving vow, a
paean of wonder, a soul-plea for peaceful renewal. Prayer is the release
of our potent will, of our life-force directed for positive ends. Our desire
for a gentler, greener, egalitarian world is just as powerful as, if not
more so than, the wish to keep things as they are, in disharmony. It is
important to remember that so many people do not actively send any
prayers or wishes, thinking that they are powerless to change the
status quo and so why bother? They passively give their accord to
sustaining things as they are whilst becoming distracted by that all the
media can throw at them. With our understanding of the energies that
flow between us all, along with the guidance of our unseen companions,
we can have a real sense of just how vital our thoughts, dreams and
imaginings are. To let go of this hopeful, prayerful attitude is to sink
back into apathy, allowing those who do believe in the power of their
more corrupt visions to triumph.

We are people who give credence to subtle affecting energies and
reject the 'quick fix' ethos. The next section will enable us to further
our ability to detect such energies as we tune into our herbal counterparts,
the green beings.

WORKING WITH THE GREEN BEINGS

This is not a book of prescriptions. In this it wholly goes against a rather
alarming trend: that of volumes which give the reader endless recipes for
spells, rites and almost anything else that guarantees a quick fix and
understanding. Any green-spirited individual would want their own
creative input and experience to be credited and encouraged and so
what follows is not a list of qualities that can be taken off the spoon
but rather a quantity of suggestions and starting points. Literally
anyone, if physically able, can take a book from a shelf and read the
medicinal qualities of herbs and wild flowers and there is a veritable

feast of such reference books currently available. But here we are not only concerned with the medicinal or healing attributes of herbs etc., although they clearly are a factual aspect of each green being, rather we are also focusing in on *how the individual herb feels to us*. How it feels and what it suggests to each of us, symbolically.

Because of this need for a rounded one-to-one relationship with the plants themselves I suggest that anyone with only a little stored knowledge of herbal lore should resist the temptation to rush off and read up straight away. Rather, it would be preferable if we could trust in our own instincts and allow the herbs to speak to us first. We can fill in the gaps with sound medicinal facts later. In a way, only relying on medical herbal books for information is human-centric, treating the green being as no more than the sum of its parts, a collection of chemical constituents for our use. An empathic relationship is broader than this and is far more respectful, which also means that when we come to work with the green being in question it will feel much more willing to work with us anyway. Such an empathic two-way rapport and energy exchange strengthens our much needed powers of sensing and feeling hugely as we need to be fully present for the herbs to hear, see and feel their subtle messages. It also allows us to compare what we pick up 'psychically', when relating directly to the herb, with that which is medical fact, i.e. it gives us an opportunity to test our psychic/spiritual skills. It will be a great boost to us if we can get much of our information 'direct from the herb's own mouth' as it were and then discover that the information we have been given, both by the herb itself and the spirits who commune with them or us, is accurate in medical terms. If this is the case then our faith in our own instincts and in our ability to hear the voices of all beings will be substantially enhanced. It will also back up the theory that all beings do have voices for us to hear! However, if we find that we are getting our wires crossed and are hopelessly off-beam then we can reassess how effectively we are relating to others. If the latter is true, and our communications with herbs etc. are poor, then our companion spirits can of course advise us on what we are doing wrong. Either way we will learn and grow from the experience of direct relating.

Obviously before we can even begin communicating we need to grow the herbs themselves. As with all our interactions, it is most beneficial to begin from scratch, or in this case from seed, so that we may oversee the process of growth from planting to harvesting; this the only way that we may truly bond with the plant and recognise its unique energy. Through this process we will learn to recognise the collective aspect of that green being, i.e. the 'world herb' aspect, as well as identifying its unique soul-song. For example, the 'world marigold' has a set of attributes we would find in a medical herbal book, such as being a local tissue healer and having anti-inflammatory qualities, while the individual marigold's soul-song enhances, or colours, those attributes. Each plant could have more potent, gentle or whimsical aspects than then next while still having the orange or golden blooms of its 'world' aspect.

To grow organic herbs from seed requires patience as many herbs are notoriously difficult to grow in this way and so it can be a long and involved process getting to know which herb needs what specific condition. However, we can establish this relationship right from the beginning by talking to the seeds themselves, experiencing them in subtle terms of smell, shape and sound, i.e. their unique resonance. We can consciously invite nature spirits in to guard and nurture them, welcoming their input. Then when a herb begins to grow we can increase our understanding of its energy by observing its requirements: does it favour full sun or partial shade, much water or little, does it move in a particular way, how does it compare/respond to other beings of its kind etc. We can more readily witness the physical attributes that reveal its resonance, experiencing its texture, fragrance, way of growing and of course its hue. As it grows we will also be able to speak more with the nature spirits associated with it as well as discussing the herb with our own companion spirit/s. By having this intensive holistic approach from the beginning, having all our senses fully open, we will be much more able to understand the soul-symbolism of each particular herb, that is, how it makes us feel and how it feels in itself.

When we have an established herb garden or collection we will be able to start working with them as green allies, calling on individual plant-beings to aid us with their healing or therapeutic qualities. When we are choosing a herb to work with, we need to use a combination of our personal experience of them, our honed perception and any specific medicinal information relating to the 'world herb' aspect of each. An informed decision can only be made on this basis; it is like a version of our 'soil, soul, society' maxim, only this time more like *'interaction, intuition, information'*. We then need to identify exactly how we wish to work with the green being and combine this with our intimate under-standing of what is in bloom or in season and which herbs have the most affinity for what we are choosing to do. And why may we work with them? Well, we may wish to work with a herb to restore a bodily function, eliminate an ailment or to help support or soothe us. There is a herb for all everyday complaints, be they emotional, physical, mental or spiritual. Herbs heal but they also uplift or subtly shift things, being excellent magical workers on the energetic levels of existence.

As a back-up we may like to engage in a small and simple trance journey to verify our choice of herbal helper or to assist us in the choosing process. Here is an example of the sort of journey we may undertake. It goes without saying that the usual routines apply before we begin and when we conclude.

'*I am standing before a high red brick wall into which is set an arched wooden door. On the other side of this lies a beautiful garden in which every known herb lives. I ask that my familiar spirit may be with me to advise me on how I may enter. When they come to me, and I have checked out their validity as my true companion, they explain to me that I must knock three times using the round brass knocker. As I knock I must express my purpose for wishing to enter the herb garden. If it is a valid purpose then the door will swing open and admit me into the green wonderland beyond. On this occasion I ask (here I fill in my own current purpose, for example, 'I come for knowledge of a healing herb suitable for my aunt's menopause symptoms').*

I wait for a few seconds and the door does indeed swing open, revealing the most idyllic garden tended by nature spirits. I step through the doorway and on to the natural stone path that leads between the thriving herb plots. Each area as far as my eye can see is resplendent in a different colour of green. As I gaze in wonder, recognising the familiar forms of many herbs as they grow in wild abundance, the door swings shut behind me, leaving my companion on the other side to wait for me on my return. I am stunned with the vibrant energy of this place; my senses are overwhelmed by its fragrance, its sounds, and its verdant energies. I take a few steps between the rows and rows of vigorous wild beings and I note that some are in bloom while some are still thrusting up spear-like shoots and still others drop their seeds. Everywhere there is the sound of bees and the barely perceptible fluttering of butterfly wings. The perfumes are at once sharp and sweet, peppery and minty, earthy and fruity by turns. I hear the hum and thrum of the land and the harmony of a thousand individual green voices singing their soul-songs.

I look about me and ask for a spirit of this place to help me with my task. After a few more seconds I am approached by the spirit guardian of that plant I need. Their appearance is suggestive of the herb that I require; it is if they have taken the herb's form and fashioned it into an approximation of a very pleasing human shape. I acknowledge them by giving them a low bow in the old way, touching my forehead with one hand while the other sweeps wide. They then lead me to their plot where I may see, feel, touch and smell the particular green beings in their care. I hear their vibration buzzing through the earth beneath my feet and moving through my entire body until my awareness expands to encompass what they have to say. I ask if the world spirit of this herb will be willing to assist me in my earthly project. I listen with my whole being for a response. (At this point I will be given any specific information by either the herbs themselves or their guardians. They will be able to tell me, for instance, if I need to work with them alone or with some other corresponding herb/s in order for a more harmonious result.)

As I speak with each herb I should ask what I can do for them in return and perhaps the nature spirits will be willing to translate their desire for me. For some herbs it will be enough to be worked with in the world but others may require a specific act of gratitude. However, all herbs will require that I treat them with great respect, picking only the parts of the plant that they ordain, returning their bodies to the earth after our work is done and, if necessary, planting more of their kind to replenish that which has been taken. After I have communed with each herb that I will be working with I pledge my continued support and respect for their ways of being and give my thanks to their guardians.

I may now leave the garden and return to my own companion spirit to discuss anything else that I need to know before returning to 'ordinary' reality. I must ensure that the door between the garden and the outside world is closed.'

When we have decided on a single herb or a mixture (up to three herbs to keep things simple) then we should pick the petals or leaves or any other parts that have been recommended to us. However, and this is important, we should only choose by consulting the plant first as it, along with its nature spirit, will direct us to the parts of it that are the best to pick at the time. These may well be those that will do the overall plant the least damage. We should pinch these off quickly, never pulling or tearing. If there is reluctance, for example, for the leaf to part company with the stem then this reveals how inappropriate it was for us to pick that particular part of the plant in the first place and we should stop immediately and re-consult with the beings involved.

Then we can begin the work. Here are a few examples of the most common ways of working with our green allies:

(a) Make a tea or infusion.
(b) Make a tonic beverage or cordial.
(c) Make an oil or salve.
(d) Make a syrup.
(e) Make a pillow.
(f) Make a bath-bag.
(g) Make a tincture.

Although this is not a prescriptive work here are some examples, for inspirational purposes, of how to create each of these in a green-spirited, magical sense.

(a) To combat stress and aid relaxation before bed, work with any of the following: lime blossom, camomile, skullcap, valerian, liquorice, clary sage, golden rod, hops, or of course any herb we are advised is appropriate (as long as it is also corresponds well, medically speaking.) We should choose a blend considering how we respond to each herb's fragrance, colour, shape, texture and, of course, energy. We should then wait until twilight or later before placing our herbs in a teapot. This pot should be specially chosen for healing brews and could have special meaningful decoration upon it or be in a shape or colour that brings us joy. Perhaps we could even make the pot ourselves in a ceramics or pottery evening class (ditto for the mug we will be using) and then as we ourselves create it we can fill the potential vessel with our intention, fashioning it with herbal healing in mind. Whichever pot we use we should then pour boiling water on to the herbs in it, breathing in the fragrance that is released. Staring into the open pot we should begin stirring the brew gently and rhythmically anticlockwise (also known as widdershins) whilst all the time repeating to ourselves '*unwind unwind unwind!*' in a soothing quiet voice which can gradually fade to a soothing whisper.

Place the lid on the teapot and allow the brew to steep for three to five minutes. As it steeps we can focus on our breathing, keeping it slow and measured, allowing only peaceful, restful imagery to surface in our minds. We should then pour the tea through a strainer into a mug that we use specifically for such healing drinks. We can then breathe in the steam, allowing it to waft and swirl around us in soothing way, before drinking. As we do so we can look deep into the liquid and repeat to ourselves '*drink deep, deep sleep!*' to ourselves. We can of course sweeten this, or any other, brew with honey before we drink. Afterwards the dregs from the teapot should be placed with respect on a compost heap or directly on to the soil. There we should offer our thanks by expressing that that which has so nourished us should now nourish the soil in return, with the hope that fresh growth will come from their demise. If we have no garden then they should be wrapped in a scrap of newspaper until we can get to a patch of earth where they can be laid to rest.

(b) To celebrate the return of health of a loved one, work with 10 to 12 elderflower heads, gathered on a sunny day from a healthy tree (with its full permission and advice on which heads to pick), one large orange, one large lemon, one and a half pounds of sugar, three tablespoonfuls of white vinegar (not white *wine* vinegar unless we want alcoholic content!) and nine pints of cold water. Take the elderflower heads and place them in a clean plastic bucket. Add the rind and juice of the orange and the lemon and the sugar and then the water and vinegar. We now need to stir the brew until the sugar has dissolved. This should be done in a positive, sun-wise or clockwise direction (also known as deosil) as we are affirming life and vitality, not banishing or reducing. As we stir we should gaze into the liquid, seeing it infused with radiant golden light, the essence of well-being. We should chant as we stir, something like

'Filled with sunlight's healing power,
The vigour of each elderflower,
Just as the sun shall rise each day,
With each sip pain shall slip away!'

When the sugar has dissolved we should cover the bucket with a tea towel and leave for 24 hours. We can then strain and pour the clear liquid into clean recycled bottles that have been painted with cheery uplifting sunny designs specific to the person we are making the brew for. These bottles must stay sealed for two weeks and during this time we should hold them for a few minutes a day, again imagining that radiant golden light emitting from the contents within as we pray for the health of the person to return as the brew becomes stronger. We may need to carefully open the lid during these two weeks to allow the gas to escape and the bottles should be resealed again afterwards. When we then pass on this gift to our loved one we should ensure that they open it with care as it is fizzy. This drink is best served chilled!

(c) To bring the sunshine back into our lives we can create uplifting oil for a stimulating or healing massage. An example of such an oil would be St John's Wort (Hypericum) which by its nature produces a beautiful vibrant fiery red oil as well as having medicinal value as a 'nervine', this being a group of herbs that help depression and anxiety. Along with being a nervine St John's Wort is also a soothing and healing herb for the skin. To double the symbolic potency we will use the solar infusion method to extract the active essence from the herb.

We should work with the St John's Wort plant to ensure that we pick the flowers correctly; this should be done when the sun is strong and high. We should then place the flowers in a clean and dry jar, such as a recycled jam jar, and cover them with a good quality olive oil. Make sure the herbs are then topped up to at least an inch above their fullest height as they rest in the jar. The jar shouldn't be too big as we should leave as little air space in the jar as possible, so it is best to find one that isn't overly capacious. As we pour the oil over the herbs we could repeat something like *'pour the oil and store the sun!'* The jar should then be placed, tightly lidded, in a warm and sunny spot where the contents can best infuse in the heat. We should then return to it each day and, using a clean dry cloth, wipe the inside of the lid and any 'head room' in the jar to avoid condensation which can cause mould. Our returning to it daily also allows us to witness the oil turning that stunning solar shade, truly a bit of magic in the midst of our lives. As it does so we can sing to it, perhaps words such as

> *'Drink the sun, become brighter,*
> *Brew to make my spirit lighter!*
> *Drink the sun, become infused,*
> *Brew to make my soul enthused!*
> *Drink the sun, within you store,*
> *The warmth to make my spirit soar!'*

Around two to four weeks is the usual time for such a preparation to brew. When we intuitively feel (or are told by our companion spirits) that the oil has steeped long enough we can then strain it into a beautiful glass bottle. As the colour of this particular oil is so evocative it seems a shame to decorate the bottle too highly and obscure the vibrancy of its contents. The finished oil should be stored in a cool place away from sunlight and will last for a few months like this. The herbs from the oil can be composted or laid to rest with a suitable prayer.

With this oil we can then massage it into our stomach or solar plexus region using a sun-wise (deosil) motion and envisioning as we do so the fire returning to our bellies, re-infusing us with an inner glow.

(c) To turn any oil into a salve (balm, ointment) mix the oil concerned with a finger-nail sized blob of beeswax and leave it to cold set for a lunar month, from full moon to full moon perhaps. A salve is easier to absorb than a cream and can be used for bites, stings, rashes etc. To make an excellent all-purpose soothing salve, for example, it would be effective at the outset to add comfrey or marigold petals (calendula) to the St John's Wort in our jar, or we can simply consult with the green beings and the spirits to find our own effective blends.

(d) To boost the immune system and protect from colds as winter comes, go for a walk at midday when the sun is strongest and pick rosehips, blackberries and elderberries, making sure not to take too many from the same tree or bush (and asking permission first obviously). On returning home boil up five hundred grams of sugar and one litre of water in a large saucepan. Add to this the rinsed fruits and allow them to simmer along with a little ginger, some cloves, a cinnamon stick and juice of one lemon. While these are simmering we can speak to our companion spirit, asking for a symbol to be given which is a special protective emblem for us to work with. Then take a clean recycled jar (the sort used to store coffee) and, using glass paints, depict this emblem alongside any other personally potent symbols which are about our own vitality or well-being, symbols that speak of our own unique, powerful soul-medicine.

When the water has reduced and we are left with a thick gloopy syrup in our pot or pan then we should stretch an old pair of tights over the neck of our chosen jar to create a strainer. Using a funnel we can carefully pour the syrup in, removing any pulp regularly and placing it on a folded newspaper for recycling later. As this is a messy operation it is better to leave our visualisation and focused chant until the jar is full.

For this, the magical infusing of our syrup with our intent, we can wait until the next day, at midday, and hold the jar up to catch the full strength of the sun. As we do so we can observe the rich red–purple of the mixture within and know it as our own life's blood, rich, dark and vital. As we do this we can sing or chant or pray something like

> *'Pulse of the land in every fruit,*
> *Blood in my veins that follows suit,*
> *Strength of the sun in every fruit,*
> *Sunny brew, make strong my roots,*
> *Wealth of the land in every fruit*
> *Health in my body follows suit.'*

This brew can then be taken, a spoonful per day, as a preventive medicine to strengthen the immune system and so keep viruses at bay throughout autumn and winter. We can up the dose to two spoonfuls as necessary if we feel run down. The pulp from the fruits etc. should be taken back to the area where we originally gathered them and so laid back on the earth that provided them, with our thanks and a hope that the trees and bushes flourish and fruit again next year, for the good of all.

(e) To promote psychic receptiveness and vivid dreams, work with a herb such as mugwort or yarrow along with sleep-enhancing, fragrant herbs, like lavender and camomile, and make a herb pillow. To do this, create (or buy) two simple cotton pillowcases, sized fifteen centimetres by twenty five centimetres. During the waning to dark moon, the time of insights or inner sight, these bags can be filled with the herbs and sealed. We can do this by sewing them up at the open end and as we sew we can chant

> *'All your power inside is sealed,*
> *So in my dreams the truths revealed,*
> *All of your power within I'll keep,*
> *So grant me visions as I sleep!'*

We can then decorate the pillow by hand-stitching or fabric painting it in purple and gold (or any other colour that suggests otherworldly connection and the mystical realms of sleep to us). We can use the second pillowcase to cover the herb pillow, thus keeping it both clean and private. This pillow should keep its power for the thirteen moons of a year and should be positioned about twelve centimetres from the face so that the beneficial properties and energies can be breathed in as we sleep.

(f) To rid ourselves of indecision and gain clarity we can create a bath-bag using a square of thin natural cotton or muslin. In the centre of this square we can place herbs with a strong fragrance and the innate ability to help us cleanse our energetic field as well as giving us clear sight. Examples of herbs that are excellent at working at this energetic level are rosemary, basil, peppermint, juniper and mugwort although obviously we need to locate our own variations on this theme using personal inter-action, intuition and information. *It is well to note that as this blend will be stimulating it is not appropriate for use just before bedtime.*

This herbal bag can then be tied to the hot tap as it runs the bath. It is best to keep the bathroom door shut as we do this so as to keep in the fragrances that the herbs release. We can then light a candle and place it on the edge of the bath, asking that as we do so we may shed new light on our situation, or gain fresh insights as we soak. As we lie in the herbally enhanced water we should focus on the fragrant steam as it swirls around us, asking that it may wash away any impurities or obstructions to our clear vision. Breathing deeply of the steam helps us to draw the cleansing energy deep within us as we relax. We can then focus on any particular issue we wish to see more clearly. As we step out of the bath and let the plug out we can envision all of our sluggish, worried or confused energy swirling away with the water.

We can then re-open the bag and return the herbs to the earth with a prayer of thanks. This can acknowledge the transformation the herbs have assisted us in and ask that as we ourselves move from inner darkness into insightful light so may the bodies of the herbs move from the light of the world into the darkness of the soil to nourish them so that new life may flourish there. Acknowledging our part, and the part of all beings, in this endless cycle is a grounding thing to do after any 'inner work' or introspective act.

(g) To create a calming potion to take after meals to reduce flatulence or stomach discomfort we can make a tincture that we can easily carry with us. We need to work with herbs that have the properties of 'carminative' and these include such well known green beings as fennel, cayenne, ginger, cinnamon, aniseed and cardamom. To do this, we must preserve our chosen herbs in alcohol, preferably a one hundred percent proof variety that provides the necessary water content. Brandy and vodka are both available in one hundred percent proof versions.

As with the above directions for creating an oil we need to place our finely chopped and blended herbs in a jar, but rather than using oil we then top it up with the alcohol. It is important to have the herbs submerged and at least another few centimetres of alcohol on top of them as the herbs may swell and soak the liquid up. If this happens we will need to top it up again. This jar should then be sealed and placed, for a whole moon cycle, in a dark place that is not too cold. We should return to our jar each day to agitate the contents gently by swirling them in an anti-clockwise motion, this being the motion of the moon which moves from full to dark to new again, allowing us to banish and move on from that which ails us. This gives us a perfect opportunity to chant, sing or pray that as we swirl the contents of the jar gently so then will the pain we feel in our guts be similarly moved on, causing us no further harm. We can instil all the soothing, removing properties we care to into the brew at this stage, working with its natural qualities (its *medicine*) by applying our own harmonious intent.

After a lunar month, or longer if it seems or is deemed appropriate, then we can decant the tincture into dark stoppered bottles (the small kind which are available through health stores and good pharmacies), straining the liquid through muslin (or old tights) by using a funnel. Our small bottles can then be decorated in soothing swirling patterns or with symbology gained in trance with the companion spirits. Remaining herbs should, as ever, be returned to the soil with a loving prayer.

To take the tincture we should follow these guidelines:

(i) For acute conditions we should use between one eighth and a quarter of a teaspoon, or its equivalent in drops, of tincture every two hours.
(ii) Ordinarily take a quarter to half a teaspoon, or its equivalent in drops, three times daily, after meals until the condition becomes less chronic (then we can reduce the dose gradually).
(iii) Tinctures can be taken in a little water or straight on to the tongue, although this may taste too strong or unpleasant.
(iv) To remove the alcohol, use boiling water to mix with the tincture, as alcohol evaporates at high temperatures. By the time the water is cooled and ready for drinking it will contain only the herbal essence.

Clearly the advice of a trained medical herbalist will be helpful as we get to know what is safe and right for us and a blend of working with the spirits and working with professional sources is always desirable, especially when we are beginning.

In the next chapter we will look at how such simple green magics as we have just been discussing can be enhanced when we work more closely with both lunar and solar energies.

4

The Greening and the Turning

As has been suggested elsewhere in this book we are all, from the most delicate daisy to the most rampant stallion, influenced by the moon. As we are beings composed of approximately sixty five percent water we will, just like the wildest ocean, feel the pull of our sky sister in our physical being. This is in addition to a more subtle, lyrical experience of the moon's moods witnessed in our innermost self. Because of this there are things we can do, magical and green-spirited acts, which will help us align ourselves further with the poetic mystery and potent pull of the moon. By so aligning ourselves we tune in to the natural flow of creation, we work with the power rather than pushing against it unwittingly and so are able to enhance our lives, becoming more effective. Similarly we are all affected, whether we are conscious of it or not, by the motions of the sun and the Earth as they create their own dance of life and death on a daily, and annual, basis. We can become more aware of these wheeling energies, of the tides of life created by the turning of the Earth and the benevolent touch of our brother sun, and so live in a more harmonious way with regards to both the greater cycles of existence and of our own inner cycles.

Here we will look at ways by which we can both identify with and respond to these solar and lunar energies, in a practical, spiritual, altruistic way from our perspective of 'soil, soul and society'. To aid us in this, the chapter will be divided into two sections although the energies being discussed are by no means separate. The solar and lunar cycles, and their corresponding resonances, work in harmony, creating a particular dynamic at any time which will affect us and our fellow beings in profoundly personal, as well as universal, ways. Such a blend of energy cannot be compartmentalised, yet for the purpose of clarity and conciseness here we will need to look at them in two different sections.

Before we begin, it would be well for us to consider perhaps how well we are able to feel such natural energies already. Are our lives geared towards nature's patterns or society's mores? By this I mean are we actually able to feel the subtle seasonal changes or lunar phases or do we live in a world where such a sensing of the wider cycles is made every difficult owing to our personal environment, home life, work pressures etc.? Are we even aware, day to day, what the moon phase is, which creatures are present or what is in bloom? We can all, no matter how well we feel we are currently doing in terms of directly linking in to the land and her cycles, perhaps do something extra now to ensure that the work we are about to do with solar and lunar energies can be experienced fully. Getting rid of some aspect of mental, spiritual or physical clutter will be a great gesture for us to make both in a material, energetic and symbolic sense. Materially speaking, when we let go of the 'stuff' we have accumulated we are then able to pass it on to worthwhile charities that can then recycle or resell it. Energetically speaking it is good as we keep the flow of letting go and receiving open, we do not hoard our thoughts and feelings but rather let them move through us and onwards in the natural way. Symbolically such a removal of excess baggage in our lives states that we wish to be free of that which ties us to our old patterns, allowing us to be more open to new input/ideas. Getting rid of our clutter allows us to be unstuck from a worn out groove and gives us another opportunity to be more in tune with the ebb and flow, the give and take, of existence.

Here are some questions that we could ask ourselves in respect of what we are holding on to, or surrounding ourselves with, and also some ideas of what we can do to help overcome the problem and let go of what we no longer need.

What are we carrying around as mental baggage?

Are we still holding childhood grudges? Do we feel resentments towards colleagues or friends? Are we jealous or bitter? Do we dwell endlessly on matters that worry us without confronting the problem? Do we constantly think about what we haven't got or what we want to have? Do we think about money, work or achievement more than is necessary? Can we honestly say we are 'in the now' very much or do we still drift off into other concerns, filling our brains up with needless babble? If the answer is yes to any of these issues, or any of a similarly mentally taxing nature, then we need to actively seek ways of ridding ourselves of this detritus. Having a session of counselling a week for a period of time will help us off-load the past grievances or current niggles that we need to air to a neutral party. If we cannot afford private counselling then some doctor's surgeries do offer a fixed amount of free sessions or else we can look into local bartering schemes where we may receive counselling in return for our favours elsewhere in the system. In the UK such systems are often known as LETS schemes and I am sure they have their equivalent all over the world.

Perhaps if the nature of our worries and constant mental babble is more practical we can get our thoughts down on paper, making a list of the things that concern us that we can then tackle systematically, thus making the problem seem less unwieldy by reducing it to its proper size. What we need to do with mental chatter and fretting is to get it out so that it ceases to gnaw away at us, taking valuable energy by its constant presence and need for attention. We can hand our worries over to our familiar spirits and ask for their assistance. We can symbolically bury them under a willing tree or rock for them to be absorbed back into the soil or drop them into an equally willing river for them to be washed away. To do this we can use our imaginations and place an imaginary bundle of our issues into the ground or water. Or, working with a stone, shell, feather or any other amenable and consenting being, we can focus our worries into their form and then bury or sink them so that they may carry our concerns back to the land that they be cleansed and transformed once more.

What do we carry round that is an outmoded belief?

For instance, do we need to hang on to that which sustained us as children, harking back to superstition that makes little sense but which makes us feel safe? Or are we still clinging to vestiges of a religious upbringing which we have somehow managed to cobble into our current spiritual stance for the sake of feeling the familiar comfort of it? Do we hark back to such beliefs when we are worried or afraid, lacking the confidence to move forward into self-reliance and trust in our spiritual companions? Do such beliefs serve us or speak to us in any way beyond acting as a reassuring touchstone? If we are able to, then we can imagine our lives free of such ties (remember the root of the word religion, discussed in the introduction of this book?). What would such a life of free-spirited seeking be like? Once we have envisioned such a thing it becomes, as we know, a reality at a deep inner level and so, by direct reflection, in a wider astral sense. Remember the maxim 'as within, so without'? Well, our internal universe always reflects the outer cosmos; by going far within our own spirits into the realms of deep trance and imagination we also touch that which is wider and universal. This paradox stems from the ultimate connection of all beings to that one source of creation; when we seek the spiritual realms within we connect with the All outside ourselves. Just as when we create an unseen (imaginary) reality, we create an energetic equivalent in the world. All we need to do for us to be spiritually free is to work towards feeding a vision of our freedom, making it real on a physical level by being honest with ourselves when we get caught in old patterns. By putting our energy into feeding that vision of freed ourselves both in the world and out of it we make it real.

Also we may ask ourselves whether our lines of communication are clear enough to receive accurate guidance from the spirits or whether we have little belief in our own ability and so have become sceptical or aimless. Perhaps we have even begun to doubt the validity or existence of the spirits themselves. Admitting this to ourselves is the first step and it can be hard to take this kind of personal inventory as it can shake us to the core. We can be filled with fear of what our lives will become without that solid foundation of belief and yet letting go of beliefs of any kind is the key to fixing this problem. We can replace belief, which limits us, with faith which instead opens us to up to all possibilities. We don't have to believe in spirits as long as what they say is valid and resonates with our inner selves. We don't have to believe in our own abilities as long as what we do works for us. As long as we can say *'what if it is true?'*, *'what if spirits are real?'* or *'what if I am good enough to hear, see or feel the spirits?'* and have hope and trust then we have opened the lines of communication with an open mind and heart. By allowing for that *'what if...?'* in our lives we become alive to possibility and therefore filled with wonder, this being at the centre of green spirituality.

We can still remain grounded and spiritually protected whilst being open; as we know from our previous work, being practical and being spiritually aware are not mutually exclusive! It is well for us to check ourselves sometimes to see if we are allowing other interference, doubt, pessimism and general malaise to allow our spiritual wires to get tangled or even broken. Or to see if we are getting slapdash in our approach and allowing ourselves to be open to any devious or manipulative spirit who may choose to masquerade as our true guide. A kind of spiritual maintainance check is a very good idea now and again so that we may remain a clear channel for the genuinely educational extraneous vibrations that are all around us.

How much unnecessary 'stuff' do we have?

Is our life so full of possessions as to make us feel uncomfortable? Do we feel burdened by what we own and does a need to get more things mean we spend less time with nature, simply being ourselves? Do we buy things to comfort ourselves or fill a void that keeps on appearing? Do we feel pressured, through the media or our contemporaries, to own things that are 'state of the art' or 'designer' when we already have perfectly adequate versions of these items? Do we worry about the loss or theft of our possessions? Do we buy what we like or give in to fashion or peer pressure? Do we consider our status or worth as being tied up with what we own in terms of clothes, home, car etc.? Do we wish we had less in the way of mementos or knick-knacks but don't want to get rid of things; just in case?' Do we find we are being crowed out by books we no longer read, music we seldom play, ornaments that just make it hard to clean or clothes that we may wear 'one day'?

We can begin by filling a bag with anything we have not worn, played or listened to for over a year. We can take any knick-knack which brings us no pleasure and any piece of household equipment which we never use and add it to the pile. We can look through our jewellery boxes, our shoe racks, our garden implements, our kitchen tools etc. and apply the same rule, bagging anything that simply lies idle 'just in case' but has certainly not been picked up, used or worn etc. in over a year. We may end up with two or more bags! These can then be taken to a local, ethical charity shop for resale. Or placed in the appropriate recycling bank where facilities exist. Perhaps we could give a quantity to friends. Or hold a bric-à-brac sale, or run a market stall, with the proceeds going to a worthwhile charity or cause. Once we have made a clean sweep of that which serves no purpose we can begin to work on our patterns of 'consuming' and make a concerted effort to buy only what we need, or truly love, that which enhances our lives by bringing creative stimulus or aesthetic inspiration. We can also consider what we buy and how we buy it, two aspects we will go into more fully in the final chapter.

How clear is our head space and our personal space?

This relates to both physical and mental detritus and also affects us spiritually because it refers to energies. Are we constantly bombarding ourselves with magazine images and words or information from radio and television? Is our head full of songs we don't even enjoy that we have heard constantly on the radio or is it cluttered with the constant twittering of a programme we don't even really want to see? Do we ever have any quiet space away from the intrusive voices of the media? Once we begin to consider this last question we may be surprised to note how much sound interference we endure. In shops we are often given piped music or radio background noise, cars are constantly thumping out bass heavy tunes, mobile phones assail us with ring tones and, if we do have the television on at home, we are often unwilling witnesses to an onslaught of advertising jingles etc.

Apart from the obvious implications of this bombardment, such as an overload of unnecessary input into the brain (much of which lodges there insidiously due to its repetitive nature), how about the energetic overload? Are we ever truly free of electronic interference or radio waves? What would happen if we allowed ourselves some free time when there had to be no such extraneous sounds and energies? What if we elected to do this permanently, being completely selective about what we see and hear, getting rid of the television completely, perhaps, or only allowing certain educational programmes to be watched? Perhaps we could just have a video or DVD player instead of a television and only watch a worthwhile film occasionally? How much more effective would we be, in terms of our observation skills, not to mention our psychic awareness, if we had less man-made energy whizzing round us, befuddling us on many levels and removing us from nature's peaceful reality? Would we be able to feel and sense things more efficiently if we removed the veil of electronic interference from our inner sight?

We can also ask ourselves this: how often do we get outside? Do we ever work with the land? Do we have any way of being directly involved, either by cultivating the soil and growing green beings, or by a soul-full appreciation of beauty, with the natural processes and the wheel of the year's turning? Do we ever go out at night and spend time under the stars, for whatever reason? What manner of activity or indulgence would we have to forfeit to make way for such meaningful interaction with the Earth Mother and the sun and moon? Is our day so cluttered that we cannot do this? What follows is a guide to doing just that, encouraging us to move with the tides more effectively and enabling us to attune to the energies available to us in the sacred round. We can then incorporate this deep understanding effortlessly into our daily lives.

WORKING WITH LUNAR CYCLES AND ENERGIES

The moon is often referred to in the feminine, in part due to the deep connection with the female menstrual cycle (known in Native American cultures as 'moon time'). The moon is also associated with traits considered womanly such as magic, seduction and poetic inspiration and so we may indeed like to think of her as Lady Luna, our sky sister. The moon, as a feminine being and solitary night-walker, is associated with that which is hidden, the inner workings of the psyche, and the mysteries found 'behind the sun'. In a more green-spirited parlance, the moon has an energy which is 'off the beaten track', connecting us further with that which many people do not seek . . . the unknown. She is the luminous face in the unknowable velvet darkness of space, casting her eerie pale light when most of us sleep, a willing dweller in an impenetrable infinity when so many of us still fear that domain. She is connected with witchcraft and sorcery as hers is the light that illumines those who work at night in secret, away from the eyes of the many and when the Earth's wild energies are less polluted by human thought and deed. Her realm is of deep indigo shadows and scurrying nocturnal creatures, her companions being far flung stars in the endless ebony ocean of night. Hers is a cold realm but it moves us because it is so beautiful, so unreachable; pristine, primal and perfect. Because of this she commands our awe and respect as well as our devotions, inspiring music and art, influencing lyrics and prose. Working with those silvery lunar energies we relate to the aspects of our lives that are enlightening and emotionally enriching; enchantment, romance, intuition, creativity, inspiration and all other deeply experienced facets of being. She is a patron of our inner worlds as she herself is solitary and introspective, an inscrutable face that shines with beauty but leaves us wanting more . . . yearning. We feel her pull in our bodies and her fascination in our souls but seldom acknowledge the truth of our connection with her.

We will begin acknowledging her relevance in our lives by considering the new moon as she waxes to full. This is the phase when we see the first slim sickle of her light emerge from the darkness, with the curve of her crescent facing to the right and the horns facing to the left. We experience this slim sky dancer as waxing until the whole of her right side is revealed and onwards to the moment when her whole radiant face is witnessed. This time is symbolic of the neap tide as it moves towards the spring, or full flood, tide. It is also a time representative of springtime as it moves into summer and of dawn as it moves towards the noonday sun. The moon in her first quarter as she moves into her second speaks to us of new beginnings, resurgence, positivity, a spurt of growth, hope, moving forward, reaching out and developing ideas etc. We only have to observe a sliver of new moon silver in the sky as it grows from fingernail slender through ripe crescent to realise for ourselves the connection with progress and innovation. This is a time for us to make plans, work towards things, initiate changes, start projects, begin making our dreams a reality and generally sow seeds, literally and symbolically, for future harvesting.

A lovely idea for a focus for any new moon magic is to make a candle and pour our intent into it at its creation. In so doing we can mark the whole moon phase, from new to dark to new again, lighting it each night with a prayer and visualising our wish, dream etc. being released each night as we burn it. To make such a candle we will need to first consider the following:

The medium we will make the candle from

Beeswax is obviously the preferable choice due to its fine colour and scent, but due to the expense we may prefer to mix this with a paraffin-type wax, both of which we can obtain in sheets from craft shops. We can also collect old candle stubs and recycle them by melting them into a single new candle (this depends on the colour blend as with too many colours, such as red, blue and green together, we may end up with a muddy brown end result!). This latter candle stump recycling idea is very effective if we do not melt the stumps down but rather place them neatly cubed into our chosen candle mould and then pour a clear melted wax over the cubed chunks. The cubes' colours then show through the clear wax of the finished candle like muted stained glass.

A mould

With our green-spirited outlook it is well for us to use a household or recycled object. This must be an item that can withstand hot wax, obviously, so a good test is for us to pour boiling water into it first to ensure its suitability. Try ice cream tubs, jars, recycled vending machine cups, long tubes used to store effervescent vitamins, dessert pots, empty spread tubs etc. or any kind of lined carton (milk, juice, soap). Cartons are good as they allow the mould to be simply torn away when the candle is set or we can use a silicone spray, again available from craft suppliers, to coat moulds so that the finished candle slides out easier (better than this may be to use tome fresh vegetable oil, just as we would grease a dish before baking to stop our food sticking to the sides).

For a good mould we can just experiment with anything heatproof that has no holes for wax to escape through. If we do find something we like but it has a hole in the bottom (like a terracotta plant pot) we can line the inside with our aluminium foil and seal up the hole with rubber putty on the outside. A candle in such a pot can be kept in there afterwards and the pot decorated suitably.

A wick

Wicks can be purchased from craft suppliers but we can also substitute a length of sturdy string soaked in boracic acid. This acid is sold in pharmacies. Alternatively we can dip the string in the wax as we melt it and leave it to dry flat.

Any symbolic colour to add a particular resonance to the wax mix

To colour the candle we can either melt wax crayons or use a variety of supplied dyes.

Any fragrant green beings that may be willing to give us their scent to enhance the candle

We need to consult with the spirits on this. We can include any flowers, leaves, crushed spices etc. we may be guided to work with, with full permission of the plant, of course. We should be aware that they may settle in the mould and produce a bottom-heavy visual effect but this will be outweighed by the fragrance and resonance they release. Essential oils that have alcohol or water added are no use for this process and using pure oils can be trial and error. However, this is obviously preferable to using the manufactured variety on offer. A little vybar, using the gauge of one quarter teaspoon for one pound of wax, helps fix any oil we may use into the candle. Vybar in this minimal quantity also helps fix colour.

Other equipment we may need to purchase

Habitual candle makers may like to invest in a small double boiler but for us green-spirited souls who like to make the occasional candle whilst retaining our green-spirited ethos we can recycle an old coffee can (or any large metal tin) and use an old saucepan which is big enough to fit the can or tin inside.

Miscellaneous useful items

These would be vybar, newspaper, aluminium foil, rubber putty and strong adhesive tape plus a suitable knife to break apart or chop up the wax sheets or stumps efficiently.

Here's what to do next.

(i) As we are creating a magical candle it is well to ask the companion spirits to draw near to us, offering their protection and any guidance we need to have. We may ask for their loving support and active input as we work.

(ii) Prepare the home-made mould by sealing the bottom if it has any gaps. There must obviously be no way the wax can leak out once it has been poured in. 'Grease' it if necessary.

(iii) Prepare the wick as described above. Take one end and attach a square of the aluminium foil to it and then glue this firmly and centrally to the bottom of the mould, allowing the glue to set. Then wind the other end of the wick on to a pencil or dowel long enough to balance centrally across the top of the mould. This allows the wick string to hang taut, straight down and centrally placed, ready for the wax. A thick wooden lolly stick can be used (if it is long enough to span the mould). This stick can then be split halfway along and the wick can be slid between the two halves, keeping it straight and tight.

(iv) Put about an inch of water into the saucepan and heat it on a low setting. Put the metal tin into the saucepan and place the wax, in pieces, into the tin. We can use three parts paraffin wax to one part beeswax.

(v) Melt the wax slowly. It should be melted at between 85 and 95 °C (or 180 to 200 °F). A thermometer can be used to take the water temperature or, if using no beeswax, we can wait until the paraffin wax melts clear and use that as an indication.

(vi) Remove the wax from the heat and add any colour or fragrance. It adds magical resonance to speak (or think) what we are doing. For example; '*I am using pink crayons and rose absolute oil to enhance my candle as I wish to increase the romance in my life*'. This adds potency by establishing our intent as a reality.

(vii) The mould should be placed on newspaper on a flat surface ready for the melted wax. Now, as we pour the heated wax remember we are pouring our intent also; we are making a symbolic statement that echoes the manifest one, doubling the power and making it a reality on both the unseen and the seen levels. We may visualise what our intent is, as the wax flows, and accompany the action and visualisation with a chant which could be as simple as

'*I pour to store my will inside,*
The wax that seals it makes it so,

148

Inside this wax my will resides,
To be released in candle glow!'

This can be repeated, building up that all important potent rhythm, as we finish our task. This is an en-*chant*-ment . . . we chant to make our vision a magical reality. We should hold that vision firmly as we work.

(viii) The candle is then left to cool at room temperature until it is cold to the touch.
  (ix) The candle can then be removed from its mould and the wick trimmed. Voilà! A magical candle with symbolic colour or scent that is imbued with our loving intent.
   (x) Do not pour any remaining wax down the drain. This is not very green-spirited and as wax and water don't mix it suggests we may get a blocked drain! Any old wax can be stored for re-use in a plastic bag, preferably a biodegradable one as mentioned in the resources section at the end of chapter five.
  (xi) The candle can now be lit nightly for a moon phase, for us to wish, dream and pray with whilst visualising our aims. It becomes an evocative focus, a reminder of what we desire to make manifest. As it burns so is our will released. This is made more effective if we imagine it to be so.

We may also like to attune ourselves more fully with the resonance of this moon-time with a simple prayer-song, offered up either as a gift in itself or with a separate heart-gift accompanying it. We can ask our companion spirits, as well as the green guardians, about suitable lunar oriented offerings. Perhaps the land, or nature spirits, where we often spend time such as around our companion tree, will ask us for a particular contribution. As an example, I have offered milk, elderflower cordial and silver jewellery at meaningful moon moments as each has a pale, shining, pure quality that is reminiscent of that moon energy. We could also bake simple biscuits in crescent shapes, topped with white chocolate and share those with the land or spirits. In my experience there are few spirits, as with people, who can resist chocolate in any form, although a good quality organic variety is best in symbolic terms. As an aside here, I used to wonder how on earth the spirits would get anything out of physical offerings such as food. I could see how the land absorbed my 'libation'; as I poured the drink on to the soil and I could appreciate how the land also would absorb the food, as would any attendant insects or small creatures, but how would non-physical beings like spirits eat? The answer I received was this, that I overlooked the fact that it is only

149

humans that do not feel the pulsing connection with all life that other life-forms do. The spirit had enjoyed the offering by osmosis through the land, for the land to be offered the food or drink was as if it had been too. Spirits experience the offerings we give by being at one with the land, experiencing themselves as part of the process of decay and absorption and re-growth. Part of what feeds the spirits is the energy of the symbolic act we make; our intent is as real to them as if it were solid to us. This is how they 'eat', drawing in the goodness of the offering not nutritionally but energetically, as being part of the land. It is always worthwhile to make such a gesture, then.

Here is a brief example of a suitable prayer offering for new moon:

'Fair one, seduce me with bright budding power,
Glide barefoot, pale candle, and quicken my soul,
Caress me, enthuse me, let me blossom and flower,
Dance into your dream of a new dawn for all.

Ripe crescent, ascendant, there's hope in your kiss,
Carry me onwards that I may begin,
Ripe crescent, resplendent on your wave of bright bliss,
I now open my spirit to let your light in'

Of course there are many other things we can do during the new through waxing moon period which are aligned with the fresh optimistic feel that accompanies new beginnings. Because we are talking about lunar influence we are dealing with the emotional or psychic realms and because the moon phase is new we are working with the theme 'start as you mean to go on'. Everything we do at this time, with regards our relating to others and to the intuitive aspects of ourselves, can be about planting fresh seeds, symbolically and literally, and turning over a new leaf. We can then flow with the moon's waxing power to sustain and nurture what we have begun. We can discuss the most appropriate new moon actions for us to take with our companions as it seems unnecessary at this stage to offer a list of further suggestions...we now have the direct link we need to pursue this individually!

As we follow the moon on her journey the new/waxing moon becomes, for one peak day and a day on either side of this, full moon. Full moon is reminicent of midday when the sun is at its zenith and of the summer solstice or longest day, when the cycle of the seasons peaks in solar intensity. Here is flood tide, the natural power of creation at its glorious height. The full face of the moon reflects the sun's strength back to us, glowing with an eerie radiance which casts long shadows as we walk in a landscape transformed by this truly magical luminosity. In terms of our feminine analogy here we have the moon as mother, the strong matriarch or woman at the very height of her physical and creative potency. She has nothing to hide and everything to give but her openness and honesty can be too much for some of us. The light she shares allows us to channel our own inner power into insightful acts but it also enables us to see, perhaps with unwelcome clarity, into our darkest corners. Because of this we have the dual nature of this phase; it is on one hand the bringer of immediate, raw, mystical power for us to work with in creative ways whilst it also makes things a bit too clear for us, laying bare all that we try to hide within ourselves and our lives. This latter aspect can lead to mental trauma as well as emotional turmoil and can, if continually left unchecked or harshly squashed down, lead to more serious health problems. This is 'lunacy', the flip side of this offered clarity being our deviousness, duplicity and lack of courage coming back to haunt us. Our response to the call of the full moon for absolute honesty, clear-sighted action and frankness is obviously a personal issue but if we are to work with that power regularly, acknowledging it and flowing with it, then the full moon enables us to turn a spotlight on ourselves and others in order that we may continue with our lives more effectively. It is, therefore, a magical time of transformation if we are truly 'up for it'.

It is a time for both revealing truths and seeing things to fruition, a time for action but not of intense physical doing. Because we are talking of lunar, rather than solar, energy it is about our thoughts and feelings; it is our emotional and mental resolutions and revolutions that we will need to concentrate on. Of course it is also about our spiritual well-being, the moon as patron of our psyches being at her optimum strength. The full moon is perfect for seeing the truth and energetically fortifying that which we need to consolidate. This consolidation could refer to a project we have worked on all new/waxing moon, or to a matter of the heart that we need to pour our energies into. Love and sexual relations benefit hugely from our attentions at full moon and it is the perfect time for any magical acts revolving around this romantic or erotic aspect of our emotional and physical well-being... more about this at the end of this section. So, full moon is about blending that inherent wild power that incites us to 'do' with calm insightful consolidation of current issues, projects, relationships etc. It is the ultimate positive push we need to get things sorted out, to move them on or see them clearly.

Symbolically, as well as physically, the full moon has a powerful relationship with water as we know. This is both in an emotional sense, affecting our watery, loving, sensitive, psychic selves but also as it affects the tides. All beings become more restless and frisky at this time, whether the moon's brilliant face is clearly visible through the clouds or not, and we can observe all green beings growing more avidly too. Therefore a wonderful idea for a green-spirited full moon project, an undertaking that combines ecological awareness, water and that essential full moon quality of honest contemplation, is a lunar pond. Not only does this serve us as a place in which we may capture, albeit briefly, the moon's magic in a silvered mirror, thus doubling her power, it also gives us an opportunity to creature one of the most valuable assets a wildlife garden can have. There is no need to feel automatically excluded if we have no garden at present as we can perhaps engage with a friend, neighbour or colleague, asking that we may work on their land to create such a pond. Our only request need be that we can sit with the water over three days of the month, to work with the energies of the time. If, for reasons of health, this is an entirely impossible idea as we cannot get out and physically create a pond then perhaps then we can think of crafting an equivalent moon mirror for us to reflect that potent lunar essence. We will come to this after we have looked at how we may build a pond.

It should be said before we move on that we need never be tied solely to that which is suggested in this book and we can always think symbolically to come up with alternative ways that energies can be celebrated in our lives. We certainly have the perfect back up if we can't think of any appropriate alternatives ourselves...we are in the excellent position of being able to ask the spirits!

So, how do we create a lunar pond? Well, the best time of year to begin this is March as the solar year waxes to full in June (at Summer Solstice). It can be as small as we like, although the larger we can fashion it the more likely we will attract diverse beings who want to dwell in it, and its shape can be rounded to echo the fullness of Lady Luna. The area we choose should be out of the shade of trees as these beings will cast their leaves on to the water in the autumn and not allow enough daylight in for the natural growth of any plants in the water.

Once we have found the perfect spot then the hole should be dug (as the moon is waxing to full) and lined with newspapers or fine sand, then thick plastic sheeting. To calculate the area needed then multiply the greatest width by the greatest depth. It is important that the liner should touch the pond's bottom at all points so that there is no danger of it ripping when the water is added. The edges of this liner should be trapped with stones and any gaps between filled with soil for the plants. The liner should, ideally, be trimmed to fit as well as possible. It is of course best for us to let the pond fill naturally using rainwater. Perhaps we can plan ahead and set up some water butts outside to catch the water we require some time before we dig the pond. Water butts are an excellent idea anyway, and we can show our respect for the water spirits, and the spirit of water itself, by not wasting valuable tap water when rain water is available to us if we just establish a means to collect it.

An irregular, gently shelving edge is a good idea as it allows for small mammals to drink safely from the water as well as providing more area for valuable waterside plants which can give food and shelter to other creatures. Stones placed into the pond provide access for toads and frogs as well as making good perches for the birds to use when bathing or drinking. Pond snails are a valuable addition as they will help chomp up the natural debris and keep the water clean. Such plants as those which oxygenate the water and lie submerged, such as starwort, milfoil and Canadian pondweed, can be included as well as floating plants that discourage unwelcome algae like duckweed and bladderwort. With time and a little research of our own we can hope to establish a thriving wildlife community in a relatively contained space as long as we are prepared to learn the workings of the food chain in this interdependent, intricately woven system.

What shall we do with the pond once we have established it? Besides our obvious duty to monitor, appropriately embellish and maintain the environment we can also spend time there, at full moon, engaged in observation studies. This will not only help us work with the pond and its inhabitants more effectively, as we will understand its ways better, it also helps us to strengthen our skills in the area of focusing, enabling us to be more effectively 'in the now'. We can do this as part of our full moon meditations at the pond in the sense that we are projecting our calm, silent, prayerful attention *without* rather than within. We can set ourselves full moon observational quests, asking such questions as does the pond seem to respond to lunar energy and, if so, how? The power of the moon as it waxes at its peak will help us enormously as we open ourselves to new experience and information, the energies being compatible with our being receptive on all levels, as well as being appropriate for any activity that needs solitary silent contemplation. Our findings from such vigils can be noted in our journals along with any spiritual guidance we receive during this time of illumination.

Before we even consider settling down to meditate in this way we should consider a heart-gift for the pond, its spirits and physical inhabitants. If we are to work with the lunar flow at this place then we need to continue our relationship as one of give and take and acknowledge the place as a living being in its own right, not something we use once a month. This gift could be a new stone we bring to the pond, or a plant, or some particular food for its creatures. It can have a lunar theme or feel, that is something silvery, pale or round perhaps. We can also leave a gift for the moon herself, pouring a libation of organic soya or local dairy milk or a fragrant decoction of pearly white elderflowers as a symbolic gesture of thanks as we toast Lady Luna and share the liquid with the land. When we know the pond and its attendant spirits we will be able to ask what gift is required, as ever. Then we clearly need to employ our relaxation and protection routine before we begin to tune in to the energies of the place/time and journey within. Remember when we attune to energies we open up, psychically speaking, and full moon's influence may well see us opening farther than we are used to so it is well to be vigilant with our protection and be certain we call on our *true* companions to guide us. We may then gain psychic counselling and spiritual visions at the full moon pond by staring into its mirrored surface as it is silvered by lunar radiance. Or, better still, we can gaze at the full reflection of Lady Luna herself as she shimmers in the pool before us, her mystical potency doubled by the watery interaction.

To moon-gaze like this we can employ the technique we worked with when we first encountered the energy fields around all beings, that is, we can stare past/through the water with our eyes unfocused but our gaze definitely focused on *the beyond*. This takes practice for most of us. Rocking gently may help to lull us into that dreamy way of seeing, that *looking beyond*, that will help us hear inner spirit-voices and see deep visions at this time. As we moon-gaze, images, words, sensations and memories will surface from the watery depths of our consciousness, emerging into the luminous clarity of the present time. The whole process of moon-gazing in the lunar pond is symbolic, the water representing our hidden soul-selves and the light of the moon representing the radiance of realisation, drawing that which is lost, buried or forgotten up to the surface like bright bubbles. The more regularly we sit and become one with the water and the moon and the velvet night the more we will find we are able to access that part of us which lies submerged, thus enabling our daily lives to be more consciously lived, with a fuller knowledge of ourselves and the spiritual aspects of being.

Just a note of warning here: the full moon is a time of intense magical potency which can sway ordinarily grounded people. As we know, all times, all places and all things have inherent magic but sometimes energies are heightened and can become overwhelming. We should not succumb, under the moon's glamour, to the temptation of listening to beguiling voices that are not of our authentic companions. Protection and vigilance are watchwords for full moon. It is easy to be carried away on a wave of winsome waffle from some troublesome impostor masquerading as a seductive spirit at full moon but not so easy to disengage from their influence after the glamour has faded and we see the truth. Many books would leave this fact out for fear of seeming negative but from my own experience I urge readers to be attentive, especially at this time. Be a conduit by all means, flow with the power but filter out the dross as, like our lunar pond, we cease to be effective if we become clogged by extraneous material.

We can, of course, offer up prayers at the pond too. Here is an example of a prayer-chant for the full moon.

'*Oh Lady may I see your face,*
Open, honest and revealed,
Oh Lady may I see my face,
May no true aspect be concealed.

Wise Lady may I know your soul,
Perceptive, inspired, revered,
May I know your vision in my soul,
May no true aspect be feared.

Mother cast your silvered light,
That all may come to fruition,
May I grow with wisdom and insight,
And glow with renewed intuition.'

This prayer asks for typical full moon traits, such as self-knowledge or psychic vision, to be heightened. We can also ask for more specific gifts to be bestowed on us, like the clarity to see the solution to a particular emotional problem or creative inspiration. If we continue to think symbolically we will discover a wealth of parallels between ourselves and our own lives and the energies of the time.

As an alternative suggestion to the lunar pond we can craft a mirror. This need not be a major exercise in glass-blowing and cutting, rather we can paint an existing mirror or fashion a decorative frame for one. To do this in a green-spirited way we can trawl charity shops and second-hand markets for a suitable lunar mirror. This should preferably be round to echo the moon's fullness. If it has a frame already we can decorate that accordingly, depending on whether it is made of wood or metal. We can burn flowing designs into wood, using a pyrographic pen, or carve into it, and paint any metal using silvery or pale pearlescent enamel paints (after we have roughened the surface to give us a 'key' to paint on). If the mirror has no frame then we can stick it centrally on to some hardboard or MDF which has been cut into a larger circular shape, leaving a wide border for the frame. We can then cover the border around the mirror with ordinary bathroom tile grout. Into this we can press shells, stones, found quartz crystals, pearly buttons, fragments of glass, shiny or silvery beads and sequins. Once the frame has dried we can *lightly* spray a fine mist of paint over the whole thing, to give a speckled lunar effect. This should not be a solid coating; rather it will just give random patches of colour to the remaining white grout between the pressed objects. The best colours for this misting would be shades of metallic light purple to iridescent greyish blue as they give the best 'shadowy moon' effect which finishes the whole thing nicely. If we choose to have no frame then a border can be painted around the mirror's edge, in watery or lunar shades, using wavy lines, flowing designs and any symbols that conjure up for us the feeling of full moon. While we are working on this craft project we can be focusing on this feeling, imbuing what we do with personal moon-influenced energy.

The mirror is, just like the lunar pond, a place of deep and clear reflection which doubles the moon's power. It can be set up to reflect the moon's full face or to catch her radiance, we can keep it in our hands, hang it in a special place or place it flat on a table or our lap. This mirror can then be blessed under the full moon and its spirit awoken that it may help us as we gaze into it each waxing lunar tide for the purpose of clarity. We can call to our companion spirits before we offer it up, asking for their support in our endeavours. Here's an example of such an awakening prayer.

> '*Mirror, place of mystery,*
> *Under my gaze you come alive,*
> *Welcome, spirit of clear sight,*
> *Behold this space where insight thrives!*
>
> *Mirror, become visionary,*
> *Illuminate the fullest truth,*
> *May your reflections dispel doubt,*
> *In blessed beauty show me proof.*
>
> *Mirror, mirror under moon,*
> *Your face is turned to catch the light,*
> *I call upon your power, awake!*
> *Give clarity in darkest night!*'

We can, at this time, collect and store some 'moon blessed' water which we can work with in the coming cycle. This is simply rainwater which has been collected in a sacred way in a specially chosen vessel. By sacred I mean that we honour the process of selecting a beautiful chalice, goblet etc. and give thanks to the water spirits for blessing us with their pure, life-giving essence as it fills over the period of a night or several nights. It is important that we collect the water at night as this is not a solar activity; we are not aiming to store up vital physical energy but rather subtle lunar emanations. The water is then left outdoors for the three nights of the full moon so that it may become infused with that potent vibration. Symbolically moon-blessed water is once again about doubling that lunar/watery connection, blending the emotional and the soulful in a powerful brew that requires no human intervention. The kiss of the moon on our naturally gathered water is enough.

A vessel to hold this water need not be grand and indeed with our green-spirited ethos it is all the better if it comes from a second-hand or reclaimed source such as a charity shop rather than it being bought new from a more impressive emporium. It can also be lovingly hand-crafted from natural materials by a local potter or woodworker, or by our own hand. A recycled papier mâché vessel, if painted and well varnished, can be a lovely way to create a cup of this type, either in standard beaker form or more in the style of a wine glass. The whole symbology of a cup or chalice for moon-water is powerful, as if we consider the suit of cups in the traditional tarot we come into contact with that deeply psychic, emotional energy we have been discussing. Here is a way of containing it, holding it in our hands, using it to anoint our foreheads to aid spiritual clarity (over the third-eye, or mind's-eye, spot between the brows). We can sip it, taking it within our being to enhance our inner clarity and visionary powers. We can wash any special symbolic jewellery in this water to add an extra dose of that concentrated emotive lunar energy to it so that when we put it on we feel more attuned to that power.

What else can we do during that magical full moon period? Well continuing with our dream diary is an obvious suggestion as here we are in the midst and at the height of that reflective, meditative energy. We can focus on having dreams of exceptional clarity at this time. Also full moon is a very *glamorous* time, in that it is a time when we may use our charm, or a charm (an extension of ourselves focused into an object) to attract others or have them do our bidding. This is in the sense of a faery glamour, that which the Fey may use to enchant us by assuming the shape of whatever it is that will seduce us or make us compliant to their wishes. Such a charm, glamour or enchantment can be highly suspect if it involves such manipulation and is not simply a way of enticing our loved ones to come to bed with us! Doing any form of love magic (focusing our intent with an act of enchantment) concerning a specific person *without their knowledge* or *against their will* is obviously an unethical manipulation of another's energy. It is fine for us to magically wish, at full moon, for the right person to come along and be illuminated in our lives but it is *not* acceptable for us to bend the will of someone who does not seem interested! Would we care to be manipulated in such a way? So a full moon glamour could be cast, with attendant symbolic love spells, for us to energetically charm the most appropriate man or woman for us into our lives as this simply means that the person most suited will appear for us (although not always straight away – more of this in a moment!) This does not manipulate but instead acts as an astral call that the most appropriate lover or partner picks up our magical scent and is drawn, like to like, closer to us in a physical or spiritual sense. Some of us have the *knowing* (or a psychic insight) that our fated lover or soul-mate is out there somewhere waiting for us to find them and this magic can just alert them to us more effectively, thus drawing them to us more quickly. This is fine to do as we are simply calling out to the person, or spiritual being, that is meant to be with us anyway, and so it is not a manipulation. We are just speeding up the process, making it more energetically feasible. Similarly if two existing partners wish to re-glamorise, or re-energise, their love then a mutual spell cast at full moon would be wildly appropriate. But to do magic against a known other's will or behind their back? I don't think so.

This is not a spell recipe book but if we think symbolically we can probably put together our own very creative, effective act of green magic to woo a soul-linked beloved to us, or enhance an existing love. Think of all that lovely pale, silvery, reflective, romantic light and the emotional resonance it sets up within us. We simply need to blend a physical aspect representing that watery, poetic, shining energy and bestow it with our intoxicating meaningful feelings through prayer, chanting etc. All we need to remember is to include the following.

(a) Before we do anything we should consult the spirits for validation and inspiration. Is it appropriate to call on this persona or enhance an existing love? If so how best may we do so?

(b) We should then gather consider the six practical aspects of successful spell-weaving. First, are we going to use any physical charms, or energetic representations of our magical love-wishing? These are things such as jewellery, ribbons, stones which may have a particular representative shape or specially carved wooden or clay talismans or amulets representing our soul-desire. All of these need to have a lunar or romantic aspect...think flowing, heart-shaped, silvery, soft pink etc. Second, we should consider if we need to make anything to support the charm such as a cotton, velvet or muslin pouch or papier mâché or wooden box to store or carry it in. Third, do we need to gather any herbs that will be willing to work with us to ensure success? Perhaps we are going to make a brew to drink and offer to the land as part of the spell-working. If so we need to ask our green companions for their co-operation etc. Fourth, we need to give a little of ourselves to make the spell powerful. This can be a physical gifting, such as nail clippings, blood or hair, or it can be an energetic offering, a gift of time and effort.

Fifth, we can think about props. By props I mean anything else that will get us into a suitably romantic, dreamy, 'moony' mood while we weave and release the energies of the spell. These are things such as evocative incense, music that rouses the appropriate emotional response, coloured candles for atmosphere, and fragrant essential oils. We may, however, decide to dispense with all of the charms, props etc. and simply choose a practical task such as combing our hair or baking a cake to combine with our simple spell-wishing. We can make it as complicated or as everyday as we feel comfortable with, the most important thing being that we commune with the spirits and do what is appropriate and then give it our all, energetically. This guarantees success, not the level of complication.

Finally we should always decide what we will give in return for the spell working. This is an energy exchange. Do we give a gift of time, of selfless generosity, of charity, of a physical present, of replenishment for the land? Again our companions can advise, as can the wise wild beings.

(c) Where and when we work on, and release, the spell will be something we discuss in our initial consultation with the companion guiding spirits. We can opt for a spell which is worked gently from full moon to full moon and added to on a daily basis or one that lasts over the three nights of the moon, or even one that is worked and released when then moon is at its absolute peak of waxing power. We can do it at the moon pond, by the moon mirror or anywhere that suggests wild power and the kiss of seductive, receptive, romantic Lady Luna on our lives. The seashore at night is a wonderful option, if possible, or by a waterfall, but as grounded green-spirited folk we are all about natural enchantment and so again if we choose to make our spell part of our daily eco-friendly chores then so be it...the living room will do just fine! It is our awareness of and attunement to the moon's energy that matters as much as our being out under her gaze. So, we may simply light a silver candle in the kitchen as we cook up a love-spell pudding or burn some sandalwood incense in our bedrooms as we paint a symbolic picture representing the love we seek. It is the atmosphere, awareness and connection. We do not need a formal temple setting!

(d) When we have created the right atmosphere or settled into our pace for doing the spell-working then we should carefully engage in the *way of the tree* protective or relaxing ritual and call on the companions.

(e) We can then concentrate on either the charm we have chosen or the ritual/symbolic everyday act we are going to engage in. As we focus our intent into the charm or the act, we can pray, sing, chant or repeat our wishes over and over. Remember that rocking and singing are excellent for taking us deeper into the energy we are creating and so is stirring, plaiting, weaving, sewing or rolling something over and over in our palm. It is the pure focus, the will and wish, the *intent* combined with the rightness of the energies involved, as we flow naturally with the tide of the time, which gives us a powerful way of effecting transformation. The repetition gets us into the rhythm of natural being and moves us beyond our usual way of seeing into a more profound spirit-full experience. It also fixes the spell, energetically, making our words into a flowing river of power that can shape the unseen stones of existence.

(f) We can also, if we are doing a more formalised spell away from everyday tasks, go into trance journey at this time whilst holding our charm. We can go to our own safe Otherworldly place and there call up our soul-love's spirit-self in the blue flame of protection. Or we can speak with their companions and liaise with them for a meeting with our soul-mate. Or we can simply send out our 'astral call' to them in the Otherworlds.

(g) We can then both release the energy and bind it to us (this is one of those magical paradoxes, allowing the spell to be *bound-free*, sent out yet kept close to us). We do this by putting on the jewellery we have poured our intent into, bagging or boxing the charm we have wished on and then carrying it with us (or whatever has been suggested we do with it, other ideas being burying it, throwing it into water, hanging it from a willing tree etc.), drinking or eating what we have brewed or baked or witnessing what we have made or done more fully. Whatever we have given our magical focus to, be it charm or actual act, we need to let it be seen, felt and known in the world whilst we ourselves experience its closeness also. We let it release its power within us and without too. As the physical object or act is let go, its energy is sent out from us. We can actually state that this is so, that we have set it free whilst keeping it with us, as we conclude what we are doing. We can say something like;

160

'That which is dear I now give wings,
Within its resonance still rings,
Fly now, dear spell, to the beyond,
I'll keep the essence of your song.'

(h) We then keep our promise and offer up our gift in return for the spell's safe passage into the energy matrix of the universe. This can include any personal thanking of herbs, trees, stones etc. involved as well as our companions who shouldn't be overlooked just because they are becoming familiar to us...pun obviously intended.

(i) Even if we have been engaged in a practical act we should ground ourselves fully in the usual ways after the spell is released.

Spells, and indeed all Otherworldly interactions, are notoriously difficult in terms of a time scale. I have known a spell take an entire solar year from its inception to become effective so we need not lose heart if what we 'put out' into the universe for doesn't come hurtling back at us at a rate of knots. We just need to be specific if we ask for something, as long as the companion spirits back us up on the feasibilty of any time scale we give. If we do not express a limit then that vague, fluid 'faery time' will be in operation and we will see our spell come to fruition in the manifest world *mañana*! A suitable time scale would be, for example, in three moon cycles, not 'by 2.30 pm on September the 13th' as we are dealing with natural energetic forces which do not pin themselves down to man-made calendars. We can try to think as disembodied souls and remove ourselves from human parameters when stating what we need. As ever the way to approach things of an energetic, spirit-full nature is symbolically; is the spell about short term effects or long term change, about developing or banishing, about gentle ripples or radical rearranging or is it about someone close or something far away? By gauging the resonance of what we are asking for we can better ascertain for ourselves a realistic pattern for its effects to be felt and the best season and lunar tide for it to come to fruition.

Moving on, the waning to dark moon is seen or felt from the point when Luna's fullness begins diminishing, from right to left. As this happens we are left seeing a mere sliver of luminescence (curve to the left, horns to the right) until that too has been absorbed into the inscrutable darkness of her shadowed face. The symbolic resonance of this is clear; the energies are all about diminishing, banishing, fading, returning, introspection and honest delving into the depths of the self and life's mystery. This is the very opposite of the new/waxing moon's vibration of positive invocation, innovation and forward thinking for here is the

161

essence of drawing back, sending away and internal retreat. The waning to dark moon is like the autumn as it moves to the stark beauty of midwinter. It is the journey to the lowest ebb tide; the still, strange beauty of twilight as it makes the transition into deep mid-night and the mysterious small hours. It terms of a woman's life we see the matriarch or person at the height of her creative and physical powers begin to fade and fail, moving into old age and the realm of the crone. This realm is a place of great mystical power and inner strength if it can be faced for what it is...the last phase before death or unknowable darkness. Here we may find strength in being stripped back, like black twigs against a blanched December sky, if we have the courage.

In the words of the late lamented English singer/songwriter Nick Drake we may 'find the darkness can give the brightest light' and gain perfect psychic clarity in the unlit period of the moon. This is not the broad illumination of full moon but more a particular kind of prophetic knowing, like that of the wise woman and cunning man of old; it is less emotive and more penetrating, and it need not be a huge personal revelation but rather a wisdom that goes beyond our physical selves entirely into the realms of eternal understanding. We may find that this happens naturally as a consequence of us being more attuned to the flow of external energies, witnessing a vast increase of meaningful coincidence, synchronicity, correct hunches and feelings, clairsentience/audience etc. in our lives at dark moon time. Or we may choose to actively work towards developing this shadowy side of our spiritual selves. Either way we can benefit greatly from the creation of our own divination tools.

In our green-spirited way we will want to get involved with the process from start to finish but before we do we will need an idea of what area of divinatory art we are best suited to. Are we likely to be accurate, empathic card readers, successful seers or scryers, astute casters of stones or perhaps adept, sensitive wielders of a pendulum? For the answers to these questions we need to engage with our companions lest we waste an awful lot of time crafting a divination tool that we have no real affinity for at a deep level. We may be very attracted by the idea of being a rune reader but be far better suited as a pendulum dowser or we may have no faith that we could be a natural scryer and so try and make ourselves read cards instead. We will discover, from engaging in a conversation with our familiar spirits, whatever aspect of divination we will be best suited to, regardless of how glamorous it seems to us; they will, as ever, give it to us straight. Our companions may divulge to us that we will have the most success from creating our own way of reading omens, perhaps in the patterns formed from the dregs of a cup of herbal tea, or maybe in the symbolic way fruit or vegetable peelings fall on to a piece of paper. We may be wonderful at far-seeing through a myriad of means which will be no less valid for being highly personalised. However, here, for the sake of convenience, we will concentrate on a few of the more standard means.

So, when we have been given the best idea of what to work with we can begin the hands-on part, bonding with the materials we are to use, infusing them from the beginning of the process with our energies and our positive healing intentions to see, vision, scry or predict for the benefit of all. For instance, if we are to fashion a wooden pendulum then we can seek a piece of wood by engaging in a specially focused walk or journey, putting out a call to the piece of wood which will be willing to assist us. If we have a knowledge of the nature spirits that inhabit and guard an area, then consulting with them will be beneficial. Our own tree friend may have some guidance for us on the suitability of the wood from his or her kin of bark and branch. Our personal involvement with this process stretches from finding the wood to working it lovingly into the most effective shape (we will have been shown this in our mind's-eye when conversing with the spirits) to oiling it and threading it on to cord so that it becomes a pendulum. Thus we have had the opportunity to become one with the pendulum, giving it life, purpose and an energetic responsiveness to us. Here is a living way that is far more satisfying and effective than buying a tool commercially; what we lose in time initially we gain in years of accurate dowsing with a pendulum we have a relationship with. Symbolically, our magical statement of intent says that we reject consumerism and embrace lovingly hand-crafted, spirit-full tools.

Similarly if we have been shown, in trance or otherwise, that we should craft clay discs with personal symbols for divination then it is for us to dig up the clay, shape it into rounds (or otherwise), inscribe our meaningful glyphs on to the surface, then find a way to fire and finally glaze them using an environmentally friendly method. This way the whole process becomes an involved quest. How do I fire clay? How do I work with it? How do I research a glaze that isn't harmful to the land and its creatures? How shall I journey to find my meaningful symbols? In what way shall I note down their meaning for future reference, or should I not write anything down and learn the meanings by heart?

Creating divination cards can be a more involved process. We could spend a whole lunar year of thirteen moons, beginning at dark moon in the waning to dark part of the year (preferably Winter Solstice) and moving through to the final dark moon of the thirteen, creating a card deck for our personal use. We can gain great insights through trance as to the nature of our deck and this need not follow the standard tarot pack but be much more of a simple, green-spirited affair. For example, we may have a deck of three suits, for the three moon phases, or thirteen for the lunar cycle of the year and the cards may be round or crescent shaped, depending on the energy involved. Maybe the whole divination set only has thirteen cards in it, each with a wealth of emotional meaning depending on how they crop up in a spread when we read them. We may choose to stick to the four elements for our suits or ascribe them to birds, mammal kin, insects, fish, reptiles etc. We may have no suits but instead have representatives of trees, flowers or herbs. Perhaps our groupings of the cards emotionally reflect environs such as desert or tundra or maybe they have a seasonal theme. We may indeed choose to follow the traditional tarot or playing card route but with our own particular twist. Perhaps all the characters depicted in the cards could be modern folk from the world around us as opposed to archaic, esoteric beings. Maybe we choose to keep to the tarot format but have no people shown in our deck, only natural forms or shapes.

We may choose highly figurative or symbolic representations for our cards, depending on both our natural abilities or inclinations and the guidance we have with reference to the way we approach this project. Perhaps if we are highly artistic it would do us good to do something different and pare ourselves down, having very simple symbols on our cards as opposed to making it a complex pictorial affair. If we usually work traditionally in oil paint we could use a limited watercolour palette or perhaps even use pastels, charcoal or ink instead. If we favour tiny detail we could revert to a fluid broad brush strokes, pushing our boundaries a little in the name of transformation. By this we are making a symbolic statement of looking beyond ourselves and our current limitations. This need not be a high art project at all and so those of us who feel terminally inartistic are not excluded. Making a deck can be an excellent way of recycling old magazines, catalogues and books as we can cut out images and collage them, pasting them in meaningful ways on to recycled card. The process of looking for suitable images is a way of further focusing and absorbing ourselves in a task, being effectively 'in the now' and not becoming distracted. Junk mail can be cut up and the colourful areas and images saved for the project before the rest is recycled into the appropriate collection point. Similarly we can use found materials such as sweet wrappings, foil, fabric scraps and thread to create our imagery. Such cards can be laminated, or coated with broad clear sticky tape when they are completed, to stop bits coming unstuck and dropping off them with prolonged use. We can also try potato printing bold symbols on to the cards or lino cutting, using a roller to cover the carved lino design with ink before printing.

There are so many approaches we can take if we wish to engage in this time consuming, but very satisfying, project. How we read the cards is just as important as how we fashion them and as we create our deck we should be very aware of how simple or complicated we wish this process to be. It is personal to us, obviously, and so we need not adhere to anyone else's prescribed formula. Perhaps we only read the cards for others, never ourselves? Maybe we never read them, as such, only meditate on them for insights as to their significance at that time? Perhaps we like to read them in a circular formation, or only look at three cards, or create a complicated spread that branches out like a tree, above and below, and this is entirely our prerogative. It would, however, be a wonderful idea to have a companion journal to our deck so that as we work with the cards we can add in any deep realisations that come to us, creating a rounded view of each card in a positive/negative sense. Our cards are not just individuals but have relevance to each other, and in this they are like a community, reflecting a microcosm of the collective macrocosm, and how they speak to us when placed next to any other card is a vital part of their message. They are best considered as an energetic whole just as we are best related to as part of a bio-network and not as an exceptional being that stands alone. This understanding of the cards is indeed an ongoing labour of love and can present a lifetime of learning all on its own, it can be aligned with our studies of nature and the associated spiritual realms, and it is a limitless observational journey.

I once made a beautiful little divination kit from found stones which was very simple and satisfying. First, I engaged in a trance journey to ascertain which qualities I should include when seeking my set of stones. Then I took a specific focused walk on a beach in winter when I would be undisturbed to look at my leisure. I then located stones that fitted all the qualities, be they emotional or physical, I had revealed in my journey. I asked each and every stone if it was willing to engage in this process with me and only took them if they agreed. When I returned home I created a basic pictorial guide in my magical journal so that I would not forget which stone stood for which quality. As examples, I had stones that stood for feelings, such as fear, and people, such as a young woman. I was able then to 'cast the stones' on to a special cloth (I had a square scarf which I would tie up as a carrying bag afterwards with a cord) and read their message. How the stones fell in relation to each other answered any question I had asked as I was casting them. As time went on I added shells and small bleached bones into my set, with additional meanings. At the time of writing my stone companions in divination have all been returned to the earth, my time with them being complete. Their presence in my life was, however, very beneficial.

We may find that scrying is our gift. This is gazing into dark water or a black mirror with the aim of seeing visions. Gazing into a still black place calms the rational, babbling self and enables us to open the mind's eye the better. We can easily craft a scrying bowl or mirror by painting an existing object in environmentally friendly paint. If we do not want to use paint then we could always line a bowl with black fabric and pour the water over the material. To begin scrying we need to employ that method of 'looking beyond' or seeing through the water, that highly focused (or directed) but paradoxically unfocused (in a physical visual sense) way of seeing.

Whatever divination tool that we create we can fashion a bag or box to keep the pendulum, cards, stones, mirror etc. safe between our working with them. We can also bless them with the power of the dark moon.

What else can we do magically, practically speaking, at this time? Well, I have worked effective banishings at dark moon by fire, water, air, and earth. By this I mean I have taken my grievances or problems and written them down on recycled paper. I stress recycled not only for its green-spirited relevance but because it symbolises the cyclical nature of being, the fact that everything can be transformed. Then I have taken the piece of paper to a hilltop where it is always windy. I have then made my outdoor space safe, asking for the protection of my companion spirits, and I have stated my intent, which in this instance was to banish the influence, idea or difficulty from my life. I would say something like

'*Spirits who walk with me,*
Spirits of this place,
Spirit of the moon which shows a dark face,
Spirits of wind and water that sustains us,
Spirits of fire and of the land that supports us,
Be with me now and work with me,
For I wish to let go, in accordance with the tides, of that which ails me.

In the still of this night,
Under the gaze of a hidden moon,
I cast my words from shadows in to light,

And may these words be transformed,
In accordance with natural law,
Just as the moon will be new tomorrow,
I shall be replenished as [name the problem] *is banished*

By the eternal mystery of the moving moon,
So shall my own life now move on,
Thank you, powers of the wildest way,
For with your help I know that it is done.'

Then I would carefully light the piece of paper with my words upon it. This can be difficult in the wind so if we do this be prepared for fun and games. This difficulty is part of the challenge for me, and that I choose to do this banishing in the midst of wild elemental power shows that I wish to align myself with that which is not of man, that which is untamed and therefore raw and potent. However, in so doing I have to accept that outdoor working can have a rather comedic aspect to it and I am careful to keep the notion of 'magic in the midst of life' to the fore as wild green spirituality is not meant to be full of solemn ritual dramas. It is always our intent and symbology that counts, not our being perfect! I then hold the paper up as it burns, letting the wind fan the flame a little.

When the piece of paper finally catches aflame and the words on it are blackened, I then douse the paper with the water I have brought with me and tear it into pieces. Some of these I let fly in the wind and some of them I place on the earth, sometimes even digging a shallow pit to bury them in. As each action is undertaken I visualise, with my mind's-eye, my letting go of the burdens. For me, what I am burying or letting fly is not just words on paper but the actual problems themselves. I know that I am not just affecting change symbolically with paper and fire, air, earth and water but that I am using the magic of imagination to reinforce my actions with clear visualisation. Thus the banishing happens within and without, symbolically and spiritually, as well as having that all important practical manifest connection involving my interaction with the land and the elements.

At dark moon we can also clear any patch of earth we have of 'weeds' (plants that choke or crowd out others as opposed to those we find unattractive), stating that as the darkness of the moon passes to the new so the bodies of those who have to die shall be transformed once more into compost and so find rebirth and newness through others. Similarly we can freshen the energies of our homes and dwellings, banishing that which is stale and negative and praying that with the new waxing moon shall become brighter, lighter energy. We can burn fragrant

167

cleansing herbs as we do this; use a charcoal disc in a heatproof dish and sprinkling the herbs on to the disc when it glows red all over. Our companion spirits can recommend appropriate herbs for us to work with, as can the green beings themselves and their attendant nature spirits, but as a starter idea good basic herbs for the purpose of cleansing space are pine, juniper and rosemary. As we carry the dish with the fragrant smoke wafting up from it we can carry it to each corner of the room, fanning the smoke around with our hands or some found feathers bound with a cord or ribbon. We can offer up a blessing prayer to banish any extraneous energies which are detrimental to our well-being. Such energies could be caused by unpleasant visitors, by bad feelings within the home between occupants, by our not being scrupulous when 'spirit-walking' and so inviting bogus spiritual presences into our space or simply by the room becoming clogged by negative thoughts and feelings due to ill-health, hard times or depression. This uplifting prayer could be something like

> *'Sacred smoke that bathes this space,*
> *Rise and raise the energy!*
> *Take that which comes with little grace,*
> *And that which is my enemy,*
> *Swallow them and so replace,*
> *With that which shines and blesses me.*
>
> *'Spirit of* [insert herb name], *of air and fire,*
> *Assist me, lift the ambience higher.'*

Here is an example of a suitable prayer-chant to welcome and attune with the dark moon;

> *'Oh Grand Mother, Mistress of All that Returns,*
> *Your sharp sickle reaping,*
> *Your ancient face turning,*
> *My own soul yearns for the secrets you keep,*
> *In the silence of shadows,*
> *In the loam of my sleep.*
>
> *May we both turn inwards in one fluid motion,*
> *May we both sail onwards, through night's darkest ocean,*
> *Oh, grant me the courage to seek what is hidden,*
> *May I welcome the wisdoms that well up, unbidden.'*

Finally a word of advice (or explanation) as regards this moon-oriented section: we shouldn't berate ourselves if we do not experience, or even understand, the moon's energy readily. Perhaps certain phases appeal to us more than others; we may be able to fully grasp the significance of a full moon in our lives but not really appreciate a dark moon's power, for instance. I personally have the reverse of this example, suffering disrupted sleep and jangled energies at full moon whilst I find myself much more aligned with that deep introspective dark moon resonance. Maybe we simply feel no real resonance with Luna's particular way at all, even if we do acknowledge and respect her influence. This is due to the fact that some of us are not so much 'moon people' (that is, overtly emotional, poetic, magically inclined etc.) as others. Just as some of us have an innate preference for one elemental way of being over another so do some of us feel little kinship with our sky sister. If this is truly the case then we can simply be aware of her movements and recognise her influence whilst not attuning too greatly to her mysteries. Maybe we will find ourselves more attuned to the solar dance, gaining more spiritual sustenance from the seasonal procession than the lunar one. Whatever, it certainly doesn't mean that we are lacking in some way, the only lesson being that we should remain true to who we are and not waste our time pretending. The same goes for anything we have discussed in this book, we can't all feel or experience everything equally and it really is no reflection on the effectiveness of our magical selves. Our awareness and respect of external energies and beings are as much touchstones of our green spirituality as our personal authenticity and integrity.

WORKING WITH SOLAR CYCLES AND ENERGIES

To begin with we will look at the cycle of the seasons as the tree does, moving through the rolling wheel of the year. For an expansion of this brief introduction we would be well served by experiencing the year first-hand through our own tree companions, observing the physical, emotional and spiritual changes they express to us and translating this into our own lives by direct reflection. We will then consider how we may create a space in our lives where we may experience these energies first hand with greater effectiveness.

Each aspect of the year's wheel segues seamlessly into the next and flows effortlessly from the former. Yet there are times, as with the lunar progression, when the energies of that particular tide are at their most potent and affecting. The Celtic peoples had names for these times, which they knew as festivals, and these I include as a point of reference for those of us who are not already familiar with them. The Celtic festivals have become synonymous with actual dates, probably imposed by the church and state when they regularised the festivals and appropriated them for themselves, and again I include these as a reference. Many modern pagan practitioners stick to these imposed dates rigorously even though they are becoming less and less relevant to us as the climate changes and now act more as a rough guide, not a fixed dictum. I do not think, with our ethos, that we would wish to hang our wild spirituality on such dates and so we will get much more of a sense, as ever, from personally feeling, witnessing and observing what is going on within us and around us at any particular time for this is our only true indicator of the peak of a seasonal tide. As we know we need to be continually awake and alert to external elements and spiritually 'tuned in' to inner patterns to be in harmony with nature's rhythms. This brings us a real sense of the Earth-tides power and only then can we grasp what it means for us personally as well as witnessing what it means for all other beings. What follows, then, is a poetic journey, not a hard-and-fast list.

Let us begin with the moment when the light of the year begins to wax.

Here, for trees, is the *Season of Stirring Sap* when there are few outward signs of life but inwardly there is an awakening, a subtle yet significant shift towards light and life and away from darkness and slumber, a sense of renewal at a deep level. Around the trees there are the first signs of this resurgence as tenacious shoots break the soil's hard crust. The trees feel their movement yet they take their time and wait. They savour the slow return of the sun's strength with each fibre of their being, experiencing a gentle rekindling of the spark of life in every cell. This time of beginnings is the Celtic festival of Imbolc, celebrated around 1 February and is or was also known as Oimelc or 'Ewes Milk' due to the first flowing of this life-giving milk at lambing. The Christians have appropriated this festival as Candlemas but their symbolism is the same as that used in the ancient celebrations: the return of the light to the awakening land is represented in the burning of pale candles. In the times of our Earth-honouring ancestors candles were even worn as a 'crown of lights' by a young woman, or maiden, whose virginal purity and tender age represented further the new life and hope and the hidden prospect of fertility in the rousing land. The land echoed the maiden, fresh and full of promise, and the maiden stood for the land so that those who lived by her generosity may offer their respects.

The Greening and the Turning

The land at this time speaks of the energies inherent if we care to read the signs we are shown; the green blades of snowdrops push through black frost-bitten soil with all the vigour and enthusiasm of youth and crocuses push through frozen ground in colourful child-like defiance of the hardness and coldness of the old bitter winter season. Triumph over adversity, of light over darkness, of rebirth after death . . . all of these things are shown in the land. The hazel puts forth its catkins long before its soft fuzzy leaves are ready to unfurl. Tiny lambs skip and skitter in snow, full of the joys of a spring that is barely detectable but can be perceived in the tiniest movement which strives to overthrow the staid, cruel grip of the winter. Off with the old and on with the new! This is a season of throwing off the outworn and outmoded, of awakening to new possibility, of purifying ourselves from that which keeps us in stasis. It is a time of stretching and reaching out beyond our limits, of regaining the vital enthusiasms and wild passions of our youth, of believing we can overcome that which currently binds us, of looking forward with hope and planning great new schemes. In this it is like the new moon at its rebirth from the dark moon and so a new moon at this time would be a perfect time for an inception of any kind, not an active forging ahead but rather the identification of, and a slow growing towards, a new dream.

We can be as the trees are at this time and simply become aware of that which is new within us after the darkness of winter. In our lives we can consider that which we wish to push towards when we have the energies of the burgeoning year flowing more strongly with us but during this season it is ours only to formulate quietly and foster fresh awareness. It is like the dawning after a long night when we may begin to think ahead again and not look back.

Equinoxes and Solstices (cross quarters) can be tied more to a day than the other four 'fire' festivals we will be discussing. This is because at an Equinox the observable terrestrial reality of days and nights being of equal length occurs and at a Solstice the days and nights are, as a planetary fact, at their longest or shortest (we shall come to this latter point when we look at the Summer Solstice). At this point on the wheel of the year we have turned from the *Season of Stirring Sap* towards the *Season of Bursting Buds* which culminates around the Spring Equinox and usually occurs on 21 March. For the trees their initial stirring has become an active surging. The sap pulses more strongly in their veins and their tingling limbs forge bright buds which positively long to open as the sun's kiss becomes more persistent, more ardent. The wise ones of the bark are thrumming with internal activity as their energies rise with the sun's climbing strength. A palpable excitement pours from them at this time, when the days and nights are of equal length, as one by one their shining buds open, allowing leaves both glossy and downy to emerge, triumphant. Bark which once appeared brittle and dull now glows with life again, each thorn becoming harder, each branch thrusting forth more twigling shoots.

Around the trees the delightful daffodils dance in the strong breezes of the time and cheerful celandines are prevalent, shining like tiny suns and gifting us with their uplifting energy. Buttery primroses bloom and gorse makes the land glow, offering its warm sweet scent to the March wind. Daisies, or day's eyes, turn their yellow centres to the waxing sun and dandelions raise their glorious golden heads again. Female hares, so representative of the season's lively fertile aspect, box their suitors in the dew soaked meadows. The thrum of the land is getting stronger and all, from toad to hedgehog, know it in their blood and bones. '*Resurgence!*' the wren calls from the hedgerow, her tiny body no longer penetrated by winter's chill. This season is the energetic equivalent to early morning and to the new moon in its first quarter, it speaks of spurting growth and joyous renewal. It is about the delight we feel when encountering sunshine after a storm, witnessing the land as pure and new in its sparkling rain-washed state and wanting to get out there and be part of it all, experiencing everything afresh. We want to get started on things!

Spring Equinox has always been the time when the soil begins to warm and the people are able to actually begin to sow seeds rather than just plan what to sow. Symbolically this holds true, now the time to actively pursue that which we conceived of in February's brisk chill. There is a buoyancy and freshness about this season, a festival which was long since appropriated by the Christian church as the time of the death and resurrection of Christ. The hot cross buns that we connect instantly with Jesus on the cross were again part of a much older tradition, the cross within a circle being a 'sun wheel' appropriate to mark the first of the cross-quarters as the sun moves through the cycle of the year. To mark Jesus' resurrection, Easter (its name taken from the old Saxon goddess of Springtide, Oestara, whose name provides us also with the word oestrogen, the female fertility hormone) falls on the first Sunday after the first full moon on or after the Equinox and therefore is a 'move-able feast'. The theme of resurrection, of resurgence, is expressed through Jesus rising from the dead after the crucifixion whereas once the country folk would have celebrated the goddesses and nature spirits of the land returning, clad in green with pussy willow in their hands and flowering blackthorn in their hair. Easter eggs (symbolic of Oestara's ovum, perhaps) continue the theme of rebirth, renewal, and suggest the actual birthing of things into the world. We have moved past the stage of plans and dreams and are in the realms of doing, seeking, making real ... preparing for a birthing. We can plant our own seeds now, literally and symbolically, working with the spirits and with the land to ensure that the things we dreamed of can be made manifest, for the good of all.

As the sun gets stronger so do we move through the *Season of Bright Blossom,* which is also remembered as the Celtic fire festival of Beltane and celebrated on or around 1 May. The time when the trees, their glad wild hearts pounding to the heartbeat of the thriving land, pour forth their praise in pearly white and softest pink and palest cream; frothy blossom crowns the hawthorn, the apple and the bird cherry. They glow with life, standing eagerly like lovers wearing glorious flowering diadems, awaiting the touch of a beloved to make them fruitful. Butterflies unfurl startling wings of fire and bees alight on the delicate sprays of tiny blooms, bold messengers of the greening. The trees without such blossoms fully take on their own green mantles during this season and their new leaves gleam like shining arrows, aiming for a sun that dances higher, teasing, and bidding all the earth-bound kin to strive for its perfection, its joy, and its glorious abandon. All of the denizens of the land are witty, wilful and winsome now, each seeking union, be that with the sun or with another of their kind. They are active, searching, seducing, displaying themselves at their best, reaching out and stating *'here I am, this is who I am, see me, experience me!'* and it is for us to follow their calling, thrusting outwards, pushing forwards, adding to our knowledge, expressing our creativity, showing our love for the land and each other. It is the time akin to the new moon waxing towards fullness and a season reminiscent of mid-morning's energetic buzz.

At Beltane, or May Day (1 May) in the elder days there would have been a celebration centring around the spring maiden, or maturing Earth-goddess, and rejoicing in her finding joyous union with the young, passionate, virile Lord of the Trees...her Jack in the Green or Green Man. We still have echoes of this traditional symbolic ceremony in some parts of England with a Jack figure wearing a canopy of leaves. Similarly the traditional May Day maypole speaks of this sacred marriage, of the land and the sun, of earth and sky, with the twining ribbons of red and white revealing the feminine and masculine principles merging as the dancers wind them around the phallic pole of life. The

173

pole itself enters the soil, the above and the below shown in union. Beltane in the past was also a time of time of revels, so revealing an unbridled lust for life and of free sexual coupling to ensure the ongoing fertility of the land on which the people depended and revered. The people honoured and echoed the land's promise of abundance, sharing themselves freely, experiencing a spiritual and physical bonding. It was, and still is, energetically speaking, a season of powerful active loving communion with the Earth which we can express by putting all our energies into green-spirited projects we conceived of earlier in the year. It is a time for loving who we are and what we do, then extending that passion to others, a time for reaching out and connecting.

We now move into the second of those cross-quarter festivals, Summer Solstice, usually observed on 21 June and experienced in the period around this time. This is the *Season of the Greenest Leaf* when days are at their longest, peaking usually on the 21st. Nights are therefore short and the sun is exultant, claiming the days and making them beautiful. The trees are at their finest, some like the elder, the bramble and dog rose, clad in a new raiment of blossoms. Each branch sings with life, fully grown leaves compete to drink the strong draught of light from the sun in its ultimate position overhead. The leaves whisper in soft breezes to one another, sharing the ebullient energy of the season, each tree speaking of the elation found in creation from their unique sacred point of view.

This season is like midday and reminiscent of a full moon, a time of heightened clarity and energy, of peak power and creativity. It is about striking while the iron is hot, that is to say, seizing the moment of optimum power presented to us by the sun to really give what we do life, energy, and adding in our own unique pizzazz to the fiery brew. Our Earth-honouring ancestors experienced the land as a heavily pregnant woman at this time, Mother Nature about to birth all that they had worked hard for, sowing and planting all year. She is heavy and drowsy in the heat of summer, to be tended by her people as they continue to prepare for the birthing of the harvest. Because of this we can experience this time as one of creative potency, of high energy and of a burst of fulfilling activity whilst we also feel the mellow, rounded, gloriously full and sated feeling of midsummer. We may have the impetus to experience life to the full in both work and play, being at optimum effectiveness within our projects whilst loving the lazy times of relaxation, thus making the most of the passionate, pendulous peak of the year. So here is another paradox for us...in terms of energies midsummer is both hot-blooded and easy going! Whatever we do, and however we express ourselves, it can be in a rounded way that balances our hot zest for life with a measured satisfied gratitude. The ideas we had back in February can really take off now, running at full creative pelt, yet we can also afford to sit back a little and enjoy what we have wrought so far.

Come early August the trees experience the *Season of the Heavy Bough*. They have all stretched themselves and grown to their fullest capacity, their sap singing as their new branches reached for the dizzy heights of the cerulean blue sky, and now they are yielding the fruits of their year's labours. Blossom has given way to hard green fruit over July and now the wise ones of the bark are becoming laden with the first signs of their maturation. That which was green is now darkening to rich red or shiny black as the sun begins its waning journey, getting imperceptibly lower and weaker even as the land is burgeoning with the harvest of the year. The land itself is a riot of colour, a patchwork of ripening crops and wild flower meadows and all is moving in a celebratory dance of deep fulfilment. The golden seas of corn ripple in hazy heat waves, the dancing scarlet poppies nod in approval on their slender hairy stalks and the cornflowers, echoing the hue of the afternoon skies, rock themselves into satisfied slumber in balmy breezes. As the season progresses there are pert blackberries on the bramble and clusters of lustrous elderberries hanging in hedgerows alongside crimson hips and haws. These juicy hedge-fruits are the first indication of how good nature's harvest will be this year. As they appear and ripen to maturity we can also begin to gauge what our own harvest may be this year, personally speaking. We can count our blessings for the gifts bestowed upon us, both by the wild land and those received through our own efforts in the world during this sun cycle. We can acknowledge the external and the internal abundance or dearth that is ours to experience. If it is the latter then we can try to understand why this is so and, on a personal level, let go of that which hindered our progress so that next cycle may be more bountiful for us.

This season is known as Lammas, or 'Loaf-mass', which is or was celebrated on or around 1 August and is the festival of the first fruits. It is known as Loaf-mass due to the ripening of the grain which may be gathered in and baked into bread around this fecund time. For the ancestors who lived and died by the land's generosity this was the time when the pregnant Mother Nature gave birth to the Corn King, her son. She then was seen to sacrifice her newborn child, the harvest, to the people so that they may live. In this we may detect another mythos, that of Jesus who Mary saw sacrificed for the good of humanity...so that they may live. Jesus is often recognised as a Sun King, his tale echoing the ancient stories of death and resurrection as the year waxes and wanes, and it is the Sun King himself that is seen to be given up as Lammastide, for in August his time is passing. As Lugh of the Celts (who gives the name Lughnassadh to this festival) relinquishes his hold on supremacy he leaves a legacy on the land, in his wake he bequeaths sheaves of golden corn to sustain the land dwellers that they may continue in good health. In return the people show gratitude for this endless cycle and recognise his gift by remembering his spirit in the corn dollies which are often made at this time and in the singing of old songs such as 'John Barleycorn'. We too can recall this endless cyclical sacrificing, this untamed and untrammelled pattern of the wild land, in our own lives. We can recognise our own time to sow and our own time to reap, flowing with the seasons to know when we should cultivate and when we should harvest, gracefully moving from new beginnings through tending and sustaining through joyous bounty and selfless reaping and relinquishing to rest and assimilation...then round again. This is nature's way and it can be our way too if we witness the symbolic significance of what is going on all around us and allow it to speak to us on a deep level.

Here is the seasonal time which is resonant of afternoon, a time which can be relaxed although the work is not yet done. It is reminiscent of the moon just after fullness as it moves towards its last quarter and is a time which suggests winding down but doing so slowly as the influence of the energetic potent peak is still upon us. We may still be creative, innovative and outward-looking whilst having a great deal of what we hoped to achieve under our belts for us to assess and admire at leisure.

For the trees, the most transitional time is that of the *Season Clad in Many Colours,* the Autumn Equinox, and the time when summer has passed and the waning of the solar year can be truly felt. This is experienced again as a time when days and nights are of equal length and as it passes the balance moves towards darkness becoming the better friend of our waking hours. The Autumn Equinox is usually on 21 September.

The trees are now glorious in their own personal relinquishing of summer's energising presence and, in their own letting go and dying back, reveal the radiant beauty of their personal medicine. As they feel, deep within their core, the pull of the land drawing their sap down, slowing their pulse, retracting their life-force, the outward signs of their slow withdrawal are seen in a final brilliant display. The sun is no longer strong enough to warm the sap in their veins and so as each leaf loses its life-blood and feels it drain back down into the tree's central body it also loses its glossy verdant hue. In this dignified death there is glorious fire, a celebration of a life well lived, as each leaf goes through its own metamorphosis from bright green being through lightest gold, warm amber, molten copper, burnished bronze, rich burgundy, burned umber and finally shades of bitter chocolate, henna and sienna. As the swallows fly gamely south, the ivy gives out its distinctive flowering scent that still has the wasps swarming in delight, showing us that things are not quite over yet! The winged sycamore seeds rain down in swirling perfusion and the fallen horse chestnuts burst glossily from their spiny casings showing that there is still time for us to appreciate the year's worth. There is still a sense of celebration for what still is, for this is a last hurrah, a gesture which begs us to acknowledge what has been, see its good points from a rounded perspective, and not dwell on what has gone from us. It is a time to remember that there are always returns in nature, and so by direct reflection, in our own lives. The land utters a long sigh, held at the Equinox, for that which is lost but also for that which has been achieved . . . it is a sigh for both things held in balance, a sigh of both happy relief and of sad parting.

Autumn Equinox is also known as the festival of Mabon by modern pagan practitioners and it is the opposite aspect of Oestara in that now is the time for decreasing and pulling back, not growing and moving ahead, a time which energetically echoes the last quarter of the moon's cycle, the time before it fully wanes but when it has moved well past its waxing peak. This is a season reminiscent of early evening which comes upon us with a sense of the majority of our own energy having been spent when the sun was high, earlier in the day. We may well relax, withdrawing from the world into our own personal space, recouping the energy which we have given out during the day's interactions and replenishing our physical and spiritual aspects through pleasurable activities or communing with loved ones. In terms of our flowing with the land's rhythms we can observe the 'second harvest' of nuts and seeds which is happening at this time and so respond to the ancient need to store that which has been bestowed upon us so that it may nourish us until the energies rise again, in spring. We may not need to gather a harvest in from the land now (although we may well have crops of our own to tend to in gardens and allotments) but we can gather our personal harvest, symbolically, and keep it with us through the waning months to come. By doing this we can assess what we have been given and what we in turn gave for this to become so. The nuts and seeds of the trees and green beings allow us to reflect on the eternal seed of truth within all beings, the spirit, and how this spirit is transformed,

177

season after season, changed by experience and environment. We can observe the brown acorns as they fall free of their dainty cups and wonder if they will have the makings of another fine oak within them, will they fall on fertile ground and find shelter over winter or will an eager squirrel make a meal of them, so transmuting their essential energy into another life? Just like the seeds we can appreciate our own ability to either grow or change now and can assimilate all we have learned, store it within us and begin to move on into a new phase.

In late September huge sunflowers, standing like wilting sentinels by the side of maize fields soon to be ploughed again, bend their heads and begin nodding into slumber even as hungry birds pick their huge seed heads clean. The damp and growing chill begin to dull their large leaves and their sunshine yellow petals, once so glorious, now lie limp and brown close to their empty faces. Any remaining apples are falling, creating a rotten feast for jealously screeching starlings, and releasing their evocative autumnal scent; cloyingly tangy and sour as the season. We are moving into the time of Mother Nature's sleeping, her final relinquishing of her fine green mantle, a process shown in the leaves which begin to fall like fiery rain from the trees. As we move through towards the end of October the trees experience the *Season of the Falling* fully as the strong winds tear at their remaining dull crisp leaves and whip and whisk them on to the ground. They are sleepy and their energy has all but gone back into the very deepest darkest centre of themselves; the sap has seeped into their roots to wait to be roused by the return of the sun. Only the holly, the ivy, the yew and the fir trees remain green as their companions are buffeted and stripped by increasingly hostile weather. Their energy is resolute and even delightfully nose-thumbing in the face of the season's relentless decay and laying bare. They stand as reminders of the evergreen nature of the spirit of all things as we move into the time of spirits.

This is time of the festival known as Samhain or All Hallows Eve, a time of wood smoke and mists, of mystery and illusion. It is a time of passing over into the unknown that darkness symbolises for us...and of death. The fields are black now and the crows, tattered and flapping inky shapes in the strange lilac light of a late October afternoon, are scavenging the carcasses of things already killed by cold and hunger. The spirit of the land is sombre, mournful and all external energies are low. However, on the inner levels there can be much activity if we follow the season and withdraw into the mists of the soul, looking for answers in the Otherworlds and the realms of the spirits. At this time we are travelling towards the dark of the moon, concerned not with worldly doing but with profound internal knowing, focused on the bigger questions that haunt us, not on issues pertaining to the personal development of this human self. Our attention can be with the immortal self and what it needs and how it feels. Like the trees our vital life force is pulled down deeply to sustain us and like the other mammals the urge is to hide ourselves away and rest. If we override these primal urges too much we will find this season the most difficult of all as a definite shift is happening, a spiralling motion drawing all beings away from an outward aspect towards the inward. It is a time for walking with spirit, both our own and others, safely and with respect. The presence of the ancestors is never felt more strongly than at this time, time ceases to be a linear process and instead our daily lives become overlaid with that which has gone before . . . memory is not discernible from current reality.

Samhain is a faery time and so we need to retain that vital rootedness which sustains us and be aware of that which is glamour and illusion in our lives. We can earth ourselves in simple wholesome activities like making fortifying stews and soups, pursuing indoor crafts and carving the ubiquitous humorously grimacing pumpkin, and, more traditionally in England, turnip lanterns to ward off any unwelcome trickster spirits who may be abroad in the mists between the worlds. It is the equivalent of twilight, a time to be inside our homes lest we get led away into the growing gloom by dancing figures and lilting music. Perhaps, with our green-spirited approach which combines the practical with the magical, we can still dance with the shining ones under the silvered trees and not feel the urge to leave this world behind us. It is the awareness of the temptation and the confusion of the time that will keep us from wandering too far from that which is everyday, retaining our sense of responsibility to the here and now and to the Mother Earth who needs us in *this* reality!

The cycle is almost complete save for the *Season of the Blackened Branch,* experienced by the trees around Winter Solstice, time of the shortest day, which falls on or around 21 December. At this time the silver birch stands denuded of its shiny bark, the remains of its delicate leaves long since trampled into cold black earth. Fieldfares, winter visitors to the British Isles, call to each other in dripping trees, trees that stand outlined like brittle charcoal sketches against the white featureless sky, denuded of all but the last few straggling leaves. The wise ones of the bark seem almost dead, their energy retained somewhere safe within, yet their silent silhouettes dominate a land cut back to the quick and pared down to its bones. This is the time of deepest dreaming when all beings experience that ultimate retreat into the velvet darkness of internal, and external, night. We are reminded of the cyclical nature of existence at this time, for even as we enter the tomb of the year's ending, witnessing the seeming extinction of life in the land, so do we simultaneously experience the rebirth of hope emerging from the womb of nature . . . for this is both the time of the shortest darkest day *and* the point when the sun's power waxes again. At the Winter Solstice the sun begins to regain its strength as we move slowly again into lighter days and warmth. The message is simple and profound, that in the midst of death there is life. The ancients who walked the wildest ways knew of this symbolic resonance, building their burial chambers and monuments to acknowledge the returning light at this pivotal time. Shafts of sunlight can still be seen penetrating the womb within their tombs at sunrise on the shortest day. New life is so guaranteed.

How do we celebrate this eternal returning? Our Christmas lights echo the age-old tradition of the Yule log, candles and fires which are lit traditionally with the remainder of the old log to show respect for the cycles of life and death in which we all live. The mistletoe, the sacred branch of the Druids, grows tenaciously on the oak and apple trees and acts as a reminder of potency even at this seemingly cold, still time. The clusters of white berries on its winged green leaves are still brought into our homes for us to kiss under in what is not just a cheeky game but an old green-spirited charm. This ensures that there is fertility for the land, and, by a direct reflection that acknowledges our deep connection, in our own lives once more. The holly, with its ever-green leaves and glossy red berries, is included in both seasonal wreath and greetings card and recalls immortality and life-giving blood; these qualities can either be related to Christ (whose birth was aligned to fit in with the Solstice) or the returning Sun King, depending on which aspect appeals to us. Similarly we can give gifts to our loved ones in cele-bration of the birth of the Son or the rebirth of the sun; the symbology is basically the same as both offer hope and renewal. Our giving, receiving and ardent feasting at this time are signs of our acknowledging, and offering thanks for, the plenty our year has yielded in both physical and spiritual terms. It is a time of holy-days, of resting and rejoicing and sharing what has been bestowed on us through our labours. At this time, so reminiscent of midnight and dark moon, we can flow with the energies of the land as the ancestors did, both reflecting and looking back and dreaming with the flickering fires of what may come. This is why the month of January, following only ten days after Solstice time, was named for the Roman God Janus who looked both backwards and forwards simultaneously.

And then, of course, we are back to the *Season of Stirring Sap*; the wheel turns and so we become what we were born to be, naturally.

But what of other, smaller, cycles? What of the wheels within wheels that we experience daily? Well, we have been mentioning the correspondences that the seasons have to times of day as we have gone along. Some people, as we discussed in chapter two, are more aligned to a certain time of day, just as they are to a certain element or moon phase, than others. It is a soul preference. It can also be a physical preference if we choose to work shifts and do nights, for instance. Any description or guide I can give is a general one depending on the usual patterns of work and most common preferences. It is enough for us to know that we are not being abnormal or weird if we feel drawn to midnight above midday or our optimum energy is found around mid-evening rather than mid-morning. Go with the flow and know your own flow!

It may be worth briefly mentioning how weather affects us quite individually too. We need not all be sunshiny summery people. We may find wind and rain uplifting and sun a nuisance due to skin type or soul-temperament. We might find low pressure absolutely unbearable and depressing or not notice it at all. It is well worth making a note of such things in our magical journals as weather often gets overlooked as a contributor to mood and energy etc. As an example of its importance, there would be no point trying to do some practical green magic at a time when the weather was influencing us adversely to the effect we were aiming for with the wish-spell. To align ourselves with the energies of weather is a beneficial aspect of what we do and can help us enormously if we come to understand our personal energetic relationship to it.

All we really need to do to be more in tune with nature is to flow with the land's experience as if it were our own, feeling the external energies wax and wane and allowing them to influence the internal, regardless of restrictive human convention. If we are able to read the exquisite, eloquent symbolism inherent in bud, branch and bark as if it were a soul-poem them we will be inspired and moved, no longer feeling *removed* from creation. When the music of nature, as expressed in this eternal wheel, is allowed to penetrate past the shell of modern society we are suddenly spun into the centre of the circle; we are glorious dancers in the sacred round, not dulled spectators waiting in a seemingly purposeless line. By becoming attuned to these cycles, *and living them,* we come to understand the personal in the universal, the within in the without, the wild and wonderful connectedness of all beings. However, to encourage this attunement we can take practical steps.

181

One of these steps is to create a sanctuary in which we can observe the wheeling of the year, meditate on it and experience it intimately as part of our own selves. It is a sacred place, both in the world and in the Otherworlds, where we may experience the seasonal energies (and their seamless flowing) to the full. This sanctuary can be created in our gardens, on our allotments, in another's garden where we are allowed access, on a balcony or even in the area around or in a window box. Our whole patio or back yard can become a sanctuary. If necessary a sanctuary can be made indoors but it is better to have the touch of earth and sky, sun, wind and rain if possible. The spirits will be with us just the same but their presence will be much stronger and more immediate if we meet them out of doors where we can smell, hear, and feel the seasons on our skin as well as sensing their energies. I do appreciate that not everybody is able to contemplate physically building a sanctuary and so please do feel free to tailor the following suggestions to suit any special requirements or, if possible, engage the assistance of a like-minded partner who can take on the more laborious tasks. It is the whole ethos of *sanctuary* that is more resonant than its setting and our green intent and loving, reverential approach are all important.

Firstly why build or create a sanctuary? Well, a sanctuary is somewhere where we can make our experience of the dance of life very personal to us and gain a much more intense relationship with the greening of the land and the turning of the seasons. We can have powerful, immediate interactions with the verdant beings that grow there and with the sylvan spirits who attend them, as we are working alongside them for the same ends. Creating sanctuary is an effective way of showing our intent to the world 'in miniature', the sanctuary acting as a microcosm of the macrocosm ... what we do there we do for the Earth in a wider sense. By tending this small area as if it were the whole of the Earth we also have the opportunity to express our stewardship; that is, our desire to be custodians or green guardians in the manner of the old wild ones, relating to the land as a living being, and serving and defending her gladly. The whole idea of a sanctuary is a space that renews and uplifts, offering peace and tranquillity as well as regeneration. Our sanctuary will therefore be a place where we may reflect prayerfully on our wishes for the wider world whilst channelling our love, hope and wisdom into the soil beneath our feet and under our fingers. We will guard and tend our sanctuary in a way that sustains us and replenishes us just as much as it does the land itself; in this it is part of a greater circle of connection, being both a reflection of the greater world and of our individual selves.

As we now know, green spirituality is not about building man-made temples, shrines or setting 'sacred space' apart from 'ordinary space' (all being sacred) yet here is a way of focusing on and *condensing* our magical will into one small area for the sake of a more effective healing for the land. We can do this whilst gaining a much needed restoration of our own energies, energies that can be so easily depleted when engaging in hectic modern life, even when we live in a green-spirited way. Yet this sanctuary is not a place set apart from 'real life' in the sense that our lives are polluted and damaging and it is pure and nurturing . . . this would run clean against the grain of our view of magic being inherent in the midst of normal, mundane life! Rather it is a space which is grounded and earthy *without being worldly in a human sense*. It gives us time away from that human aspect so that we may reconnect with the eternal spiritual aspect of ourselves and the land. By doing this we are better equipped to see the spirit in all beings we encounter back in the world and so be more patient and compassionate with them. We create a new cycle, that of personal replenishment for the sake of the replenishment of wider society . . . and back round again.

In our building, or creating, of a sanctuary we are referring back to our magical life-motto of 'soil, soul, and society'; offering something ongoing to each of these vital interconnected aspects. We will tend the soil and feed the green beings there, we will engage with the nature spirits and give our own spirits a boost through our intimacy with the essence of the land and we will offer back our work to the world by

(i) becoming stronger, calmer and more response-able in ourselves through our healing time in the sanctuary,
(ii) reflecting out our prayers, intentions and actions for this one part of the Earth to the wider world, and
(iii) allowing anyone else in need of healing, a quiet time or solitude to respectfully spend time there so that they too may go back into the world as more able, peaceful and focused beings.

Sanctuary brings together the *green* and the *spirituality* aspects of who we are and allows us to share it with the world. Encouraging any green area to flourish is a worthwhile thing in an increasingly built-up world but here we have the added benefit of making it a soul-full experience that does not divorce the practical manifest aspects of being from the spirit-led. This project shows in perfect simplicity how one feeds the other, mirrors the other and dances as the perfect partner of the other. Here is a true act of gentle eco-activism that states '*this small space is how I wish the world to be*!' whilst also knowing that such a statement, said with a

183

full heart and a knowledge of the power of unseen energy, is a magical prayer and a green healing spell for the good of the All.

To begin, we can identify where we should create our sanctuary by asking the spirits for their advice on the most resonant place. We can then en-vision (that is, psychically *see*, through trance journey) what our sanctuary should be like, obtaining visual guidance for its optimum benefit. For this purpose I first suggest that we engage in a trance journey to meet the old wild ones again, perhaps meeting them one-to-one as we did in chapter two. We can then allow them to take us to the best possible space for us to create a sanctuary in. For example, if the best place for the sanctuary is at the bottom of our large garden then we will find ourselves there in spirit during the journey, looking at the manifest place with our insightful spirit-vision. When they have shown us this we can begin to see, with their help, what our sanctuary should look like and what it should contain. We can ask them such leading questions as the following.

- Which spirits already dwell here and how can I work with them harmoniously? How may I best create an atmosphere of peace and healing calm which will please them as well as me?
- Which spirits should I encourage in to the sanctuary, if any? And how?
- Should I clear away what is currently there and start again? Or work with what there is?
- How may I represent the four elements in the sanctuary? Which elemental theme, if any, would suit the land I am to work on? Is it a predominantly 'watery' area or one more suited to stone, rock etc.?
- Should there be a shape or pattern to the overall place? How shall I demark its boundaries, if at all? Is there a doorway of some sort, denoting a shift of energy, through which one needs to pass in order to enter?

Once we have formed a clear mind's-eye picture of the sanctuary as it should be, complete with any mental notes of things that cannot be seen but need to be done, we can ask for the green guardians' continued blessing on our project, taking care to ask them if we can show our gratitude to them in any way through this project. We can also check to see if we may visit them again as the work progresses for any further inspiration or practical advice as regards the land or space. As we begin to create our sanctuary we can converse with the nature spirits in attendance too and no doubt we will begin to pick up mind's-eye imagery and physical omens resonant to what we are doing as we are actually working the land there. Our own spiritual companions can help us with personal issues as regards what would be best for us to have there to ensure it is a place of gentle rejuvenation and soothing calm. Remember that our companions are there for guidance on personal matters and the old wise ones for advice on more general green issues while the nature spirits can advise about individual aspects of nature such as plants or rocks.

There are no 'should be's' attached to this project and that is why it is impossible to do much more than suggest its worth as an endeavour and offer some guidelines for approaching it. I cannot list all the things to include as we each have differing tastes and will choose markedly different sites for our sanctuary. However, there are some aspects it would be pleasing to include, if we feel guided to do so. Our sanctuary can become a wildlife haven, for example, perhaps even a specialist habitat for a certain species. We can include wild areas to encourage bees and butterflies, trees and shrubs to feed birds along with providing nest boxes, feeders, bird baths etc. Perhaps our lunar pond could be a central focus, with all of its attendant creatures and green beings. We could devote the area to growing native wildflowers or fragrant herbs which would be visually stimulating, gloriously life-affirming and deeply soothing as we breathe of their perfume. The spirits may have suggested a strongly earthy or watery or airy feeling and so we could create a stunning, flowing water feature using local stone. The vesica pool at the Chalice Well Gardens in Glastonbury, UK, could be a fine inspiration for such an endeavour. Or we could build a simple seat from wood recycled from our willing tree companions and maybe even a gazebo-style structure for all-weather meditations. If we feel so moved (and it fits with our guidance on the area) we can create rockeries, labyrinths or monuments which flow with the energies of the land. For inspiration we can have a look at the stunning work of either Chris Drury or Andy Goldsworthy, creators of sculptures and structures which nestle into the landscape in the manner of the dwellings of our ancestors. Based around organic forms and patterns and using entirely natural materials they are evocative pieces which at once express the tranquillity and vitality of the wild land. The essence of their work is the way it is in total harmony with its surroundings whilst making an individual statement about the energy there. The sanctuary can be aesthetically lovely, a sensory treat *and* an ecological statement; it is for us to learn how to balance the unworldly with the worldly in this way with the help of the spirits.

We can, in seemingly complete contrast to making beautiful sculptures, create a compost heap at the site of our sanctuary, if it is appropriate. This may seem unrestful and ungainly but in fact is an eloquent gesture which will bring deep and lasting satisfaction as it is a constant reminder of the sacred round of growth and regeneration in our midst, as well as it being a wonderful living system to show our commitment to the ethos of recycling and replenishment. Our compost can be used to feed the green beings we grow in the sanctuary while we continue to donate our organic kitchen waste to its pile. We can include everything from tea-bags to vegetable peelings, just omitting anything diseased or meat-oriented as these obviously cause problems of their own. If we find the idea of heaps or piles a little too messy for a sanctuary we can purchase a ready-made bin although it is relatively simple to create one of our own with just a little effort. The main thing to remember is that the bin should not be totally solid as air is needed for the process of decay to occur most effectively. Something without corners is preferable as the air then circulates more freely and therefore any manner of large barrel that can be cleaned and pierced with holes will suffice. If we do decide to build a box then remember that it will function best if the air can also pass beneath it and so something raised on blocks or bricks and constructed of slatted wood will work well for us (but only if we then line the constructed box with chicken wire so that the gaps between the slats won't allow for bits of waste falling out!). One side of any bin does have to open, however, so that we may turn the material inside it, thus encouraging an even breaking down of its contents, and so planning how this will work should not be over-looked . . . perhaps hinges or nuts and bolts that need to be unscrewed can be used. No practical problem is too mundane for the spirits who will gladly advise us of such matters even if we consider it to be too human a task for them to be bothered with. If it's green-spirited in ethos they will help! There are also plenty of excellent books that can be used to back up this basic idea and any volume on wildlife gardening usually has a section on successful composting.

If we do have to create our sanctuary indoors then it is for us, in league with the spirits, to work out how we may grow things and flow with the energy there in a similar way. It is perfectly possible for us to create miniature water features, labyrinths, herb gardens etc. in a suitable corner of our homes. Symbols of rebirth, regeneration, growth and dying back should feature, to ensure that we are fully immersed in the cycle of life within the internal sphere of our sanctuary. The aim is to create as natural a space as possible and not to be caught up in buying props; this is not an altar in any sense but rather a place of reflec-tion and renewal that reveals our inherent green-spirited way and commitment to the land. With our 'do it yourself' ethos we can make and create what we need just as effectively indoors as we can out . . . in fact the challenge may be that much greater and so our ingenuity and contact with the spirits is strengthened more by the experience! The only thing that will be missing from our indoor sanctuary will be the blessings bestowed by nature herself, the wildlife, the wind etc. We can do a great deal to invoke the wild land within, however. Opening a window with an invocation for the green essence of the Earth and the four elements to come into our lives can be effective if repeated daily. Covering the walls with stunning photographs or paintings of the land in all her storm-tossed, sun-soaked, wind-chilled, moon-washed elegance, with a soul-prayer for each to bring a little of the real power of nature within, can be transformative. Undertaking regular meditative trance journeys to the Otherworldly wild realms in our sanctuary space can assist us in bringing a little of the green back with us each time we venture there. We can ask the old wild ones to regularly infuse our space with their potent organic spirit too. I myself have been housebound for periods of my life and have found all of these things helpful.

As a final note on indoor space it is well to regularly cleanse the energy by offering the smoke of herbs that help us in this task and burning organic essential oils of similar green beings in an oil burner. Opening the window will obviously help, with invocations that the stale energy should leave just as the fresh wild energy pours in. Allowing the energy in our sanctuary to be kept pure and raw is a matter of our own custodial duties as they will not be regulated by nature's cleansing hand.

It would be nice to have an 'opening' ceremony to mark the occasion of the sanctuary's completion so that we can acknowledge the fact that the place is now energetically different and dedicated to green-spirited qualities such as replenishment, reflection and observation. This can just be between ourselves and the unseen ones, or perhaps we can share our intent with a few like-minded others who will be invited to enter the sanctuary themselves, if they feel the need. We can then take on the title of steward–guardian in their presence and make vows to affirm our role as custodians, both in the place we have helped to create and in the wider world.

We can bless the sanctuary with a loving soul-prayer such as

'*I acknowledge you, place of purest power,*
I stand by you, place between the worlds,
I honour you, space where knowledge flowers,
I will bless you, space where peace unfurls.

I respect you, place of green rebirthing,
I will tend you, place where spirits dwell,
I will serve you, space of soul's earthing,
I now bless you, space where silence swells.'

We can also affirm our vows by saying something like

'I, [insert name], *do offer myself,*
As both a transient human and an eternal spirit,
As both a dedicated person and an honourable soul,
And as an integrated being with a wild green essence,
In the service of this sanctuary.
May I know the sanctuary as a place that represents all places,
That I myself may come to represent all people,
In working for a sustainable future,
Praying for restoration and renewal in the gift of the present,
And searching for the truths buried in the past of the ancestors.
May I walk gently in truth and beauty here,
Just as I vow to tread lightly on the Earth Mother,
And may all I do here be so reflected out and ever onwards
For the good of all beings.
May the spirits that come for my highest good now witness me,
As I step into the sacred circle, flowing with the tides of life,
As keeper, guardian and custodian of this blessed verdant space,
May I know response-ability and shoulder it gladly,
And so may my green mantle be proudly worn in celebration,
In a sign of my stewardship and kinship with all that live
alongside me.

At this time, by this place, and with the grace of the Wise Wild
Old Ones may the healing begin . . .
And let it begin with me.'

This is the point when our green mantle should be felt clearly around us, a protecting presence that gives us strength of purpose, vitality and clear vision. We can experience, in trance, the reality of this verdant mantle and reaffirm our vows so that they resonate in the material world *and* in the Otherworlds. We can know by the creation of a sanctuary, with our new understanding of both the ways of the land and of the spirits, that we are transformed. Nothing will ever be the same for us. Perhaps now we can take on a secret magical name, in consultation with the spirits, that affirms our life-choices and our wild path. Or maybe we can buy a piece of symbolic jewellery to wear that reflects this transformation. Or perhaps we can even choose to mark our skin permanently with a tattoo that symbolically echoes our internal intent. At this time of completion we can also offer up gifts as a gesture of our allegiance to the spirits who attend both us individually and our sanctuary space, to honour and celebrate what has been created with their help and to pledge our energies for our ongoing union. The completion of the sanctuary and the taking on of the role of guardian means there is much cause for celebration for we are now truly part of the solution for a better world, not just a dispirited, disconnected, apathetic part of the problem. It is now time for a new cycle to commence for us, one that is richer, fuller and more beneficial to the All.

We now know how to live in a green spirited way, walking with the spirits of the land as well as with our own familiar companions and the other beings we share the bountiful land with. We know how to live magically from moment to moment, in tune with the Earth, sun and moon. We have a good rooted understanding of energies, in terms of the correspondence to what we do in the spiritual or unseen sense as a reflection in the manifest levels and vice versa. We are looking *beyond*, into the green, whist staying 'in the now', experiencing life as empowered, en-souled and impassioned people. All that remains in this work is for me to share some more inspirational ideas for us to consider when going on with our daily existences; existences that are now realms of wild enchantment, no longer mundane but rich with possibility and the power we have found in our own hands.

5

Deeper into the Green

It is easy to think that the authors of books such as this one lead charmed existences as perfect examples of outstanding moral fortitude. Not so, I am sure, or at least not in this particular case! If the book is in itself inspirational and helpful it is largely irrelevant what the authors themselves do in their own life but here I thought it may be beneficial, in the open and green-spirited way I am expounding, to briefly share with you a little of my own struggles. This is so that the work we have shared here doesn't seem unrealistic but rather grounded in real experience, coming from a place of wholehearted authenticity. By explaining a little of my own striving I hope I impress upon the reader that we are in this together, finding new ways of being at one with the land, finding our wild selves amongst the debris of modern living and looking beyond the superficial into that which is gloriously ethereal yet utterly eternal.

So, here's my confession.

Due to a chronic and painful set of physical diseases I have still got medicines in my box which I know have been tested on our four-legged creature companions at some stage. For a long while these tablets have provided me with instant pain relief but now the very real understanding of how these unnatural drugs came into existence is enough to render them ineffective for me. I am working hard towards replacing them with kinder herbal alternatives and I understand that if I can remain patient with their gentle touch the herbs will be far more effective in the long run. Part of my own healing will now come from being part of a compassionate future; my pain can no longer be eased by products that are themselves steeped in the pain of other beings. Also I still have a few unethical products in my cosmetic bag . . . old habits die hard but our kin die harder and sooner or later I will be ready to sacrifice every last item so that they may live in freedom. What else? Well, even though I know that my energies are everything I still continue to pollute myself with addictive substances, knowing that what I do to the land I do to myself, within always finding an echo without. Such an understanding is a grave responsibility and I can only own my actions for today and hope that one day I will be strong enough to walk my truth fully.

Furthermore I still panic when I see a spider in my home even though I know, and truly *feel*, that this creature teacher is my kin. It seems so foolish but there it is. Some behaviours are deep-rooted and, like the insidious knotweed so detested by gardeners, it puts out runners that we need to locate and remove every last bit of lest they spring back up when we least expect them to. And finally I confess that during the writing of this book I have allowed my communication with my own dear companion spirits, the trees and the spirits of nature, to lapse. They haven't ceased but they've been blocked from that nourishing flow that I usually enjoy on a daily basis. Why? Well, as a writer it is easy to get tied up with words and have one's brain permanently wrestle with concepts and ideas and this is to the detriment of more gentle, meandering spirit dialogues. I fully intend to let the full flavour of life in all its energetic, spirit-full glory flow through me again once I have completed this manuscript as I feel the poorer for my self-imposed removal from the essence of my being . . . and that of others.

Being green-spirited is a hard road that leads to places of unparalleled beauty. Just because we veer off that unbeaten track occasionally, never wilfully but always with sadness, doesn't mean we are unworthy of its ups and downs, its hidden treasures and moments of breathtaking clarity. My advice to myself, and so to you, is honour yourself as you honour all beings and *be kind to your mistakes*. We should only ask ourselves if our intentions are good, coming from a place of deep love rather than old fear, ignorance or prejudice. I myself intend to keep on growing in beauty, striving for the light just like the tiny sunflower on my patio which has struggled through frost and dismal dark days to produce its golden flowers in late November this year. I hope that each of us will find our own reasons to keep striving.

So, to finish let's now look at some more activities that we can engage in, for the good of all. These are everyday things/tasks that allow us to be magical in the midst of life!

Firstly, we need to ask *are we a consumer?*

One of my own pet hates is the word 'consumer' which the media love to label us all as. And there is truth in this loathsome label for we do *consume*, we devour new things with little thought for the consequences. But are we replenishers in as much as we are consumers, do we replenish rather than consistently use up? Do we see ourselves as a part of a cycle of give and take, of flowing energy passing from one to another, or do we not think of where things come from or where they go to when we throw them away? Do we consider ourselves to be the end of the line or are we but links in a chain? In a world which calls almost everything a 'product' from toothpaste to a tomato, how far have we bought into the buying in? Which of us can answer this honestly now and assess the levels to which we consume? If we are willing, in true full moon style, to look at ourselves clearly then we can see what we need to cut back on or develop within our lives. Then we can tackle how we may actively change the ingrained patterns of modern 'throwaway' society.

Here's how.

Become a charity shop, thrift store or jumble sale goer!

The former allows us to get a real feel for being a link in a chain, acting as a recycler of unwanted items so that more 'things' need not be manufactured on our behalf, and doing so whilst actually helping other charitable causes. The latter allows us to be a recycler of other folk's discarded 'stuff' whilst perhaps contributing to the organisation or school that ran the event in the first place. Second-hand shopping for a worthy reason is a double edged act of compassionate green awareness. We can extend this awareness to actively selecting charities which are ethical in themselves, boycotting those which support animal experimentation (many cancer charities do this) and favouring those with a more holistically caring approach. We could opt to help only local concerns such as hospices or shelters for the homeless or unwanted animals. This is making a statement of intent which shows that we do not support, actively or passively, the depleting of the world's resources in the needless churning out of yet more items such as fashionable clothes or attractive kitchenware.

At the time of writing it is coming up to Christmas and as I check my e-mails I am being reminded by every company that has been able to get its hands on my details that there are 'only so and so shopping days left!' Wouldn't it be a wonderful act of green magic for us to buy all our presents, be they birthday or Christmas, through such charitable shops? By buying gifts there and then passing on our purchase to another we are keeping that energy of giving, not taking, flowing. For everything we buy we can donate something else of our own to the shop so that we contribute to the chain. By actively opting to do this, even if it makes life a bit harder for us by our having to search out appropriate items rather that having them neatly displayed for us in a superstore, we are being magical. If we add in a prayer or wish as we donate, buy and give away then we are truly connecting with the spiritual aspect of being as well as stating our allegiance to the Earth. The wish-prayer could be as basic, but heartfelt, as

'I stand against society's tide,
I flow instead with nature's way,
I borrow from the Earth and so,
I contribute and give away,
My energies move round and on,
May others flow with me today.'

Or even more simply

'Round and round the giving goes,
My tide, like nature's, onward flows.'

Just a word of rather humorous warning about charity or second-hand shopping . . . it can be addictive if one is that way inclined! As charity shopping is much, much cheaper that supporting major chain stores, I have in the past found myself a sucker for a bargain of any sort, thinking that something was too good to be left behind at such a reasonable price! I ended up with bags full of 'stuff' that I had convinced myself would come in useful one day as a present as I had been unable to resist whatever it was at such a low price! This rather defeats the object of fighting against the consumerist flow and I ended up donating most of it back to the charity shop where I had bought it! It's far more fun to go shopping seeking a specific thing and aiming to find it rather than going with no notion of what we need and being swayed by a ridiculous bargain! I find that I am able to clearly visualise what I need to find a few days before I go shopping and I am usually able to locate it . . . this is rather like sending out an astral call for the right item to come along which someone then answers by donating it to the shop in question!

Note the stress on the word *need* used here. Identifying a genuine personal need helps us reject the 'consumer' label which promotes the *'I want!'* mentality. We should consider what we really require above what we are exhorted to want. The phrase *'must have purchase'* is one of the unnecessary claims of the consumerist society we are turning against; it panders directly to the *'I want'* side of human nature and not to the *'I need'* aspect which is far more measured and green-spirited. The way of replenishment we aim to actively live with our second-hand shopping is about restoring a balanced attitude which cannot be easily manipulated by greed or desire. It holds the Earth first and takes pleasure from being in tune with what Mother Nature needs. If we can adhere to this then we are not at the mercy of any quick pleasure fixes that come from purchasing 'consumer luxuries'.

Mend what is broken and make things ourselves!

This first point is a tough one as the consumer society does not encourage fixing things *at all*! It is usually cheaper to replace a faulty electrical item with a brand new one than it is to have it fixed by a repair person. Because of this price discrepancy the temptation to throw whatever it is away and start again is overwhelming, even for the green-spirited individual. Yet think for a moment about the things that languish on tips and dumps (and even, disgustingly, in hedgerows and in lay-bys). What happens to the thing we discard when it is out of sight and mind? Does it cease to be? By throwing away something, say a television or hairdryer, which could be fixed we are divorcing ourselves from the chain of responsibility and turning a blind eye to the desecration of the land. We are making our contribution to the growing mounds of unwanted consumer fare that lies barely rotting all around us and we are symbolically stating that we don't care, that it someone else's responsibility to deal with the mess we make. Everything we do has an energetic implication and the energies of our not caring about this issue, or any other that seems like hard work, cannot be confined to one area of our lives!

This 'throwaway mentality' is about us putting ourselves into a supreme position at the end of a line of production. It allows us to look no farther than our own immediate desires and conveniences. We need to step back into the loop and take responsibility. This may be annoyingly expensive and time consuming for us and the repair people themselves may try to persuade us otherwise, but we need to keep what we have running well so that we do not keep demanding and discarding more and more non-biodegradable things. Consuming strains the Earth's resources, contributes to the non-sustainable status quo and it adds to the ever growing unnatural mountains of man-made detritus which one day won't be so easy to hide. We may bury the evidence of our short-sightedness, or we may sink it, but whatever we do we are fouling up the Earth with monstrous pointless examples of our excess and flaunting a flagrant disregard for nature. To stand against the human tide and flow with the natural way we can know that every time we choose to get our old tape recorder or washing machine fixed we are making a magical statement of intent. Living magically can be, as we know, that simple. We can be fully aware of our actions, their seen and unseen implications, and if we act with green-spirited care, full of an Earth-honouring intent, then our lives are touched by wild enchantment even if what we do seems unconnected to the land or unimportant in the scheme of things. *It never is!*

In previous chapters we have already looked at ways we can build simple things, like a bat box, to save us purchasing another item which is overpriced and unnecessary. The best thing about making things is that we can put magic into the act of creation ourselves. It is a biological fact that if food is prepared with love and eaten with care, free of guilt and fear, then it has a greater nutritional value for us. What we put into things, the unseen emotional aspect, the spiritual dimension of our being, does make a difference. Therefore the jumper we knit for a nephew with the visualised, prayerful intent of it keeping him warm, safe and happy will always seem cosy to him, like an old welcoming friend. The papier mâché sun that we fashion to hang above a sick child's bed, with the visualised and spoken intention of it spreading healing light and uplifting warmth just as the sun itself does, will bring them much joy and give them daydreams of better days to come. The quilts we sew, the cupboards we build, the toys we fashion, and the clothes we make . . . all of these can have a resonance which we ourselves add in to the mix. It is in our hands, as well as in our imaginations and through our directed will, that we can transform a craft or homespun act into a truly enchanted *living* thing. Not only do we add our spiritual essence, but we can work with the *soul* of the material and thus make a piece empathically. For example, if we work with wood we can relate to the essence of the contributing tree's spirit and that of its attendant nature spirits and if we work with fabric we can relate to the resonance of the contributing cotton plant that once grew in the soil. It is well do to all that we do with this awareness, knowing that our energy goes into what we do and is reflected from it again, combined with the energy of the being that contributed itself that it may exist.

So, here's a challenge for us all . . . to learn how to do something practically or creatively that we cannot already do. This could be carpentry, metal work, pottery, sewing, crochet, cooking or any other craft considered as everyday. We can do this in order to save ourselves money as well as helping the Earth's resources by committing to work with recycled or basic materials for the good of the All. The thing about doing it ourselves, the D.I.Y. ethos, is that we have the control

over where things come from and we know what went into making
them! When we are back in control with first-hand knowledge we
become more empowered as green-spirited individuals and so are more
able to contribute positively to the whole.

Ethical trade . . . think global, act local!

Here's another potentially difficult area . . . that of buying fair traded
goods and not those created through the misery or poverty of others
that we cannot see, in far off places. It is easy enough these days to
purchase all manner of foodstuffs marked 'fair trade' in supermarkets,
goods such as coffee, chocolate, fruit juice and sugar, and, if we are
willing to pay a little extra for these, it is easy to show our support for
such ethically produced fare. This fairness usually means that, for
example, the coffee growers or pickers themselves receive a fair
wage for their labours and are not 'ripped off' in the market place.
Fairness also means the suppliers of the goods are not expected to work
unreasonable hours in terrible conditions and child labour is not
condoned. These are the things we are guaranteed by 'fair trade'. But
what of the things we unwittingly buy without looking at the labels? I
have been shocked to discover how many items of clothing I own,
even if they are second hand, that have been made in a country or
region renowned for its sweat shops or its unfairness as regards the
above conditions. It is now well known that such luxury items as some
expensive training shoes are made in such a way. The difficulty comes
again with our responsibility, as green-spirited folk, to other beings. In
this case, our responsibility is to care for other human beings who are
possibly being demeaned and forced to work in brutal conditions for
the sake of our fripperies. The effort we have to make, as a magical act
to facilitate change, is to reject such standards and to cease buying
goods that come from a place that allows us no way of knowing if
they were ethically produced or not. We have to put our energy into
supporting locally produced goods wherever possible.

How may we do this magically? Well we can make a start by
attending farmers' markets for fruit and vegetables grown in our area,
seasonally. Farmers' markets also sell butter, cheese, eggs and other
produce which we can guarantee has only travelled down the road and
hasn't been hauled over thousands of miles in a refrigerated truck. We
can also talk to the actual producers and get a feel of how they grow/
produce their foodstuffs. When we buy like this we know we are

living prayerfully, within the way of replenishment, in the time-honoured way. It is a sustainable act based on the natural harvest of the land we live upon. Again we opt back into the loop, knowing where our food comes from, knowing we will compost it after we have finished with its remains and return it to the soil. It is empowering for us and good for the Earth. In this way we can also shop in grocers that provide a range of locally produced fare such as bread or pies. We are putting our energy, the money we have worked for, into that which is wholesome and ethical. Each time we buy in this way we can pray that the spirits of the land witness our behaviour and pass on the message to others as they sit in parks, gardens and in the fields. Pray that people's senses and spirits should be opened to the call of the land on which they walk. Know that what we do makes that call stronger as we feed the land.

This 'buy local' approach doesn't end with food – it applies to any other item we need. We can check out small independently owned craft shops or look at adverts in the newsagent's window to see what services are being offered in the area. It is a worthwhile quest!

Bartering

Just a quick note here to remind us to consider any local scheme that there may be that supports swapping skills and goods locally! Perhaps if there isn't one at present we could set up our own? To help us we can type **LETS scheme** into a search engine on a computer and see what comes up in our area. If there isn't one, then perhaps one of the existing branches could advise us on how to establish one?

Become a recycler!

Even if we live in isolated rural areas these days we usually have access to some sort of basic recycling scheme or centre which we can take such items as glass, paper and aluminium cans. It would be preaching to the converted to suggest we have overlooked these facilities. However, it still amazes me to see rubbish sacks on the street, awaiting collection, which visibly contain bottles and cans. We can be brave if we see this and have a word with our neighbours, even offering to take their recycling for them if that's what it takes. There can be no excuse as it is being made easier all the time for us to recycle our bit, in the most basic sense, because the amount of detritus we dispose of is growing ever more unwieldy. This is why it is well for us green spirits to go a little farther, or a lot farther if we are again willing to take responsibility and take the difficult route along the wildest way.

So, what else can we do? Well, I have long since adopted the position of refusing plastic carrier bags in stores. It is astounding how assistants in chemists seem to think I need a tiny plastic bag to carry my tiny bottle or box home with me! It is truly exhausting sometimes to keep repeating 'I don't need a bag, thanks!' in every shop, at every check out, when the cashier has already assumed that a bag is needed and started to pile my goods into one. It is easier not to bother but then the thought of all that non-degradable plastic from all of those purchases, every minute of every hour of every day of every shop across the world, is enough to make me take on my green mantle a little more and say 'no!' I have also discovered that if I inadvertently end up with a bag (through someone else leaving it with me) that there are carrier bag recycle points outside most supermarkets. I suppose that this acts as a sort of band aid for what they are constantly responsible for giving out. I always take my own shopping bag with me, a canvas rucksack with a second fold up holdall inside just in case, and this I count as a way of refusing to keep the flow of unnecessary plastic coming.

Talking of unnecessary plastic we are also faced with ludicrous packaging every day. Think of mushrooms in giant plastic boxes with polythene over them for instance. Mushrooms sweat and so far prefer a paper bag anyway! If we buy locally at markets or in small groceries we are far more likely to get paper bags of vegetables and fruit. I have endless plastic containers left from the days when I still shopped at a supermarket and these I use for seed trays. The rest I have recycled where facilities are available. I have also found that any old plastic bottles, cut in half, make good cloches in the growing season. Yet beyond these gestures it is still unspeakably sad when standing in a large shop to look at the shelves and shelves of packaging and wonder where it will all end up. I am eternally aiming to focus on practical magical works to change the tide on this one and not get too despondent in a sea of plastic boxes and drinks bottles. The more we avoid large shops the better we are able to focus on all the positive things that we do and so we avoid getting overwhelmed. We can think globally and act locally, knowing that change begins with us, today, now, that we have the power. No ocean was ever formed without the action of tiny raindrops.

Moving away from food shops, a friend of mine always writes *'recycle, re-use, re-create!'* on the reverse of her envelopes when she writes to me and so here is another way to use our power. We can collect envelopes, and any paper we have that has been used on one side only, then simply tape the blank side of the paper over our name and address on the envelope and create a new space for us to write the next address in. A bit of effort and a lot less paper wasted and we have a conscious act for the trees themselves. If we too write the message of recycling (I put '*please recycle me!*' on the reverse of my envelopes) with a prayer that for each envelope recycled, not wasted, another tree is saved then we are again feeding magic back into life, actively.

We may not think of recycling natural elements but we also need to think this way about water. Rain butts are an excellent answer to watering the garden in summer, avoiding the senseless squandering of this life-giving element which results from using a hosepipe or constant sprinkler. Similarly using a washing up bowl and tipping the water out from this on to the plants or bailing out bath water in a bucket, are both good ideas if we have the physical strength to do these things. The quality of the water we use leads me on to the next point which is . . .

Are we polluters?

Would we be able to use our recycled water on the land or is it full of chemicals? It is easy to refuse to pollute the water and opt for using household products that are biodegradable and harmless instead. Such products are suggested in the resources section which follows this one. This polluting aspect extends to shampoos and soaps . . . do we opt for simple, hand-made products which have basic ingredients or do the labels of our toiletries read like some kind of laboratory report? Even creature-friendly toiletries can have chemical constituents included way above the quantity their natural ones so it is worth checking out. Perhaps it is time for us to learn how to make our own soaps and shampoos, using only pure essential oils etc.?

And it may seem highly obvious but it took me a long time to abandon my use of bleach. I know many green-spirited folk who seem to have a blind spot when it comes to this noxious chemical liquid and refuse to relinquish its super-cleaning properties. It is true that eco-friendly products require a lot more muscle-power to get the stains off things but if I may just gently remind us all that we are pouring something down our toilets and sink drains that would kill us, let alone any other being who drank it. We are feeding the waters, and so the land, poison. It doesn't sit well with our green spirituality at all! Perhaps when we have relinquished such cleaning products and toiletries we can stand out in the rain, feeling it on our faces, on our fingers and on our tongues, knowing we now do as little as possible to pollute its purity. We can pray to the spirits of water that as we have relinquished our hold on these toxic things so may others. We may say something like:

'Spirits of water, by droplet and rivulet I now know you,
Take my message and let it be transmuted
As you yourself are transformed
From trickle to torrent, from vast ocean to vapour,
Let it flow as you flow, let it grow and swell as you grow.

Oh, may my message be as pure as you,
Taste as sweet as you,
Refresh the spirit as you do,
May the world know you as I do now,
May the truth well up, as you do, in all things.

Spirit of water, I hold you now, reverently, with love,
In my quiet hand I cup you softly, drink of you gladly,
That you may be held gently by a healed land,
That you may give life to all beings that thirst.

By sparkling river and shimmering rill, may it be so!'

Are we organic?

This final question may seem ludicrous; of course we are all organic! Yet is what we put inside of us so? Does it sustain the soul as well as the body, being resonant of nature's way, or has our food become 'product', a chemically enhanced genetically perverted thing that has been mass-produced and then dragged half way around the world to our plates? There are many reasons for eating organic produce centring on our own health and well-being and these again are obvious as who wouldn't prefer to feed themselves with a gloriously misshapen parsnip grown without pesticides and with much love in a local allotment as opposed to munching on one of those well-scrubbed regular vegetables that last saw natural light thousands of miles from our home and which is permeated right though with chemical fertilizers etc.? The only thing that puts most of us off buying organic fare is the price when compared with the cheap mass-produced fare next to it, but it cannot be stressed enough that it is worth the extra money to choose food that has the energy of the soil about it, something that is wholesome and *real* as opposed to soulless and bland. Our bodies need fuel which is full of vibrant life-force and which we feel confident about. It makes sense to feed ourselves with that which is local, untreated, unprocessed...that is to say, *whole* food. It shows a respect for ourselves that is echoed by how we feel about the land; as within, so without.

But why else choose organic produce?

Well, there is the other human-centric argument that says that we should leave a better world for the next generations to enjoy and therefore we should support that which doesn't destroy the environment. If this tenet allows people to support natural, ethical farming then I have no gripe with it as it at least opens people to a different way of perceiving existence which doesn't centre around immediate gain/quick fix mentality of modern society. It takes us a step away from short-sighted destructive irresponsibility and helps preserve the Earth's bounty too. Yet there is a problem with this human-centric way which can lead us up a blind alley after a few well-meaning steps. If we do not stop thinking of the Earth as something which is there for the benefit of humanity, be that for us or other generations, then we do not see her as a living organism in her own right. *We negate her as a being and instate her as a backdrop.* We do this every time we call her sacred land 'scenery', as if we humans were in a play and she was the stage, there solely for our benefit. If we do this we are not relating to her as she is, as the living mother of our physical life here. A wilful, independent, beautiful, strong, generous mother whose patience may seem limitless but clearly isn't. Here is the key to green-spirited thinking on this issue...*we do not need to placate her so she is nice to us, we need to respect her because we love her.* And beyond that there is no other reason to eat organic.

It is better for *her*.

So when we buy our knobbly muddy carrots in a paper bag we can pray for *her* health as well as that of all beings who reside on her, by her grace.

I rest my case!

*　　*　　*

We have, perhaps, come a long way since beginning this book. We may have moved well away from the concept of spirituality being apropos of religious affiliation and also from the idea that spirituality is only a means of self-improvement in a very human sense. In fact we may have moved away from human-centric thought entirely into a new way of seeing based in the deep understanding that *all* beings, not only all men and women, are equal even if they do not speak/think/behave as we do. We may be becoming more response-able, that is, able to *respond* with all our being focused 'in the now' rather than our *re-acting* with an old reflex employed because we were not fully aware of what is actually happening at that moment. We may well know now that living a life of green response-ability means that we are committed to remaining uncluttered by the debris of modern living, proceeding with all our senses open to spiritual as well as manifest influences. We may accept that when we respond to life in this way we strike a balance between the rational and the instinctive, between that which is deemed purely scientific and that which is simple, earthy and raw...we walk in balance. Through this new balanced perspective we may have found that we no longer need to be solely influenced by the physical world nor do we have to lose our grounding and spend our entire lives away with the faeries.

We are no longer victims to cold logic nor are we bound by unfounded second-hand dogma; the physical realm and the ways of spirit are no longer separate for us, nor are they remote from us, and we know that we are protected and guided within the framework of the realms in which we walk daily. We understand that we are a law unto ourselves yet realise that if we do not acknowledge the greater natural laws within that realm of free choice we do not function effectively, in harmony. Accepting this wider connection we may then have taken on the maxim 'as within, so without' and feel our own spirit as being but an expression of All That Is, not a struggling separate being but a part of Its seamless beauty. By this we may accept that we no longer need gods of any kind as we may know that *we are all the creators*, unstoppable and vibrant forces of nature, and response-able steward-representatives of the creator energy. Our link to the Creator/Source may well now be strengthened and our purpose as a facet of that Source enhanced. As compassionate creators we can imagine a verdant world, alive with spirit, and nurture that vision wholeheartedly, feeling the power of our visioning rippling out from us because we accept that everything is energy and our energies are everything...what is done by one is done for the many.

Since reading this book we may well have accepted that it is up to us to reach out alone, if that is what it takes, as a trailblazer and a champion of verdant values and the rights of our kin. Even as soul-warriors we can continue to walk a path of peace, with faith, yielding like the sapling in the wind to the truth that needs no beliefs, ready to take gentle, effective action and use the shining weapon of our imaginations when we are called upon to defend that which we hold dear. We need never feel lonely for we have all our relations, spiritual *and* physical, human and non-human, to walk that wild way beside us. We can choose to live our lives in support of a cause that is greater than we ourselves are, even as it remains profoundly personal to us. We have maybe decided that we will do this not just the sake of human generations to come, as we may have considered previously, but for *all* beings and, more importantly perhaps, because it is respectful and right to do so. We can then wield the only weapons we will ever need, these being the transformative power of our imaginations and the realisation of our environmentally sound, compassionate actions. We cannot change the Earth Mother, for she is an independent sentient being just as we are, but we can change the way we live upon her in accordance with her principles. We can do this, as we have seen here and as we have found in our own lives, every single day...in thought, kind word, and soul-song and loving deed. As we walk onwards from this point, as magical beings united by a common bond of love for all creation, we can continue to find joy in the mundane, acknowledging simple pleasures without expectation, experiencing enchantment in the commonplace. This is a good way to worship; this is our prayer in action.

We can now go on to be as creative as the bower bird, as versatile as the chameleon, as receptive as the bat and as free as we were born to be, all of us walking our own individual tracks into the untamed heart of being, solitary yet supported by many presences.

Here is a final green-spirited challenge for us all and I am going to imagine hundreds, maybe thousands, of us doing it. Today let us reject the captivity of convention and plunge deeper into the green, for this is our wild spirituality in essence.

The rest is an unfolding dream that we all may share...*if we dare to live it.*

6

Resources

What follows is a far from exhaustive list of organisations that we can support and gain farther information from. These are predominantly in the UK although each one can help us locate similar organisations in our own countries, I am sure. Each name listed may lead us to others not mentioned so it is a start for our own research into a green-spirited lifestyle. Imagine if everyone who reads this contributes a small amount to one of the charities listed with a prayer for a re-greening of the Earth and all her children...*what a collective wild magic that would be!* (If we have no money to donate then there are always campaigns being run by these organisations and we can contribute our valuable time and energy to those instead.)

BUAV
British Union for the Abolition of Vivisection,
16a Crane Grove,
London N7 8NN, UK
Telephone: 020 7700 4888
E-mail: info@buav.org
Web: www.buav.org

ANIMAL AID
Web: www.animalaid.org.uk

NATIONAL FEDERATION OF BADGER GROUPS
2 Cloisters Business Centre,
8 Battersea Park Road,
London SW8 4BG, UK
Telephone: 020 7498 3220
E-mail: enquiries@nfbg.org.uk
Web: www.badgers.org.uk/nfbg/

RSPB (Royal Society for the Protection of Birds)
The Lodge,
Sandy,
Bedfordshire SG19 2DL, UK
Telephone: 01767 680551
Web: www.rspb.org.uk

WILDLIFE TRUSTS
National Office,
The Kiln,
Waterside, Mather Road,
Newark,
Notts NG24 1WT, UK
Telephone: 01636 677711
E-mail: wildlifersnc@cix.co.uk
Web: www.wildlifetrust.org.uk

THE FOX PROJECT (charity dedicated to the wild fox)
The Old Chapel,
Bradford Street,
Tonbridge,
Kent TN9 1AW, UK
Telephone: 01732 367397
E-mail: vulpes@foxproject.freeserve.co.uk

THE WOODLAND TRUST (a charity that protects and manages Britain's ancient woodlands)
Autumn Park,
Dysart Road,
Grantham,
Lincs NG31 6LL, UK

BAT CONSERVATION TRUST
15 Cloisters House,
8 Battersea Park Road,
London SW8 4BG, UK
Telephone: 020 7627 2629
E-mail: enquiries@bats.org.uk
Web: www.bats.org.uk

GREENPEACE
Canonbury Villas,
London N1 2PN, UK
Telephone: 020 7865 8100
E-mail: info@uk.greenpeace.org
Web: www.greenpeace.org.uk

SUSTRANS (the sustainable transport charity)
Web: www.sustrans.org.uk

WILD FLOWER SOCIETY
68 Outwoods Road,
Loughborough,
Leics LE11 3LY, UK

SPEAC (campaign to stop primate experiments at Cambridge, UK)
PO Box 6712
Northampton NN2 6XR, UK
E-mail: info@primateprison.org
Web: www.primateprison.org

PETA (People for the Ethical Treatment of Animals)
Web: www.peta.org

BRITISH TRUST for CONSERVATION VOLUNTEERS
36 St Mary's Street,
Wallingford,
Oxon OX10 0EU, UK
Telephone: 01491 839766
E-mail: information@btcv.org.uk
Web: www.btcv.org.uk

HUNT SABOTEURS ASSOCIATION
PO Box 5254,
Northants NN1 3ZA, UK
Telephone: 0845 450 0727
E-mail: info@huntsabs.org.uk
Web: www.huntsabs.org.uk

HDRA (charity to improve organic horticulture)
Ryton Organic Gardens,
Coventry CV8 3LG, UK
Telephone: 024 7630 3517

SAVE THE NEWCHURCH GUINEA PIGS (campaign to close breeding camps for doomed guinea pigs destined for research laboratories)
S.N.G.P.
P.O. Box 74,
Evesham,
Worcs WR11 3WF, UK
E-mail: info@guineapigs.org.uk
Web: www.guineapigs.org.uk

The following are some ethical companies who can help us maintain a cruelty free, Earth-friendly magical existence:

CO-OPERATIVE BANK (ethical investment)
Customer services,
P.O. Box 200,
Delf House,
Skelmersdale,
Lancs, UK
Telephone: 08457 212212

CO-OP (animal-friendly household cleaners/toiletries)
Web: www.co-op.co.uk

ORGANIC GARDENING CATALOGUE
Riverdene,
Molesey Road,
Hersham,
Surrey KT12 4RG, UK
E-mail: enquiries@chaseorganics.co.uk
Web: www.OrganicCatalogue.com

VEGETARIAN SHOES (for those seeking an alternative to leather)
Web: www.vegetarian-shoes.co.uk

THE BODY SHOP (cruelty-free cosmetics, toiletries etc.)
The Body Shop
BN17 6LS, UK
Web: www.the-body-shop.com

HEMP UNION (for all Earth-conscious, hemp-related products and information)
Web: www.hemp-union.karoo.net

SYMPHONY ENVIRONMENTAL LTD (makers of totally bio-degradable plastic bags etc.)
Elstree House,
Elstree Way,
Borehamwood,
Herts WD6 1LE, UK
Telephone 020 8207 5900

ECOVER (animal and environmentally friendly cleaning products available through most supermarkets and health food shops ... check out the excellent refill service which saves on buying more plastic bottles!)
Web: www.ecover.com

ETHICAL WARES (ethical mail order for products supporting animal and human rights as well as environmental concerns)
Cargwyn,
Temple Bar,
Feinfach,
Lampeter,
Ceredigion SA48 7SA, Wales, UK
Telephone: 01570 471155
E-mail: vegans@ethicalwares.com
Web: www.ethicalwares.com

*   *   *

Here are some green-spirited authors/artists/creators that are well worth checking out for the reasons suggested below. However, this is a list I could just keep adding to so there are bound to be many omissions!

RAE BETH
Rae's books and talks are gentle yet potent, encouraging as they do both personal transformation and green-spirited action. She is a great

one for making the reader feel at home instantly. Her books are centred in witchery but this is of the most lilting and earth-honouring kind; uncomplicated, effective and without pretension. To keep up with her newest contributions, ideas etc. see www.raebeth.com

POPPY PALIN
Poppy's writing and illustrations (as seen here in *Green Spirituality*) stem from the same source as this work, that is, she focuses on the simple soul poetry of nature and the wild spirit inherent in all beings. Her latest book, *Craft of the Wild Witch* (Llewellyn 2004), can be experienced as a companion to this book as its emphasis is on everyday enchantment; a way of living lyrically and magically which leads us deeper into the green. She is also a sacred skin artist, a tattooist working in a way that effects transformation, and examples of her inspirational work can be viewed at www.poppypalin.com

NICK AND JAN WOOD
These two publish an excellent quarterly journal, *Sacred Hoop*, and have between them in print a couple of beautiful and informative books. See their website at www.sacredhoop.org or E-mail: Editor@sacredhoop.org. Jan's stunning green-spirited artwork can be seen at www.maytreegallery.co.uk, or write to BCM Sacred Hoop, London WC1N 3XX, UK.

JAMIE SAMS
Ms Sams is my all time favourite on spirituality and earth energies. She never fails to challenge me and make me aspire to her unerring standards when it comes to working respectfully with the land, the creature teachers and the ancestral spirits. She is published by Thorsons.

SATISH KUMAR
This man is such an inspiration, he lives and breathes green spirituality and I cannot recommend him highly enough. He is the editor of the journal *Resurgence* which has an integrated ecological/spiritual ethos and he writes marvellous books such as *No Destination* published by Green Books.

JULIETTE DE BAIRACLI LEVY
The classic works on herbalism are written by this wonderful woman from a Romany perspective. See the Amazon.co.uk/com website for farther information.

ANNA FRANKLIN

Anna produces a plethora of excellently researched volumes on all sorts of magical subjects which can be relied on to inform and entertain. She is also an artist and creatrix of the *Silver Wheel* magical journal. Her work can be seen at Web: www.annafranklin.net and www.silverwheel.net, or contact by E-mail at annafranklin@lycos.co.uk

MARC POTTS

I have already mentioned Marc and his fabulous fine art featuring nature-spirits. Do have a look at his website at www.marcpotts.com, or contact him at 12 St Sidwells Avenue, Exeter, Devon, UK.

CAROLYN HILLYER

Part of the 'Seventh Wave' musical partnership with Nigel Shaw, Carolyn produces some stunning, moving work based around the subject of the wild land. She works especially with feminine energies and ancestral spirits to great effect. For a catalogue of her artwork, books, workshops and Seventh Wave's music/performances contact Carolyn or Nigel. Telephone: 01822 880301. Web: www.seventhwavemusic.co.uk

SUSUN S. WEED

Susun is a wonderful herbalist, writing about the very spirit of the green beings that we ourselves seek to identify and honour. Her hands-on approach is inspirational. She is published by Ash Tree.

GREEN MAGIC

Green Magic are the publishers of this book and of many others on thought-provoking, ecological, magical themes. Much recommended is *The Faery Faith* by Serena Roney-Dougal, published in 2003. They can be contacted through Counter Culture book distribution who create an excellent catalogue. Their address is The Long Barn, Sutton Mallet, Somerset TA7 9AR, UK. Telephone: 01278 722888. E-mail: info@counterculture-books.co.uk. Web: www.counterculture-books.co.uk

MARY SUMMER RAIN

I include Mary because of her lyricism in writing about both the land and her spirit kin. Always passionate and thought provoking she is published by Hampton Roads.

LISA TENZIN-DOLMA
Author/artist of the much praised *Glastonbury Tarot* and two popular works on dolphins published by Foulsham, Lisa is one to watch! I highly recommend any of her new works, when they are published, as her books will always be excellent soul and brain food!

KHALIL GIBRAN
For a pure spirituality without beliefs there can be none better than this soul-speaker. His compassion and deeply grounded wisdoms are timeless. Although *The Prophet* is his best known work it is well worth seeking out his other contributions to modern spiritual understanding, including his biography. His work is available through several publishers so it is best to see Amazon.co.uk/com for further details.

GLENNIE KINDRED
Glennie creates accessible and powerful little books full of practical information on country-lore and sacred energies. Her work is published by several houses and can be seen in the Counter Culture catalogue or through the usual booksellers.

GAEL BAUDINO
Gael's novels, especially *Strands of Starlight*, were instrumental in my own initial interest in the Fey and the Old Ones. She manages to combine the earthy and the unearthly in a believable way as does Charles de Lint whose magical fiction is well worth checking out.

JILL SMITH
As an artist and writer, Jill is in tune with the energies of the land, expressing her connection to the wild essence of place powerfully. Her work has been seen for many years in pagan journals and she has published two books about her special spiritual empathy with the Hebrides. Please contact her for more details at 20 Monington Road, Glastonbury, Somerset BA6 8HE, UK. Telephone: 01458 831953.

ROSA ROMANI
Rosa is a soul-poet, singer and animal rights activist. She can be contacted through the link at www.poppypalin.com and details of her other projects can be obtained via her publishers, Green Magic, at the previously given address. PLEASE enclose an SAE! Her own website is being set up at www.rosaromani.com

*   *   *

Finally here are another few creative enterprises that deserve your attention!

INANNA'S FESTIVAL (pagan/green-spirited gifts in a treat of a shop, ask for Naomi Kosten!)
11 Pottergate, Norwich, Norfolk NR2 1DS, UK. Telephone: 01603 626133

TRIPLE SPIRAL MAGAZINE (independently run and lovingly fashioned, this green-spirited bi-annual magazine is aimed at Earth-conscious families)
Germaine Helen, 14 Maxwell Road, Winton, Bournemouth, Dorset BH9 1DJ, UK. Telephone: 01202 519388

PENTACLE MAGAZINE (another independently run magazine for pagans of all paths)
Marion Pearce, 78 Hamlet Road, Southend-on-Sea, Essex SS1 1HH, UK.

*   *   *

In conclusion, the following was written as a symbolic gesture that all of those who read this book may be so touched to carry on the traditions of our creative, intuitive, response-able kin, be they spiritual or ancestral. May the energies embodied by this work flow on into a receptive world with the blessings of those who walked before and those who, unseen, still tread the wild ways alongside us.

Cloth of Gold

A Blessing

Oh, where may we find splendour?
In another's valour, in our own honour,
Standing as they stood for wilder ways,
Keepers of the shining thread that runs through all our days.

May the cloth of gold that covered their world cover ours also.

And where may we find glory?
Twined in the silken weave of another's story,
Reverence across the years reflected,
In a gleaming shield, wielded for the land's protection.

May the cloth of gold, smoothed by ancient hands and hands unseen,
be smoothed by our hands also.

And, tell me, how may we know home?
By the fissures in each standing stone,
Cracked by the fires where once their visions came,
Now fires within warm our bold intent the same.

May the cloth of gold that illumines the sun illumine us also.
And may it warm their sacred bones.

Green Magic Publishing

Green Magic Publishing is an independent publishing house based in the South West of England.

We hope you enjoyed reading *Energy Secrets of Glastonbury Tor* by Nicholas Mann – our other titles are:

Advanced Wiccan Spirituality by Kevin Saunders (ISBN 095429632x)
Book of Shadows Large (ISBN 0954296389), Small (ISBN 0954296303)
The Faery Faith by Serena Roney-Dougal (ISBN 0953663175)
Wiccan Spirituality by Kevin Saunders (ISBN 0953663167)
Teenage Witch's Book of Shadows by Anna de Benzelle & Mary Neasham (ISBN 0953663159)
Underworld of the East by James S Lee (ISBN 0953663116)

Our new titles for 2004 include -

Spirit of the Green Man by Mary Neasham (ISBN 0954296370)
Green Spirituality by Rosa Romani (ISBN 0954296362)

All Green Magic books are available from your local bookshop.

Green Magic is always interested in receiving manuscripts, especially in the fields of Magic and Wicca, Sacred Landscape and Spirituality.

Green Magic Publishing
The Long Barn
Sutton Mallet
Somerset   TA7 9AR
TEL/FAX 01278 722888
www.greenmagicpublishing.com
email: info@greenmagicpublishing.com

Avalon, a site of great power, revered since ancient times as an entrance to, and exit from, the Otherworld. *Isle of Avalon* illustrates and describes the physical and sacred topography of the Isle as well as its symbols, architecture and history. It gives detailed explanations about the Tor, the Glastonbury Zodiac, the Abbey, the Tor labyrinth, the St Michael leyline and much more.

This is an updated and revised edition of the first book to provide a coherent context in which to understand Avalon's many mysteries.

"*Nicholas Mann explores Avalon in impressive detail.*" **Geoffrey Ashe.**

"*Everything you wanted to know about the sacred mysteries of Glastonbury.*" **Third Stone.**

"*Mann provides an impressive overview of Glastonbury's history and mythology. An enjoyable and valuable read*" **Fortean Times.**

Nicholas R. Mann is the author of many books, most recently *Energy Secrets of Glastonbury Tor* (Green Magic 2004). Other titles include *Reclaiming the Gods* (Green Magic 2002) and *Druid Magic* (Llewellyn 2000). He lives in Glastonbury, England.

The Isle of Avalon by Nicholas R. Mann.
King Arthur / Celtic Wisdom / Sacred Landscape.
Price £9.99 / $16.99 ISBN 0953663132 Illustrated.

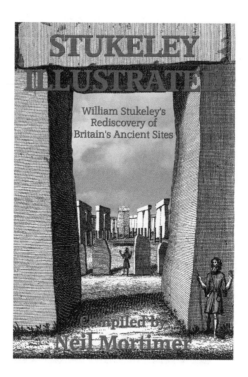

STUKELEY ILLUSTRATED

William Stukeley's
Rediscovery of
Britain's Ancient Sites

Compiled by
Neil Mortimer

William Stukeley was the first man to chronicle the greatest prehistoric stone circles in the world, Stonehenge and Avebury.

One of the eighteenth century's most remarkable characters, he was friend and colleague to some of the most gifted men of his time, including Sir Isaac Newton.

Stukeley's work laid the foundations for the modern study of prehistoric monuments, influenced the Druidic revival and inspired some of William Blake's most celebrated paintings.

For the first time *Stukeley Illustrated* brings together over 100 of the best engravings from his most brilliant books. It shows how this meticulous and inspired draughtsman changed the way we look at ancient sites. It is a tribute to an increasingly relevant figure, and is indispensable to anyone interested in the sacred sites and landscapes of the British Isles.

"A fine tribute to a great man" - **John Michell** (Author of *View Over Atlantis*)

"Highly recommended" - **Avalon**

Stukeley Illustrated Compiled by Neil Mortimer
Biography / Archaeology / Sacred Landscape.
Price £9.99 / $16.99 ISBN 0954296338 Illustrated.

Reclaiming The Gods
Magic, Sex, Death and Football

Nicholas R. Mann

In the same way as the Goddess has been reclaimed in recent years, this book reclaims the God. Nicholas Mann in this vibrant work shows how the figure of the God has become monopolised, marginalised and corrupted, to our great loss.

The restoration of the God in our lives will liberate our individual spiritual experience, enabling us to see with new insight the reality of good and evil. To understand the true nature of our sexual passions, our relationship to others and the world in all its true beauty.

Here we revisit the Trickster, the Hunter, the Shape-Shifter, the Protector, Craftsman, Lover - the Gods of Wisdom, Fertility, Wealth and Laughter that still resonate in our lives today.

"*A valuable and original work by a popular writer of contemporary spirituality*" - **Avalon**

"*Offers an intriguing and useful resource for the male psyche*" - **Sacred Hoop**

"*This could become one of the classics*" - **Pagan Dawn**

Reclaiming the Gods by Nicholas R. Mann
Mythology / Spirituality / Sexuality
Price £9.99 / $16.99 ISBN 0953663183

Handfasting
A Practical Guide

Mary Neasham

This is the first book published in the UK about handfasting! It will take you on a historical journey, starting with pre-Christian times. It describes the customs and traditions associated with betrothal from times and places in the world where our forbears were in tune with the changing seasons and the natural rhythms of the world they lived in.

The increasing popularity of handfasting is recognition that the current alternatives of church or civil ceremonies offer little in the way of deeper meaning in our increasingly pagan times.

In this book, Mary Neasham offers practical advice on creating your own handfasting ceremony. A very modern way to commit to another person based on the lore and customs of our ancestors.

"A treasury of information, useful and wise" - **Glennie Kindred** (Author of ***Sacred Celebrations***)

"An excellent book written to suit the initiated, the curious and the layperson. Highly recommended" - **Avalon**

"A very accessible, yet comprehensive guide" - **Pentacle**

Handfasting by Mary Neasham
Marriage / Spirituality / Customs
Price £9.99 / $16.99   ISBN 0954296311

Lost Magic of Christianity is a startlingly original study of the Ancient Wisdom Tradition and Celtic Christianity in Ireland and the West. It unlocks the secrets of Stone and Bronze Age metaphysics that influenced the Gnostic practices of the early priesthood. These priests were vibrant seers, healers and highly skilled astromathematicians, expressing the oneness between human beings, nature and the living spirit of the Christ principle.

However this pagan Christianity magic was soon to be eroded and destroyed by the patriarchal dogma of a debased male priesthood. Our inner mythology and folk memory were taken from us in order to control us.

Lost Magic of Christianity offers enlightened explanations as we begin to shed religion and take responsibility for our divine self in the new millennium.

"An innovative and unusual study of the Ancient Wisdom Tradition. A unique book" - **Celtic Connections**

"Seriously thought provoking reading" - **Pagan Dawn**

"Poynder's fresh look at our ancient heritage suggests a few more pieces of the puzzle that we can put in place" - **Nexus**

The Lost Magic Of Christianity by Michael Poynder
New Age / Spirituality / Ancient Mysteries
Price £9.99 / $16.99   ISBN 0953663108   Ilustrated